The Separated Ones

THE
SEPARATED ONES

Jesus, the Pharisees and Islam

Ruqaiyyah Waris Maqsood

SCM PRESS

British Library Cataloguing in Publication Data
Maqsood, Ruqaiyyah Waris
The separated ones : Jesus, the Pharisees
and Islam.
I. Title
296

ISBN 0 334 02498 6

First published 1991
by SCM Press Ltd,
26–30 Tottenham Road, London N1 4BZ

Typeset at The Spartan Press Ltd, Lymington, Hants
and printed in Great Britain by
Billing & Sons Ltd, Worcester

For Waris Ali

CONTENTS

INTRODUCTION

I began to write this book about thirty years ago, when I was eighteen and still a hopeful, youthful, know-it-all. I seem to have been writing it ever since.

I was originally a Christian, and when I left school, I went to study theology at university. There, however, I became very impatient with the intricate maze of doctrinal axioms I was supposed to accept by faith (because they did not fit in with 'reasons') in order to grasp the meaning of the Holy Trinity, the belief that there are three Persons in the one Godhead – Father, Son and Holy Spirit, all equal and co-eternal: separate entities yet not separate.

In fact, I discovered that the doctrine of the Trinity was to be found nowhere in the Bible, and was not formally accepted by the church until the fourth century CE. It was not taught in either Old or New Testament. Jesus certainly never mentioned it. He never left any instructions that we were supposed to believe any such thing: we were to love one another, feed the hungry, clothe the naked, and so on (Matt. 25. 31–46); in his view, it was on our actions and good lives that our judgment would be based.

If people were to read the Bible from cover to cover without any preconceived idea of the Trinity, they would come to no other conclusion than that God was One, separate and distinct, and that whatever Jesus was, he was separate and distinct, and subordinate to the Father! The *only* place where I could find an 'explicit' trinitarian reference was in the baptismal formula given in Matthew 28.19, but even there the three persons are as distinct as Peter, James and John.

At the same time as I was grappling with all this, I continued to read on world religions. I developed an impatience with those who thought that comparative religion was 'all right' so long as it was always done to the detriment of that other faith. I found that

I had a great deal of sympathy for *all* believers in God, *all* seekers after truth – so long as their beliefs were based on honesty, integrity and piety – even if I did not personally agree with everything they believed. As it said in the Bhagavad Gita, a Hindu scripture: 'People come to me along many roads; I will *always* find them, for all roads are mine.'

I thus came to believe that no matter from what angle one approached God, the nearer one got along the various paths, the more clearly it could be seen that God was only one. It may surprise Muslims to know that I thought this even of the paths to God through Hinduism and Buddhism, systems not 'of the Book'. Indeed, they are totally different. My only logic was that of the Jain story of the blind men feeling the elephant and each trying to identify it from a different part. All were right, and yet all were wrong in that all were limited.

In paradise, I prepare for the righteous believer what no eye has ever seen, no ear has ever heard, and what the deepest mind could never imagine' (Hadith Qudsi – and shades of St Paul?).

I always seemed to be on the side of the 'heretics' I was studying, whose systems were usually based on logic and love and had grown out of some dissatisfaction with 'the creed'. Maybe I just had a natural sympathy for the underdog, but all I was doing was trying to understand God as best I could.

In the light of all this it seemed ridiculous for one sect of Christians to condemn all other sects of Christians to eternal torment, because they differed in some detail of their faith. My experience had been to 'taste' several varieties, find good in all of them, but feel at home in none. I could not accept that *any* one group of believers could take upon itself the right to specify by what criteria God alone would judge his people. Their grounds seemed purely subjective and speculative; and they had appropriated for themselves the role of judge, which I humbly believe belongs to God alone. When Jesus was asked straight – as other rabbis had been asked – what a person had to do to enter the kingdom of God and receive eternal life, what was the greatest and most important commandment of all, he replied: 'This is the first commandment – You shall love the Lord your God with all your heart, soul, mind and strength; and the second is this – you shall love your neighbour as yourself. There are *no other commandments greater than these*'

(Mark 12.28–34; Luke 10.25–28; Matt. 22.24.20). We find exactly the same words attributed to Rabbi Hillel, who said that this was the *whole* of the Law of God. All the rest, all the detailed minutiae, was commentary.

As a historian, I had also become suspicious of some of the bias contained in the Christian texts. For example, having made some study of the contemporaries of Jesus, I felt that the constant Gospel vilification of the pious Jewish sect of Pharisees was blatantly incorrect. I became firmly convinced that Jesus must have been a Pharisee himself, of the school of Rabbi Hillel. The fact that I was not the first to have thought this was no problem. Perhaps, if there was any real criticism of the Pharisees, it came from within – when they were hypocrites and fell short of their own very high standards of faith, love and belief. My interest in the Pharisees had begun, and my initial enthusiasm led to the first draft of a book. However, things were not be be as easy as that.

I spent many more years on research while working as a teacher, bringing up a family and writing a variety of textbooks. I continued to go to church, falling silent over some of the words, but suddenly some of them actually seemed blasphemous. I think it was when I finally admitted to myself that God did not need any 'sacrifice' to make him more merciful than he already is, that I realized that I had become a Muslim. Around the same time I idly let the Bible fall open at a text and for the very first time read this:

> Why do you keep believing the descendants will be punished for the sins of the fathers? Behold, all souls are mine . . . only the soul that sins shall die . . . The son shall not suffer for the sin of the father, nor the father for the son . . . And if any wicked person turns away from sins and keeps my law, that person shall live and not die. Any sins committed will be remembered against them no more . . . repent and live . . . I have no pleasure in the death of anyone' (Ezekiel 18).

The words seemed to be directed straight at me, and suddenly the famous parable of the Prodigal Son made perfect sense. 'This my son was dead; he is alive again.' That is how I felt too.

So having served God all the first part of my life to the best of my ability as a Christian, I became a Muslim, and Rosalyn Kendrick is now Ruqaiyyah Waris Maqsood, since I have recently married a Muslim man.

True to the principle that everything is guided in life, I can now see why this book has taken so long to reach completion. I offer it to Christian, Jewish and Muslim readers with love.

Note
A description of the Jewish, Christian and Muslim holy books referred to in the text will be found at the end of this book, along with a brief chronology, to enable readers to give events referrred to an approximate date.

They who have died in grief shall arise in joy;
and they who were poor for the Lord's sake shall be made rich;
and they who have been in want shall be filled;
and they who have been weak shall be strong;
and they who have been put to death for the Lord's sake
shall awake to life.

(Testaments of the Twelve Patriarchs, Judah 25.4)

What is hateful to you, do not do to your neighbour. That is the whole of the Law. All the rest is commentary. Go and learn it.

(Hillel, *Shabbath* 31a)

1 · Introducing the Pharisees

The teachers of the Law (scribes) and the Pharisees are the authorized interpreters of Moses' Law. So you must obey and follow everything they tell you to do. Do not, however, imitate their actions, because they don't practise what they preach. They tie on to people's backs loads that are heavy and hard to carry, yet they aren't willing to lift a finger to help carry them. They do everything so that people will see them. Look at the straps with scripture verses which they wear on their foreheads and arms, and notice how large they are! Notice also how long are the tassels on their cloaks! They love the best places at feasts and the reserved seats in the synagogues; they love to be greeted with respect in the market-places, and to be called 'Teacher' (Rabbi). You must not be called 'Teacher', because you are all brothers of one another, and have only One Teacher . . . the greatest one among you must be your servant (Matthew 23.1–12, Good News Bible).

The only knowledge most people have of the devout Jewish sect from the time of Jesus known as the Pharisees is gleaned from the pages of the New Testament. Pharisees appear frequently in the Gospels, and they also occur, though to a much lesser extent, in the Acts of the Apostles and the letters of St Paul. One can hardly read these books without becoming acutely aware of an attitude towards them that could hardly be described as friendly. Other prominent groups – Sadducees, scribes, and priests – also come in for a good measure of criticism, if not antagonism, but it is the Pharisees who seem to be singled out as the especial enemies of Jesus.

Yet, if you turned back a few pages to the books of the Old Testament, you would search in vain for any mention of the Pharisees at all. There is nothing there about them, even in the sections that were written last, despite the fact that during the lifetime of Jesus they had become very much a force to be reckoned with. Where had they sprung from? Were they a completely new religious party, or had they grown out of a previous sect, and if so, which one? And why did the Christian church by the turn of the first century CE consider them to have been such intractable enemies?

This is not an irrelevant academic question. Up until comparatively recent years, it has not been common practice for theologians of any one faith to make much of a study of the dogma, holy books and subsequent literature of systems of beliefs other than their own. It is still rare, for example, to find a Christian or Muslim scholar who has read the Talmud and associated literature, or a Jewish or Christian scholar who has studied Qur'an and hadith.

Jews, Christians and Muslims all claim to worship the same God, whether the deity is known as Yahweh, the Trinity, or Allah. All three claim the same line of prophets for their stream of revelatory knowledge, and are regarded as the 'people of the Book'. The recent furore over the Salman Rushdie affair has revealed clearly how the Jewish faith is protected under the archaic British blasphemy laws because their Old Testament is counted as a Christian scripture, although obviously it was all written long before the earthly life of Jesus. Muslim lawyers in the case at law have pointed out how they, too, share the same veneration for the Bible and its Messengers – all they have done is to accept a further prophet after Jesus, the Arabian Muhammad (peace be upon them). They claim that the revelation given through Muhammad – coming from the same God – was the *same* as that revealed to all the other prophets, but in this latest case it was still preserved in its exact words, without any tampering. Muslims point out that after the perfect life, example and message of Jesus there might never have been the need for another prophet – *had it not been for one thing*. Somehow or other, Muslims believe, the message revealed through Jesus the Christ had been misinterpreted, or corrupted. They maintain that what is taught now as Christianity was *never* the message given by the Nazarene. His words had not been written down verbatim in his lifetime, and somehow, by the time the Christian holy books were written, a shift of doctrine had not so much crept in as swept in.

This book is not the place to analyse in detail what Jews, Christians and Muslims have in common, or the differences between them, and the reasons why. But it is an attempt to do two things: to puncture the unjustified, centuries-long feeling of superiority harboured by Christians when comparing their faith to that of any other of the world's religious God-fearers, and to make Christians square up to the necessity of asking a few deep questions.

To return to Jesus: it goes without saying, of course, that whereas many Jews or Muslims might be quite happy to accept Jesus as a prophetic figure, Messiah of Israel, even perhaps a martyr, none would be shaken for a second in their belief that there was only one God, the Absolute. Christians have always been known for their love and devotion to God, to their example – Jesus – and to humanity: they have died for that love in their millions; they have earned the gratitude, admiration and respect of the millions who have been helped by their urge to live in service of God.

But Muslims and Jews, who share this devotion and submission to God, are alike in condemning trinitarian beliefs as a tragic error, a misunderstanding of reality.

Muslims maintain that *all* the world's believers in God the Supreme, present and past, who have consciously submitted their lives to him, *are Muslim*. Hence Adam was Muslim; Noah was Muslim; Abraham, Moses, David, Solomon; Jeremiah and all other prophets and those who followed their 'path' were Muslim; and *so was Jesus*. And so, for that matter, were all the followers of all these prophets who were conscious of God and had submitted their lives to his service. Non-Muslims tend to scoff at what they perhaps regard as rather a grandiose claim, and wonder if the motive behind it is to 'filch' the good material from other faiths.

My aim is simply to take and examine the theme that the Pharisees of the time of Jesus have been misrepresented, perhaps unconsciously, or perhaps deliberately. Such an approach suggests that the 'enmity' between Christianity and 'the Jews' arose from a specific doctrinal cause, and reveals the possibility that what the Muslims have claimed is in fact true: that the Jews of old *had* the revelation, but mistakenly presented it as limited to a 'chosen' nation and not as universal to the world; and that Jesus also *had* the revelation, but his followers (out of an exaggerated devotion to his person) had elevated their guiding Master and Prophet to the status of being himself part of God.

Muhammad was therefore sent, as the 'Seal' of all the preceding prophets, to reaffirm their teachings, and to correct the errors.

Islam was in no sense an attack on those preceding faiths but an attempt to bring them into line. Probably one of Muhammad's most bitter disappointments was that so many Jews and Christians, when presented with the Qur'an, did not instantly see their errors and become Muslim.

It is a commonplace nowadays that those who *have* taken this step, as I have, know a very strong feeling of satisfaction and 'rightness'. All sorts of niggling problems roll away; logic and reason sweep in; there is the most powerful sensation of not rejecting one's 'roots', not being disloyal to an old love in seeking out a new, but of returning to source. Many such new Muslims do not call themselves 'converts' but 'reverts'.

So let us begin. Who were these Pharisees, the so-called enemies and rivals of Jesus? In searching for an answer, perhaps we should not make the New Testament our first port of call. It is now a well-known fact that the motives and interests of the various writers and editors must be looked into very seriously in any Gospel study. The authors were not the simple, unbiased historians of Jesus, the naive eye-witness disciples, that they might have appeared at first blush. The days have long since gone when an innocent reader, opening the New Testament at page one, could believe that the first Gospel was the work of Matthew the tax-collector, one of the twelve apostles called by Jesus, or that the last Gospel was a meditation written in his extreme old age by the apostle John, the fisherman.

Early Christian writers in the Roman world obviously considered the Pharisees to be dangerous rivals to their movement, and were intensely of the conviction that they themselves were in the right, and the Pharisees sadly in the wrong. They gave the impression that the Pharisees regarded Jesus as a charismatic but misguided leader, who certainly had great power over people, but whose influence was a major threat to the beliefs and practices which they cherished and regarded as fundamental. A very great deal of scholarship down the ages in the Christian church has assumed this to be the case. But is it true? It is surely insulting blithely to assume that all members of this venerated sect of scholarly people were violently jealous hypocrites.

Both Jesus and the Pharisees possessed intense religious convictions, and neither side was apparently prepared to compromise in any way. Yet, if they were both devout servants of the same God, and upholders of his will as revealed through the Law, how was it that they were 'enemies' and not allies in the battle against sin and unbelief?

There is a real problem here. If we can assume that the character of Jesus was everything it was claimed to be by the Christian church, then the Pharisees ought to have had had *no reason whatsoever* for persecuting him. This is sometimes the first thing that strikes a Jew who opens the text. Jesus was so obviously such a good, devout and lovable person, with such a loyal and enthusiastic following – including a fair percentage of unlikely successful converts amongst such people as fishermen, tax-collectors and harlots! – that surely only very evil people with warped and insanely jealous minds would call for his death. Were those colourful and sometimes cantankerous scholars, who had given their lifetimes to the service of God, really no more than monsters?

Supposing his teachings differed from theirs? So what? No Pharisee would have been unduly alarmed by this. Anyone who studies the Pharisaic material of the time can see that there was plenty of room within the movement for a vast range of differences of opinion. Pharisaism positively thrived on argument and debate, and it was the various opinions of numerous rabbis that formed the basis of their later collections of teachings.

Debate was more important to them than dogmatism. Far from discouraging it, Pharisees were actually very wary of accepting the opinion of any one person, no matter how enlightened, to the exclusion of other opinions. No scholar could give the final word on any subject; to do this would be to invite the charge of tyranny – what Muslims call *tughyan*.

Pharisees positively welcomed discussion and the addition of new ideas. So Jesus would never have been condemned by them for attempting to widen peoples' interpretation of the Torah, or Jewish Law, as set down in the ancient scriptures.

He would have been condemned by the Pharisees only if he had been guilty of something quite different – either inciting the people to act *against* the Law, or teaching theological dogma contrary to what was accepted as axiomatic: that God was One, and that it was the duty of the believer to love him with all the heart, mind, soul and strength.

The revelation given throughout the Old Testament by the long line of prophets was quite specific: there was only one God, the Father, the Absolute, the Creator, the Compassionate, the Just.

Everything else in the universe was separate in essence and in kind from God alone. He was divine; everything else was non-divine, created. He was creative principle, everything else was a contingent thing: something which might never have existed, but did simply because the original mind willed it so. To elevate any other entity to the status of God was to commit the one unforgiveable sin: to fail to be aware of the nature and significance of God's uniqueness, a sin that was only unforgiveable because any human stuck in such blindness was completely impervious to the call of the divine Father. Even if such a call came, they would not recognize it; the seed would simply fall on stony ground and be wasted.

Throughout the Old Testament we have numerous examples of the struggle of the monotheistic prophets to resist the people's inclination to be superstitious, to worship nature-spirits, or the trinities associated with Baal-worship – trinities which usually provided a male fertilizing force (symbolized by water in some shape or form) with a virgin bride (often the earth, with a name etymologically derived from *mara*, the womb) and a dying and rising son (representing the eternal changing of the seasons).

Did the conflict between Jesus and the Pharisees really lie in their differing interpretations of the Law of God? Or does the previous sentence strike a worrying chord? It should. It is not adequate to defend trinitarian Christianity as it was defended in the Middle Ages, by claiming that the Devil had invented all the previous many trinitarian mystery cults in order to confuse and deceive the faithful!

The written Law consisted of the first five books of the Old Testament: Genesis, Exodus, Leviticus, Numbers and Deuteronomy. In addition to this, the Pharisees had created a vast series of supplementary rules known popularly as 'the Hedge'. Pharisees, as we shall see, were 'separated people'. They were very conscious of the presence of God in their lives, a consciousness Muslims would today refer to as *taqwa*. They had made a conscious decision to submit every aspect of their everyday lives to God. Every thought or action was to be, so far as possible, in accordance with the will of God, and their extra rules were intended to guide their every waking moment. Pharisaic scholars referred to this 'hedge' as 'the tradition of the elders', or the 'oral tradition'.

According to the Gospels, Jesus seems to have held different opinions from theirs on such issues as sabbath observance and ritual cleanliness, matters pertaining not to the written Law but to the

Hedge. Even if this was so, it should not have excited enormous animosity. Many people did not, or could not, adhere to the strict tradition of the elders. Very many religious people did not chose to be Pharisees. Why should they? A life of purity and separatism cannot be foisted on to anyone not accepting it with love in their heart. There cannot be compulsion in true religion (Surah 2.256).

Therefore, if Pharisaic vehemence against Jesus was genuine, it leads one to consider the possibility that maybe Jesus himself was actually reckoned to be *one of them*, in which case his actions might have been criticized for 'letting the side down'. If Jesus was *not* a Pharisee, and did not claim to be, then the grounds for much of the supposed criticism are cut away.

In any case, the actions and teachings of Jesus that were in opposition to those of the Pharisees were not of the sort that would lead them to conclude that he was a blasphemer, or that would make them wish to see him put to death. Blasphemy was a specific offence, consisting of the actual pronouncement of the *Shem Hamme-phorash*, the hidden name of God; even then, it only counted as a punishable offence after a warning of the consequence of uttering it was directly given (M. Sanh vii.5).

We have at least two statements that suggest Jesus' complete and loyal adherence to the Law, 'Think not that I have come to destroy the Law; I have not come to destroy, but to fulfil it' (Matt. 5.17), and 'Whoever relaxes one of the least of these commandments and teaches men so, shall be called least in the Kingdom of Heaven' (Matt. 5.19).

Jesus was welcomed into synagogues to speak, and addressed as 'Rabbi'. He collected about him and trained a school of disciples, although he was not noticeably interested in making them into the same kind of experts in the Torah as were the Pharisaic rabbis. Jesus was far more a preacher of the charismatic sort, one who had the gifts of a prophet, a figure similar to Elijah or Elisha – with whom he actually compared himself (Luke 4.26–30).

There is a striking similarity between Jesus and the Pharisees, for those who have eyes to see. It may well be that the relationship of his teaching to theirs is much closer than the Gospels in their present form would lead us to believe, and that shifts of application in oral transmission may have obscured the essentially Pharisaic character of his tradition.

New Testament hostility towards the Pharisees presents numerous problems. We are faced with several possibilities. The first is that Jesus genuinely did set out deliberately to oppose Pharisees. Perhaps he saw himself as the champion of the *Amme ha-Aretz*, the 'people of the land', who found the regulations of separation imposed by the Pharisees to be oppressive, and not demanded by God. If he did, he would have been a people's hero, and the Pharisees might well have regarded him as a danger – a serious rival from the ranks of a class of people they were said to despise for their lack of concern for 'the things of God'. The theory is that the scholarly élite would not have taken seriously a person from this class who stood up and proclaimed himself as a champion of God. However, this is much too simplistic. There is one outstanding near-contemporary of just such a man who became the leading Pharisee: the great Rabbi Akiha, who was originally an illiterate shepherd.

Also, since indifference to the tradition was the hallmark of the *Amme ha-Aretz*, the notion of Jesus as their champion does not entirely ring true. Jesus obviously took the Law as the Pharisees understood it very seriously indeed, and on no occasion treated it with contempt.

A second theory is that Jesus' movement must have been originally connected closely with that of John the Baptist. It is implied in Mark 2.18–22 that he broke with John over the latter's strictness of Pharisaic ceremonial observance, which was a hindrance to his policy of going out to the common people. John's disciples and those of the Pharisees practised fasting, but on at least one occasion when a fast was obviously expected, Jesus' disciples did not fast, and were criticized for it. (Mark 2.18–22). Jesus replied to the criticism by comparing his movement to the ferment of new wine that would burst old wineskins that had already been stretched to capacity.

A third possibility is that by the time the Gospels were written, the church had become anti-Jewish in sympathy, and had begun actively to oppose the leaders of Rabbinic Judaism. This may have led the Gospel authors, writing some decades after the actual events, to read back into the time of Jesus a later hostility and ill-informed antagonism towards the Pharisees he actually knew. In other words, the Pharisees may not have been nearly so far separated from his ideals and teachings as the Gospel writers of those later decades would have us think. A subtle motivation behind the wording of the texts might have crept in.

A fourth, and most interesting possibility, is that Jesus was criticizing the Pharisees from within. The teaching of Jesus is basically Pharisaic in tone and outlook, usually following the school of the Rabbi Hillel. Perhaps Jesus had been a Pharisee, but had broken with them because of his attitude towards the non-Pharisaic population. One could argue that Jesus' supposed predilection for countering what are presented as Pharisaic excesses actually stems from a Pharisaic base, since anyone who was not a Pharisee would not have been concerned with the minutiae or the legal aspects raised.

Who were the Pharisees?

Many people assume that the Pharisees were the direct predecessors of the rabbis, and that the two groups can be more or less safely identified. The evidence leading to this conclusion, however, is by no means simple or direct. It just so happens that 'Pharisees' are attacked in the rabbinic sources as vigorously as they are attacked in the Gospels, and often for similar reasons.

One major problem is raised by the language of the various source-materials. The Greek sources – mainly the works of the Jewish historian Josephus, and the New Testament – refer to *Pharisaioi*, whereas the Semitic ones, the rabbinic writings, use the word *Perushim*. *Perushim* or 'separated ones', was the term often used to signify 'heretics' or 'extremists' (cf. Sotah 15.11; Baba Bathra 60b; Pesahim 70b; Berakoth 3.25; Sotah 22b). It was not a complimentary title at all, but one that implied bigotry and fanaticism.

When one examines the evidence, such as it is, it seems that the *Pharisaioi* of Josephus and the rabbinic *Perushim* differ so radically that one should certainly question whether these references are really to persons of the same group, or whether the word *Perushim* might not have indicated a party at all, but only a certain type of individual.

It is an awkward fact for those who wish to identify Tannaitic rabbis with the Pharisees/*Perushim* that the rabbis themselves scarcely ever referred to their predecessors by this name. They certainly regarded themselves as 'separated' from the ranks of the wicked, in that they had submitted totally to God, but they much preferred to use the expression '*Hakamim*', or 'Wise Ones', of their forebears. The word *Perushim* indicated that an individual was a separatist from themselves, a dissenter or extremist.

In one passage, the rabbis actually accused the *Christians* who were still included within the fringes of Judaism of being *Perushim*. They were cursed in the so-called Eighteen Benedictions of Samuel Hakaton, composed some time after 70 CE (Berakoth 3.25). In another passage (Tos. Berakoth 2.4) the Jewish-Christians, or *Minim*, are the 'wicked' – suggesting a thought-link between the three words wicked, *Minim* (Christian) and *Perushim* (extremist). A passage attributed to the great Rabbi Joshua lists seven types of *Perushim*, all bad except one (Sotah 22b; 3.4).

So perhaps the *Pharisaioi* whom Josephus so obviously admired should really be identified with the rabbinic *Hakamim*, and the term *Perushim* should be relegated to those whose fanatical intolerance had caused them to offend and be strongly criticized by that body of élite sages. If this were so, it would offer one very strong explanation as to why the rabbis at that later stage did not choose to call themselves Pharisees, and reveals the possibility that the *Hakamim* and Jesus were both critical towards the same type.

However, we must note that the term *Perushim* was sometimes applied to the *Hakamim*, usually by their opponents. The Sadducees apparently often referred to them as such (P. Yoma 1.5f; Tos. Yoma 1.8 B. Yoma 19b; Tos. Yod 2.20; Baba Bathra 115b; Tos. Hag 3.35; P. Hag 3.8).

There is one particular passage that occurs both in Josephus and in a Rabbinic source, an account of King Jannaeus giving advice to his wife Alexandra Salome from his deathbed. Here, Josephus refers to *Pharisaioi* and B. Sotah 22 a-b refers to *Perushim*, and the two are quite clearly equivalent. What is extremely interesting, in the light of what will be said later, is that the danger Jannaeus was warning Salome of was specifically that of the *hypocrisy* of her opponents, who gave the outward appearance of virtue while acting wickedly.

Since there is no uniform use of the word *Perushim* in the rabbinic sources, it probably should not be translated uniformly, or automatically taken to refer to the predecessors of the rabbis. *Perushim* were probably originally an identifiable group of Pharisaic extremists, later a type.

Hakamim, *Perushim* and Jesus; how are we to compare them, or their attitude to the Law? Here's an example. The *Hakamim* taught that for God to grant forgiveness to an individual, the Torah must be *intended to be kept*, even if the individual found it impossible to keep in actual fact. As long as the intention, or *niyyah*, was there, God would understand and forgive. The *Perushim*, those 'hard-liners' of piety, insisted that every detail *must* be kept, particularly since the oral tradition had made such details intelligible and possible. Jesus extended the principle of the *Hakamim*, and taught that God would forgive, even when the detailed conditions of the covenant promises had *not* been kept, even when no attempt at all had been made to implement what God had commanded in Torah, so long as there was belief and repentance. This notion was certainly preserved in the teachings of St Paul. It seems to have been an extreme deduction from the Hillelite tendency (the school to which St Paul belonged), and in this sense Jesus could himself have been called *parush* or extremist.

Most scholars accept that Mark's Gospel was the first to have been written, probably between the years 64–73 CE. In this Gospel, the Pharisaic practices described seem far too extreme to apply to the majority of *Hakamim* of this time, but they might not have been unlikely for certain extremist *Perushim*.

In the Gospels we do see evidence of an attack on extremism, occasions where Pharisaic attention to the minutiae of the tradition were pressed home to such an extent that they actually defeated the spirit of the Torah. In Mark 2.16 ('Why does he eat with tax-collectors and sinners?') they take a more extreme view of the *Amme ha-Aretz* than did even the Shammaites, the most 'severe' of Pharisaic schools. In Mark 2.18 their extreme asceticism is condemned, and in Mark 2.24 and 3.1f. their over-vigorous attitude to the sabbath is rejected. In Mark 7.3, 5 an extreme point of view is mentioned on the practice of hand-washing. The *Hakamim* certainly accepted the principle of this washing as an intention of holiness. The exact extent of it was one of the topics under discussion in that very period, as we shall see.

Many Christians take it for granted that the malice of the Pharisees lay behind the arrest and trials of Jesus. In fact, rather surprisingly, the *Perushim* do not figure in the accounts at all. This may be due to the fact that they did not hold official positions, or that their numbers may have been far too small for them to have any effective role. However, they may very well have been those extremists who had used devious means to alert the authorities to the dangers implicit in Jesus' position. Christians should rethink their attitude, since it is entirely possible that the *Hakamim* had nothing at all to do with setting Jesus' trials in motion. The investigation was carried out by the chief priests and the scribes (Mark 8.3; 10.32; 14.1). The Pharisees/*Hakamim* should probably be exonerated.

During those trials, the religious authorities strongly rejected the destructive implications of Jesus' apparent way of by-passing Torah. The deliberate silence of Jesus, and his refusal to participate in the proceedings by offering any sort of defence, might well have been interpreted as a defiance for which he could legally have been condemned as a 'rebellious elder', a term applied to any sane and competent person who refused to accept the judgment of the highest court, and who thereby brought upon himself the death penalty for his own recalcitrance.

Unlike Christian scholarship, the consensus of erudite Jewish opinion has laid stress on the possibility that the extremist *Perushim* were *not* to be taken as typical Pharisees. To them, the Pharisees were a group who accepted the Torah as the binding word of God, who had dedicated themselves to a lifetime of submission to God in accordance with God's wishes as expressed in it. Pharisees considered that existence had meaning only if it provided the opportunity to serve God by total submission to him. This submission was not to be limited to worship of holy days, or the reading and studying of scriptures, but had to be carried over into every minute of one's waking life, and be intimately concerned with every action. At every moment of the day the Pharisees were engaged in a contemplation of what was the right thing to do to serve God properly.

They possessed a reputation for their piety and wisdom, and also for their tolerance and love. They were involved in the interpretation of civil and criminal law as well as religious practices, and were well-known for their self-restraint, their unwillingness to impose heavy punishments for crime, and their general humanity. They were regarded as being mild and temperate to their opponents.

They despised people who had accumulated great wealth, particularly the Sadducaic hierarchy amongst the priests. They themselves lived simple lives. They were sometimes fiery, but had an affectionate disposition towards each other. They were generally very understanding of the difficulties faced by people who were struggling to keep the Law according to their abilities, and gave people credit for their good intentions even if their practice fell short of the ideal. The historian Josephus, who had himself been a Pharisee for a time, was full of admiration for their virtues and the conduct of their lives.

Despite hints in the New Testament of their vainglory and greed, the controversies between the Pharisees and their opponents mentioned in the rabbinic literature reveal that *not one* was based on a desire for self-advancement or an interest in wealth or power. The things they were concerned about were the correct performance of rituals, and the care to differentiate between what things were clean and what unclean (and therefore to be scrupulously avoided).

The main charge laid against the Pharisees by the Christian Gospels seems to have been that they were hypocrites. In several places, notably Matt. 23, we have the uncompromising expression 'scribes and Pharisees, hypocrites!' The *Oxford English Dictionary still* gives the definition of a Pharisee as a 'self-righteous person, a formalist, a hypocrite'. To what extent the sect as a whole could be regarded as an organization of hypocrites is one of the problems we shall attend to shortly.

Did Jesus really mount a frontal attack on the movement as a whole, or was he referring to a certain type of person who approached religion in a particular way; or even to certain specific individuals within a movement? Could he, indeed, have been thinking of particular Pharisees of note and influence in the school of Shammai – or maybe some with whom he was most intimately in contact, the Pharisees of Nazareth or Capernaum and Bethsaida? Or, on the other hand, considering the work done by form critics, should we ask whether it is likely that the views expressed in the Gospels were really those of Jesus at all? Could they not have been instead the attitude of the Christian church as it developed in its two main directions?

First, there was the community of faithful Jews who had accepted Jesus as Messiah of Israel, but who drew the line at certain beliefs they regarded as innovative, and ignorant of the facts of Christ's true manhood. Secondly, there were the views of the rapidly spreading Gentile trinitarian-Christian community that had decided to dispose altogether with the Judaistic framework, and interpreted the significance of Christ along the lines of the common 'saviour' cults.

Gentile Christian groups had an increasing awareness of the
rabbis after the débacle at Jerusalem eliminated the Temple
priesthood and dispersed eminent scholars to other countries; but at
the same time there was probably an increasing ignorance of what
the practices of Pharisaism of the time of Jesus had actually been, or
what the relevance was of their sectarian arguments to the Christian
world. The doctrines of Pharisaism attained much greater clarity
and currency during the transitional period between 70–100 CE,
when the Pharisaic party was emerging triumphant at the council
held at Yabneh to reorganize Judaism after the fall of Jerusalem. In
this same period, controversies between Pharisees and the sect of
Nazarene Christians were of immediate concern. In short, Christianity and Pharisaism were really emerging side by side as two rival
faiths in the same period.

As the Gentile trinitarian church grew, the Jewish–Christian
church, under the leadership of surviving relatives of Jesus, suffered
a decline. This was partly because it clung to the Jewish interpretations of the Law and its practices, and still considered it necessary
for a person to become a Jew before becoming a Christian, but
mainly because Jewish Christians refused to accept the divinity of
Jesus in the trinitarian sense, and insisted that his birth and early
manhood were quite normal, and that he was 'elected' or 'adopted'
by God as his Messiah-Son on the occasion of his baptism – an
interpretation that obviously rendered the trinitarian doctrines of
the Incarnation and the atonement for original sin as the only means
of human salvation untenable.

The whole business of the sectarian beliefs that divided the early
church is still subject to a great deal of confusion in the absence of
adequate records, but we know that the Jewish-Christian groups
who *were* the original church gradually found themselves outnumbered, and were eventually marked off as heretical. With the
tremendous and influential expansion of the church in the West,
they lost their position of importance. By the second century they
were being castigated for their 'poor' beliefs about Jesus, and the
use of the word 'poor' in the derogatory sense has suggested at least
one of the meanings of the word 'Ebionite' (the name of a major
Jewish-Christian group).

It is for scholars to pick a careful way between Pharisees,
Essenes, Zealots, Ebionites, Nazarenes, and so forth. In doing so,
they may find that the Pharisees were not by any means the black

villains they have been painted. They may find that the theology and the way of life taught by the Pharisees then (as the heirs and successors of a whole long line of prophetic revelation) was actually that taught by Jesus himself. They may even, on the way, pause and consider whether the church as we now have it bears any relationship whatsoever to the church founded by the close friends and family of Jesus himself.

They may, in the end, discover that in the sixth century CE the same beliefs and way of life were revealed yet again, to yet another prophet: the Arabian Muhammad, who was chosen for a ministry intended to set the seal on all the revelations of God that had gone before, and specifically to put right the 'error' of worshipping a Trinity, into which so many well-meaning Christians had fallen.

In short, they may discover what Muslims actually mean when they claim, and firmly believe with no hesitation, that Jesus and all the prophets before him were *Muslim*.

2 · Where Did the Pharisees Come From?

'To God Alone I submit, and to Him I return' (surah 2.156)

Every act, every moment, every smallest detail of the Pharisaic day was spent in submission to the will of God, in conscious separation from the normal secular life of people who had not chosen to submit in this way. The very name 'Pharisee' refers specifically to this policy of *separation*. It was a deliberate choice, and it was a way of life chosen with love.

First, the Pharisees desired to cut themselves off from the Gentile world, and the Hellenizing Jews who had accommodated themselves to it. Secondly, once the successors of those priestly-military leaders who arose out of the nationalistic fervour of the Maccabean Revolt turned their attention away from religious to specifically nationalistic policies, the Pharisees remained single-hearted and disapproved of this new departure and all who tolerated it. Nationalism was not their cause, but a life dedicated to God – so they separated from the nationalists. Thirdly, they also sought to be differentiated from their opponents the Sadducees, especially during the reign of Hyrcanus – and this feature was still prominent in the time of Jesus.

Their prime aim, however, was the desire not to be contaminated or made impure by 'the world', and therefore they adhered to strict rules of life that literally cut them off from Jews less pious than themselves, who were either not able or not prepared to follow their rigid standards.

The history of Pharisaic separatism seems to have begun as early as the time of Ezra the Scribe, when the leading Jews were in exile in Babylon. Here, Ezra had realized that if the Jews were to retain their identity as a nation, a 'chosen race', and not become integrated and therefore lost amongst the people with whom they had found new homes, then a 'barrier' would have to be created to protect Jew from Gentile. It was not a forced matter. Anyone was at liberty to choose what they would do. They could either forsake their Jewish identity by intermarrying with Babylonians, or they could make their conscious decision to stay separate. It was up to them – there was no compulsion.

For some people, who had married and had children in exile, it did involve hardship, for if they wished to remain 'pure', then they had to divorce these foreign wives.

The Torah, for these people, was the supreme guide to life. However, it was of very limited usefulness if it was not fully understood, and therefore people qualified to interpret it were of prime importance if the will of God was to be communicated to the masses. Thus there arose an elite class of priestly 'guiders', the *Sopherim*, or scribes. These were a special category of scholar whose duty it was to search out the full meaning of the Torah in all its richness, and to expound it. It was from this activity that the word *midrashim* arose (*darash*, to seek; *midrashim*, the interpretations sought out). The *Sopherim* were thought to have formed what became known as the Great Synagogue, composed of such eminent persons as Simeon the Just, who died in c.270 BCE, and who was regarded as one of its greatest scholars.

During the third century BCE, the age-old conflict between the prophetic and priestly modes of devotion to Yahweh (the Hebrew name for God) began to come to a head. It seems almost inevitable that religious persons fall into two major types: those who favour the *right performance* of special ritual to procure a communication from the Divine Entity, and those who put their faith in *mystical experience* to achieve the same end.

Certain people have always had what one might call a talent for realizing the Divine Presence. This could manifest itself in numerous ways, from the dramatic awareness of a voice or 'presence', or a vision, to the 'simple' ability of being able to detect guidance in one's daily life. Occasionally these 'psychic' gifts extended as far as precognition of future events, resulting in the tendency to interfere with politics, as is said to have happened in the case of prophets such as Elisha. Along with these phenomena came the whole plethora of the allied psychic repertoire:

telepathy, psychokinesis, healing, exorcism, levitation, out-of-the-body experiences.

It is obvious that this kind of 'talent' is not shared or desired by everybody. Some regard such things with enormous distaste – usually people who have not had their lives disturbed by unlooked-for outbreaks of these phenomena. Although the experiences can certainly be faked, they cannot be 'learned', or bought. Of the entire priestly class – many of whom would doubtless have enjoyed the prestige such talents bestowed – only a few were credited with being 'prophets' (in the sense of 'fore-tellers') as well. A notable example was the famous priest Samuel, successor to Eli of Shiloh. It was far more common for priests and prophets to enjoy a hearty contempt for each other.

Priestly awareness of the presence of God tended to follow very different lines from that of the prophets. Priests were rightly suspicious of the fringe members of the prophetic movement, and had a dislike for charismatic excesses. Certain forms of prophetic behaviour were closely akin to frenzy and madness, and in primitive days a lunatic was often thought of as a person of whom some occult force had taken possession – not necessarily a good one! (One word for such a 'holy man' was *makhutash*; a lunatic was *makhush*!)

Nevertheless, the priestly rituals were for a specific purpose: to discover the real existence of God and find out his directives for themselves, the nation, or the individual. Sacrifices were intended to please or placate him. The use of sacred lots, the Urim and Thummim, were intended literally to give in advance the outcome of a battle or guide a specific course of action (I Sam. 14.3; 23.6,9; 30.7–8; etc.).

The priests *expected an answer*. If no answer was forthcoming, there was a specific reason why not. For example, the story goes that when the Israelites had not been able to get answers concerning the capture of Ai (during the bloodthirsty conquest of Canaan after the Hebrew escape from Egypt) it was soon discovered by use of the sacred lots that the fault lay with a certain Achan, who had not devoted his spoils to Yahweh honestly, but had tried to keep them for himself (Josh. 7.1–26). Once his misdemeanour was put right, the answers – and success – followed. During the regime of Samuel, scarcely a move was taken without consulting divine guidance first. It was specifically because Saul, the first king, acted impatiently and without the usual consultation that Samuel rejected him and anointed David to replace him.

Naturally enough, one could never say with absolute certainty that what actually lay behind the phenomena, whether the inspiration of the prophet or the entity communicating through the ritual of the priest, was truly God. It might not have been. The only possible way of judging must have been that suggested later by Jesus himself: you know the character of any person or entity 'by its fruits'. Those bringing forth good must of necessity be good, and vice versa.

Nevertheless, the priests guarded their prerogatives very jealously, and insisted that they *did* know what entity it was that inhabited their sanctuary. And this specific function of a priest was passed down by training from father to son, within the tribe of Levi.

However, many influential Jewish laymen began to be extremely well-versed in the knowledge of the Torah, and there were those who considered – with justification – that perhaps some of their better brains knew a great deal more about it than many of their priestly rivals! To be a priest did not automatically indicate ownership of a first-class brain: you got what you were born with. Many priests were simple souls, and some doubtless found it a struggle to grasp the minutiae of the Law. It was perfectly conceivable that brilliant members of non-priestly families should begin to resent the privileges and authority of the priests as interpreters of God's Law, when they knew they were better qualified to expound it themselves. In an argument between a brilliant lay-scholar and a mediocre priest, there would be little doubt as to who would 'win'; yet the priest could still pull rank, and draw the bulwarks of the movement around him.

Lay scholars inevitably expounded the texts that they could use to justify their own position as valid interpreters of the Law. For example, did not Exodus 19.6 state that Israel was to be 'a kingdom of priests and a holy nation'? That did not imply a limitation of the priesthood to a certain family alone. Rather, it suggested that it was the duty of *every* member of Israel to live a life of priestly service and dedication to God. Again, Deuteronomy 33.4 suggested that the Torah given to Moses was intended to be the inheritance of the entire congregation of Israel, and not just the exclusive possession of one privileged class. Numbers 16.3 declared that 'all the congregation are holy, every one of them, and the Lord is among them'. Such texts as these were used as the basis of the Pharisaic movement, which sought to enrol all Israel as 'priests' devoted to Yahweh. In short, there was fundamental objection to the limitation of the priesthood as the sole authoritative interpreters and official administrators of the Torah.

This Pharisaic attitude came to fruition with the new revelation given to Muhammad, in the sixth century CE, when all who were called to dedicate their lives anew in complete submission to God did so on the basis of *their own priesthood*. There were certainly individuals who by merit of the quality of their lives, and the efforts of their study, might be recognized by those who knew them as people fit to lead the congregation in prayer, or to discuss their knowledge with others, but all Muslims were equal in the sight of God, all 'chosen', all 'set apart', all totally dedicated to a life of submission to God, using such talents as God had given them.

No person was to be considered a better or worse Muslim on the basis of brain, intelligence, family background, rank, and so forth. These were matters decided by God even before the person's birth, and no person could claim to be more than the recipient of whatever qualities God had chosen to impart to them, for their lifetime. It had nothing to do with the choice of the individual; God bestowed riches or poverty, beauty or ugliness, intelligence or dullness, strength or weakness, as God willed.

What mattered was how individuals, as their own priests before God, reacted to each test with which they were confronted, and how they used whatever was given to them. In the language of schoolteachers, the important part of the assessment report was not the column for academic ability, but the one taking account of the effort put in. On *that* would come the judgment.

The true Jew, like the true Muslim (for they *were Muslim*) believed that it was not for a priest to rule, nor even for a king. The only acceptable ruler was God. God alone gave instructions through the Torah. Hence, if the Torah was to rule, then it was knowledge of it and expertise in it, and not inherited family privilege, that should qualify a person for participation in the government and guidance of the community.

And so the pious Jewish lay scholars deduced that the priests had never been intended to enjoy any special dispensation or privilege for ever. Certainly in ancient times they had been given the right to speak for Yahweh, since at that stage they alone knew the Law and had studied it. But now that situation no longer applied, so there was no reason why their position of privilege should not be extended to any other person who happened to have adequate knowledge.

In about 196 BCE, tradition has it that the new Sanhedrin, the Gerousia, was established. To the great satisfaction of the lay-scholars, they won the concession they sought. The Gerousia was an assembly composed of 'men of understanding from Aaron' (the priests) and *Hakamim* or 'wise teachers from Israel'. The authority of these sages was at last accepted and recognized.

The Sanhedrin was led by 'Zugoth' or 'Pairs' of eminent scholars, one of whom would be the Nasi, or President, and the other the Ab-Beth-Din, or Vice-president. The first of these leaders were Jose ben Joezer of Zeredah and Jose ben Johanan of Jerusalem. Ben Johanan did not last long; he was an uncle of the renegade priest Alcimus, and was actually murdered by him along with fifty-nine other eminent persons in c.162 BCE.

In the period between 196 and the Maccabean Revolt in 165, the Sanhedrin threw itself into earnest inquiry as to the correct interpretations of the Torah. It was realized, of course, that the simple commands as they had been given to Moses were no longer sufficiently comprehensive to deal with their present situation. Even the later régimes laid down by Ezra no longer sufficed, since conditions were now very different.

Basically, the debate centred on whether or not one should ground one's submission to God on the strict *letter* of the Law, or the *spirit* of it. A simple example of how the letter of the Law could be interpreted in direct opposition to the spirit of it can easily be given in terms of a person's will. Suppose a man has two sons and two brothers, and £1,000 to leave between them. He might decide to leave £400 to each of his sons, and the remainder to be divided amongst his brothers: £100 each. But, if by the time of his death, his amount of money had increased to £5,000 for some reason, yet he died without altering his will, his sons would still only receive their £400, but the brothers would now have £4,200 to divide between them. Obviously, this would not have been the original intention of the will – the *spirit* of the will was to leave the bulk of the inheritance to the sons, not the brothers.

Thus the interpreters were able to show how those who clung too rigidly to the 'words of God' could actually end up doing the very opposite of God's intended will.

The same kind of principle applies to this day in Muslim considerations when trying to deduce the will of God in any given situation. Muslims believe that the world has seen countless societies that have made attempts to establish justice and fair living without recourse to divine law, and without God's help – and that none of these attempts have worked.

True justice can never come about – as the Pharisees certainly agreed – until not only individuals, but the whole of society, follow the will of God. Muslims, however, do not believe that people trying to live submitted lives should shut themselves off from the world; that is regarded as a form of selfishness. They are to live within the community, with all its problems and irritations, and try to make it a better place. They must find the *shari'ah*, which means the 'path', and follow it.

> The basis of Shari'ah is wisdom, and the welfare of people in this world as well as the Hereafter. This welfare lies in complete justice, mercy, care and wisdom. Anything that departs from justice to oppression, from mercy to harshness, from caring to misery, and from wisdom to folly, has nothing to do with the Shari'ah (Ibn Qayyim).

The same problems faced the Pharisees. How can any law laid down in centuries past meet the complex demands of another time and place, another culture? How can a person know whether any 'modern' course of action or detail of everyday life is right or wrong? Why should any person in fact bother to look for guidance outside the human level? And why should God, if there is one, condescend to bother with such trivial matters? No Pharisee, or Muslim, would think like this. For any person submitted to God, the idea of a society without God is nonsense; the Compassionate One *cannot* be unconcerned, uncaring, or unable to help humans in the task of living their lives for their maximum happiness and benefit.

Working out the principles in Islam is called *ijtihad*; it means using reason and judgment to decide on a course of action most in keeping with the spirit of the Law. Decisions made in this way are called *ijma*, but they are never regarded as totally binding, since they are based on human opinions deduced from the God-given Law. They can be accepted as guidelines, but it is possible to replace them by others. In this way fresh thinking can always be brought to bear on past decisions, and so keep pace with the ever-changing world. In making decisions, account always had to be taken of the opinions of the respected and learned scholars and holy ones, previously accepted decisions, the concern for the public good, justice, and the willingness of the masses to accept the decision. In Islam, the technique for working out *ijma* is known as *fiqh*, from the word for 'intelligence' or 'knowledge'.

Pharisaic principles followed very much the same lines. However, the Pharisees' attempts to solve the problems of interpreting the Law brought out very sharp divisions amongst them, and the contrasts of tendencies and outlooks became gradually more pronounced.

After the Maccabean revolt, these conflicts were brought to a head when the loyalty of the Jews to the Law of their forefathers became literally a matter of life or death to them.

The defenders of the Torah gradually crystallized into two parties, one 'extreme' and the other 'moderate'. The extremists gave themselves the name of Hasidim. The moderates, who formed the greater majority, had no distinctive name, but found that they were often at loggerheads with the sometimes fanatical views of the extremists. The Hasidim had no real interest in the political aims of the revolt, except in so far as it fulfilled their desire to be allowed to practise the Torah unhindered.

Once this freedom had been achieved, they were eager to bargain for peace and return to 'normal' living. However, the revolt had thrown up a family of leaders, the priestly family of Mattathias of Modin, later known as the Maccabees, and it became their ambition to win political independence as well as to restore the rights to freedom of worship. Under Simeon (142–135 BCE) this aim was achieved, and although he was never crowned as a king, he was certainly king in all but name. His son John Hyrcanus (135–105 BCE) also never took the title of king, but issued coins bearing his name, the usual prerogative of a kingly ruler.

The new political nobility had no wish to have its freedom restricted by the Hasidic interpretations of the Torah, which entered into every aspect of everyday existence. They resisted the claims that the Torah should be extended beyond its written word in order to find its spirit, and in Hyrcanus' reign the non-priestly teachers were actually banned from the Sanhedrin, branded as a divisive influence.

They became known as 'Separatists'. This title may perhaps have originated as a taunt – the 'Expelled Ones'. Pharisees, however, saw it as a title of honour, and wore the 'badge' proudly. They congratulated themselves on being the truly pious few, with the correct attitude to the Law, and despised what they regarded as an illegitimate and political priesthood. The clan Joiarib, to which the Maccabees belonged, was not even mentioned in the list of those returning to Palestine in Nehemiah 10.3–9, and only appeared in a subordinate position in Nehemiah 12.1–7, 12–21. In I Chronicles 24.7, however, it had been elevated to first place – but then, this passage was probably compiled in the Maccabean period! So, they decided for their part deliberately to stand aloof from all those who 'compromised' and would not follow in their way.

The challenge went out for all individuals to decide exactly where they stood over commitment to the Law. All those who pledged themselves to submission, in total ritual cleanliness, became *Perushim* – separated by choice from those who did not. The movement was officially launched when all *Perushim* made a voluntary pledge to separate their tithes in accordance with the Torah. Those Jews who would not or could not sign themselves to this pledge were automatically classed as *Amme ha-Aretz* – commoners, or 'people of the land' – and treated with either pity or contempt, according to the circumstances which had led to their denial of the pledge.

So, all who had 'cut themselves off' from normal living and became especially dedicated to submission to the minutiae of ritual cleanliness were *Perushim*, or Pharisees. The priests were also within the fold of those separated off, since of necessity they accepted the tithe. The grades of strictness were quaintly defined as: ordinary Pharisee, those entitled to consume the Terumah or tithe-offerings, the 'eaters of what is sacred' and those who 'used the water of the sin-offering'. Hence, all priests, Levites, Sadducees and Pharisees were 'separated' and lived in ritual purity, all Sadducees being *Perushim* but not all Pharisees being Sadducees, as those were followers of particular doctrines. It tended to be only the rich high-priestly families that were Sadducees. The priests, the hereditary caste, were all forbidden to own land, and lived on tithes. They had no teaching role, nor power to pronounce on matters of doctrine or practice – that became the province of the wise man, or rabbi. So it can be seen that although there was conflict between

Pharisee and Sadducee, because of their specific beliefs, there was no conflict between rabbi and priest.

John Hyrcanus himself seems to have had Pharisaic sympathies, which caused much annoyance to the priests who were Sadducees. However, his son, the ruthless Alexander Jannaeus, began to persecute the Pharisees, and during his reign many of them fled the country. On one occasion some 800 Pharisees were crucified, and Jannaeus ordered that the throats of their wives and children should be cut before their eyes, as they hung on their crosses. Fortunately his wife Alexandra Salome, who took the throne on Jannaeus's death, was a sympathizer and during her reign the Pharisees poured back into the country or emerged from hiding, and instantly began to make their presence felt in high places. The Sanhedrin was given a large injection of Pharisaic members, and the exclusive jurisdiction of the Sadducees in criminal and civil law came to an end. Pharisaic principles began not just to filter through but to flood in. Even the Temple ritual was subjected to their scrutiny, and the Saducean high priests suffered the indignity of being compelled to carry out the Pharisaic amendments – all intended to make the concept of God less anthropomorphic, and more symbolic and spiritual.

The Pharisees, of course, insisted that these were not innovations, but the proper and correct ritual based on the close study of the Law. The Jewish historian Flavius Josephus commented that

> practically nothing was done by the Sadducees; for whenever they attain office, they follow – albeit unwillingly and of compulsion – what the Pharisees say, because otherwise they would not be endured by the people (Antiquities 18.1,4).

It was during Salome's reign that Herod the Great was born, in Nabataea, and Roman power in the East really began to make its presence felt. When Herod took the throne, relations between the hierarchy and the Pharisees became very strained, but Herod – who was basically a pious man – seemed to avoid outright defiance of them. He deferred to their views when rebuilding the Temple, training thousands of priests to act as labourers and stonemasons, so that no ritually unclean feet ever soiled the sacred precincts. He avoided putting his image on coins, unlike his predecessors and successors, and the Romans. The Pharisees, for their part, would not give in an inch to him!

Herod's conflicts with the Pharisees began in his youth. On one occasion during his rise to power Herod had been put on trial for his high-handed conduct in executing an important Zealot rebel and his followers. The Pharisees had expected to subdue Herod, but his powerful presence, not to mention his military escort, cowed the Sanhedrin and turned the tables. All were terrified to speak out against him – except one man, the Pharisee Samaias. Samaias stood up and faced Herod, condemning him in a speech that he must have believed would have signed his own death-warrant. Herod, however, admired honesty and courage, and Samaias lived to tell the tale. Years later, when Herod became king, he executed the entire offending Sanhedrin, sparing only his brave enemy, the fiery Samaias.

Many Pharisees refused to take the oath of allegiance to Herod, but instead of punishing them he fined them, turning a blind eye while the fines were paid by one of their supporters – one of his own sisters-in-law! However, the Pharisees never appreciated his tolerance. Even as he lay on his deathbed, a gang of hotheads pulled down an imperial eagle Herod had just erected over a Temple gateway. Herod was not so merciful this time: he had them all arrested and burned to death, a particularly terrible penalty since they believed that the condition of the human corpse at the moment of death affected their chances of resurrection.

Yet fanaticism was not the usual practice of the Pharisees by any means. The real extremists believed that the Pharisees had gone soft, that they no longer represented the old spirit of defiance against the secular world. Such extremists formed the 'new' parties – the Essenes and the Zealots. Even during the revolt against Rome in 70 CE, the Pharisees did not join the extremists, but attempted to placate and conciliate. (A notable, but very late exception, was the patriotic Rabbi Akiba at the time of Bar Kokhba's revolt in 132 CE.)

After the dust of 70 CE settled, of all the sects and rival holy men only the Pharisees survived. They not only survived, but gained enormous strength and throve. The Judaism that gradually emerged and became a strong world faith was essentially Pharisaism.

3 · Why Were the Pharisees Opposed to the Sadducees?

If you were none the wiser, you would get the impression from a casual reading of the Gospels that the Pharisees and Sadducees were the best of friends (Matt. 3.7; 16.1, 6, 11, etc.). However, in spite of this rather extraordinary juxtaposition of the two parties almost hand in hand in the Gospels, they were actually engaged in quite vehement and fundamental opposition to each other, and were often enemies.

For a start, whereas the Pharisees were a movement of pious and scholarly laymen, the Sadducees were a priestly caste, a 'family', claiming descent from Zadok the Righteous, the high priest elected by King David.

The third and second centuries BCE had seen a prolonged struggle between two completely different concepts of religion, two quite opposite views of its aim and purpose. This was by no means a new struggle, but one that had been the basis of antagonism between priest and prophet since the very earliest of times.

How does one define a holy man? Is it a person who gives up his whole life to the meticulous service of a shrine, who divides his day up by prayer and ritual, and whose two major functions are to intercede for the masses who do not know how to pray for themselves, and to impart knowledge of God to them in return? This role of mediator, or heavenly go-between, is obviously one of enormous responsibility and requires personnel of a particular calibre of devotion and tireless compassion. If a religious official had simply been thrust into the job by accident of birth, and had no compassion towards those for whom he interceded, and no awareness of the Merciful Being who heard him, it is patently obvious that a shallow ritualism would ensue.

Or is the holy man the person from *any* walk of life who has been illumined by awareness of the presence of the Divine Being? Surely God, by the very fact that God does permit self-revelations to be made to individuals according to his will, is setting the seal of approval on the devout and mystical *layman*? This was the argument used by St Peter to justify the expansion of the Christian church beyond the limits of Judaism. The Jerusalem-Christian hierarchy had challenged him for admitting the household of the Gentile Cornelius (Acts 10). However, Peter pointed out that he had not been responsible for their conversion, but the Holy Spirit itself had poured out upon these people, showing that God was no discriminator of persons.

As the Qur'an states: 'God chooses for Himself whoever He pleases, and guides to Himself all those who turn to Him' (surah 42.13).

However, any talk of the gifts of the 'spirit' being granted to the 'masses' makes a ritual priest suspicious. The mystic, or prophet, or psychic, may *claim* marvellous things, but who is to say for certain that they might not simply have been deluded by the inner imaginings of their own minds? Worse, they might have been duped by the beguilements of something far less than God. It is patently obvious that enslavement to the fanaticism of a madman becomes a possibility all too real. (All too recently, a UK mass murderer heard voices 'from God' instructing him to go and cut the throats of prostitutes! How is a person to know the source of these voices? Jesus surely gave the clue – by their fruits shall ye know them!)

We see the dangers, and must take them into account, and we must be aware how difficult it has always been for the ordinary person with no enlightened experience of God other than his or her family faith to know which way to turn for guidance. One must serve God with all one's *mind* as well as heart. This difficulty is as apparent and divisive now as it was when the people witnessed the prophet Amos challenging the priest Amaziah head on (Amos 7.10–17). If we alter the picture of Jesus creating havoc in the Jerusalem Temple – the incident of the overturning of the money tables (Mark 11.15–19) – to that of a charismatic rebel carpenter with a mob-following physically attacking the premises of Canterbury Cathedral just before the Archbishop's Easter celebration, with whom would we have identified? The ecclesiatical hierarchy, or the enthusiastic reformers?

There would, however, probably have been little doubt which side the Pharisees would have been on! The discomfiture of the priesthood would have delighted them. At the time of Jesus the priesthood was in the grip of the Sadducees, the older, conservative, primitive party, formed largely from the Jerusalem hierarchy and various landed gentry from the country estates. After the death of Herod the Great they had become increasingly wealthy and corrupt. The Pharisees, on the other hand, were progressive liberals, not priests but laymen actively engaged in improving and spiritualizing the Temple worship.

As most Pharisees were generally reluctant to cause unnecessary turbulence, they would probably have disapproved of the violent manner in which Jesus and his followers made their point. Nevertheless, they were perfectly well-versed in the prophetic acted-parables of their forebears, and would have approved of the points that Jesus was attempting to make – to turn the holy precincts back from being a 'den of thieves' into a 'place of prayer'. It is noteworthy that following this dramatic incident, the Sadducaic party were quick to question Jesus' authority for acting in the way he did ('the chief priests and the elders and the scribes came to him and said: "By what authority are you doing these things?"'), whereas the Pharisees were more interested in knowing how far Jesus' challenge was prepared to go ('They sent to him some of the Pharisees and Herodians . . . "Is it lawful to pay tribute to Caesar or not?", Mark 11.27 – 12.17).

Although the Pharisees sought a more spiritual worship in the Temple, they did not go so far as to condemn the ritual practices as such. There was a sect even more extreme and more separated – the Essenes – who *did* take this step, and criticized the Pharisees for tolerating the Temple *status quo* whilst attempting to improve it from within. Essenes condemned the whole system outright, claiming it was not only corrupt but also illegal, and had withdrawn from it altogether in disgust and set up their own rival priesthood.

The Essenes were quite prepared to work actively for the destruction of the Temple, even identifying the Roman army later as the instrument of God in bringing about its downfall – but then, they were convinced that a new order and a new age were just about to dawn, in which a new priesthood consisting of themselves would reform the new and purified Israel. *They* were the righteous remnant spoken of by Isaiah, the ones who had remained true and would do so to the end (Isa. 10.20–22). It is a sad irony that the early Christians also regarded themselves as this righteous remnant, and very likely the Pharisees did too.

If the Christians had remained within Jewish orthodoxy, they might actually have emerged with the strongest case. As it happened, of course, few ordinary Gentile Christians within a hundred years of Christ's death had any deep knowledge of Judaic scholarship, and would probably not have understood the concept of true Israel. The Essenes seem to have aligned themselves at the last with the Zealot movement, and to have perished with it. The Pharisees, on the other hand, emerged virtually unscathed, convinced that their views had been vindicated by God, in the sight of the whole world. The Temple and its corrupt hierarchy had been destroyed, never to rise again, and spiritual Judaism was free to flourish and spread throughout the globe.

But *why* were the Pharisees so opposed to the Sadducean Temple hierarchy? What were their views that so uncompromisingly conflicted with each other? Both sects were composed of people who had devoted their lives to the service of God. The whole basis and ground of their disunity was one thing only, their concept of God as expressed in their attitude to the Torah. Both sides were at least in agreement that God did certainly exist, and that God's will had been made known through the sacred scriptures; but there the similarity ended.

The Sadducees revered the first five books of the Old Testament as priceless relics, the repository of rules by which an Israelite was obliged to live. They had a very keen respect for the powers of their God, and from their study of the scriptures they knew very well that it did not do to arouse God's anger. God had proved time and again throughout history that his wishes would be carried out, whether humanity agreed with them or not. It was futile for anyone to oppose God, or to attempt to thwart or hoodwink God. God knew a person's secret, innermost thoughts, and had the power to direct even foreign nations to bring about the state of affairs that he intended.

> God speaks to everyone . . . He speaks to the ears of the heart, but it is not every heart which hears Him. His voice is louder than the thunder, and His light is clearer than the sun – if only one could see and hear. In order to do that, one must remove this solid wall, this barrier – the Self (Mevlana Jalal ud-Din Rumi).

Three men cannot talk together in secret, but He is the fourth . . . Neither fewer than that or more, but He is with them, wherever they may be (surah 58.7).

Wherever two or three are gathered together in my name, there am I in the midst of them (Matt. 18.20).

We created Man, and We know what his soul whispers to him. We are nearer to him than the vein in his neck (surah 50.16).

God was a benevolent fatherly guide to his people, so long as they remembered their obligations to him and did not attempt to anger him by their deceit, ill-will, or seeking after other psychic entities. These entities might well prove irresistibly attractive to certain people, because they were not bound by the same elevated moral code, and could be influenced to act according to the wishes of the worshipper. If God's people did so stray after the desire to harness psychic powers for their own benefit, then God's retaliatory action was swift and strong. He was El Qana – a jealous God. A wise man would therefore not deliberately antagonize God.

God could be consulted about the advisability or profitability of a particular course of action, or prosecuting a particular war; and if the seeker's relationship with God was correct, guidance would be given. The priestly Sadducees had no doubt whatsoever as to the real existence of their God. God had communed with Moses on Sinai, and under Aaron and his priestly descendants, had continued to direct the nation from his tabernacle, the sanctuary.

Scholars have inevitably offered different accounts of the beliefs of the priests, and their suggestions have ranged from the possibility that God resided in a meteoric stone that was carried about in the Ark of the Covenant, to the thought that God only visited the sanctuary when summoned, when God's invisible Presence would somehow be made manifest between the two cherubim at either end of the thick golden slab that covered the Ark, thus making the Ark a kind of throne, or even a focus or 'condenser' of the divine power.

The early priests knew when the Presence of God was within the tabernacle, because it would fill with smoke. (God's Presence guided the wanderers through the wilderness after the Exodus in a manifestation of a pillar either of fire or smoke, depending on whether it was day or night, Exod. 13.21.)

Any part of the impedimenta associated with God's Presence was imbued with 'holiness', a quasi-magical property that was extremely dangerous to those not suitably purified. There was a famous instance of the unfortunate Uzzah, a man who had devoted his whole life to the service of the Ark, putting out his hand to steady it as it lurched along on a platform swung between oxen. His 'reward' for touching it was instantaneous death, as if from a tremendous shock (II Sam. 6.6–8).

It was also well known that closeness to God caused a kind of aura to appear around the priest. Exodus 34.29–34, for example, gives the narrative of how the skin of Moses' face shone so brightly after communion with God that he was obliged to wear a veil over it whenever he spoke to the people (a reference picked up by St Paul in II Cor. 3.13).

It was also axiomatic that if a human came in too close to the Presence of God, and in particular if he happened to 'see' God, instant death would be the result. Moses, perhaps, got the nearest. Exodus 33.18 records Moses' very natural but rather brazen wish to see God's 'glory', God's physical manifestation. God obligingly reminded him that he might not see God's 'face' ('for no man shall see me and live'); but if he climbed into a cleft of the rock God would place some kind of shield over him (it says God's hand) and God would pass by. The shield would protect Moses from death, and after God had moved away to a safe distance, Moses would be allowed to look out and be able to see God's 'back'.

Another group of passages recounts the appearances of God to the prophet Ezekiel (Dhulfikl) as he meditated by the river Chebar. There, God appeared complete with UFO, a flying-machine the prophet found virtually impossible to describe – although it appeared to have a clear crystal dome through which one could see the pilot, and came down on four legs that seemed to have been controlled by helicopter blades (Ezek. 1.4–28, etc.). Once down on the ground, it apparently had the sort of wheels that could roll either forwards and backwards, or sideways, without having to turn. And yet another prophet encountered a strange flying-machine – Elijah was whisked away, never to be seen again, in a 'chariot of fire' (II Kings 2.11).

When Solomon built the first Temple, it was naturally believed that as soon as the Ark was carried into the innermost chamber, the Holy of Holies, where no man might tread save the high priest on one solitary day of the year, God took up residence there. As before, it was known when God was 'at home', for the Holy Place in front of the inner sanctum would fill with smoke in the same way as the cloud had covered the tabernacle (Exod. 40.34–38; I Kings 8–10). Incidentally, it is quite obvious from these descriptions that the people were not talking about the normal puffs of incense smoke – whose origin was obvious, even to the village idiot!

Extraordinary precautions were taken to shield the priests on duty from any of God's 'fall-out'. The incense in the Holy Place had to be lit, and a good volume of smoke produced *before* entry within. This was precisely one of the rituals that the Pharisees at the time of Jesus had managed to have changed, much to the alarm of the Sadducees. Pharisees insisted that the high priest should only light his incense *after* he had gone into the Holy of Holies.

It is so easy for non-believers to scoff at the passionate heat raised by those who would even die for the principle of whether the flame on a table should be lit before or after a priest entered a room. It seems so laughable, so divorced from reality, from the 'important issues' of the 'real world'. Yet, to a Pharisee, such an act was of fundamental significance. It meant the total and un-superstitious acceptance within one's heart, one's unshakeable faith, that God's presence was *not anthropomorphic but spiritual*.

Another precaution, this time one the Pharisees did not alter, was the weaving of a stupendous curtain in special threads, to hang over the doorway of the Holy of Holies. This curtain had the thickness of a man's fist. According to the Gospels it was rent in two by an unknown force at the moment Christ died, a fearful omen indeed that suggested God had deserted Judaism at that moment (Matt. 27.51). However, the Sadducees did not accept this interpretation at all; they believed that God did not desert the sanctuary until 70 CE, for the phenomena of the inexplicable manifestation of smoke continued until the last stages of the capture of Jerusalem. Then, according to Josephus, a terrible voice was heard saying: 'Arise, let us go hence', and with a mighty rush of wind the Presence deserted the Temple and left it, empty, to its fate (*Jewish War* 6.3).

The fall of the Temple, and God's desertion of the Sadducean priesthood, was the blow from which that movement could not recover. The defeat of the Sadducees meant that they had been shamed before the eyes of the whole world. Some of the Pharisees, on the other hand, were no doubt smugly thinking to themselves 'I told you so', and enjoying a certain satisfaction.

However, at the time of Jesus, the fall of Jerusalem was still some forty years away, and the Sadducees had no reason to suppose that their opinions of God were at fault.

Once enfolded within the sanctuary, God was considered almost as a kind of oriental potentate or genie, who should be kept warm and comfortable and occupied with things he enjoyed doing, well away from interference in the private lives of the people serving him. Behind God's 'back', one could get on with one's normal, self-centred living, and God would not be involved. All that concerned God was the right performance of the various rituals. These had to be performed, day in day out, meticulously and without deviation.

This kind of thinking the Pharisees found intolerable. To them, God was a spiritual Being to be conceived of in terms far higher than a domestic power-source. God was 'omnipotent and just, all-wise and all-knowing, all-merciful and like a father in loving all his creatures'. God was not to be pictured in any image or likened to any other being. God was not limited to any place, but was present everywhere.

> To God belong the East and the West; wherever you turn, there is the Presence of God; for God is all-pervading, all knowing (surah 2.115).

God was in the heavens above and on the earth beneath. The whole earth was full of God's glory, and there was no place in the whole universe where God could not be found.

> Thus says the Lord: Heaven is my throne and earth my footstool; what is the house which you would build for me, and what is the place of my rest? All these things my hand has made, and all these things are mine (Isa. 66.1–2).

> The sons of Adam complain about the ravages of Time; but I am Time, and in My hand is the night and day' (Hadith Qudsi).

In the New Testament, Stephen, in complete accord with the Pharisees, cried that 'the Most High does not dwell in houses made with hands . . . the heaven is my throne and the earth the footstool of my feet (Acts 7.48–50); and Paul declared on the Areopagus in

Athens that 'the God that made the world and all things therein, he, being Lord of heaven and earth, dwelleth not in temples made with hands; neither is he served with men's hands as though he was in need of anything, seeing that he himself giveth life to all' (Acts 17.24).

Basic to Pharisaism was the idea that God was One. The Pharisee could argue that the status of the Sadducaic God was not clear. God might be a great power, but could arguably be one of a species, one of many. To the Pharisee, submission to God required the acceptance in the heart and mind that there *was no other power besides God*. God was not subject to any weakness. Everything depended on God, but God did not depend on any outside being. He was not in need of anything, and asked nothing of humanity but to walk in his ways, to do justly and to love kindness.

All the laws which God gave were to direct and guide people in these right ways. Even when God chastized, he did it with the love of a father.

> And you must consider in your heart, that as a man chastizes his son, so the Lord chastizes you (Deut. 8.5).

> Whatever God the Merciful does is for the best (Berakoth 60b).

The Pharisees insisted that passages in the Torah that seemed to be anthropomorphic at first sight were not to be taken literally. The Torah was the truth, and it could therefore not be self-contradictory. The utterances of the prophets under divine inspiration were revelations from God also, and so if God was Truth, the teachings of the prophets should never contradict the Torah. So, when the Torah said 'and they *saw* the God of Israel' (Exod. 24.10), it must be remembered that the Torah also stated 'You shall not see me and live' (Exod. 33.20). The first of these passages was speaking figuratively only.

Similarly, the Qur'an presents a spiritual concept, beyond the limits of human understanding:

> No vision can grasp Him, but His grasp is above all vision; He is above all comprehension, yet is acquainted with all things (surah 6.103).

Presumably the many descriptive passages concerning the after-life in the Qur'an should also be taken figuratively and symbolically and not literally, since in eternal life the faithful are not subject to physical limitations at all. It is a completely different dimension, and we are created afresh in a form beyond our knowledge. It is clearly stated that

> No person knows at this time what delights of the eye are kept hidden (in reserve) for them – as a reward for their good deeds (surah 32.17).

In our present state we can scarcely imagine the real bliss that will come in the future.

> In Paradise I prepare for the righteous believers what no eye has ever seen, no ear has ever heard, and what the deepest mind could never imagine (Hadith).

Marital and family bonds will not necessarily continue, since individual eternal souls *outside time* are not bound by the relationships that belonged to the world of time.

> There will be no relationships between them that day, nor will they ask after each other (surah 23.101).

> We have created Death to be in the midst of you, and We will not be prevented from changing your forms and creating you again in forms you know not (surah 56.60–61).

Another example of a statement that should not be taken literally is the one that God made the universe in six days and then rested on the seventh (Exod. 20.11). Prophecy taught that God *never* wearied. 'By a word of the Lord were the heavens made' (Psalm 33.6), and not by labour.

> Have you not known? Have you not heard that the everlasting God, the Lord, the Creator of the ends of the earth faints not, neither is he weary? (Isa. 40.28).

> My help comes from the Lord who has made heaven and earth. He will not suffer your foot to be moved; he that keeps you will never slumber. Behold, he that keeps Israel shall neither slumber nor sleep (Psalm 121.2–4).

> Allah, there is no God but He – the Living, the Existent in Himself, the Absolute. No slumber can seize Him, nor sleep. To Him belong all things in the heavens and on earth. Who is there

can intercede in His presence except as He permits? He knows everything, and no-one can know the least particle of His knowledge except as He wills it (surah 2.255).

One thinks also of Jesus' defence of his setting aside of a rule about working on the sabbath day in John 5.16–17. God never rested: 'My Father is working even now, and so am I.'

In short, the conflict between the Sadducees and the Pharisees was one of two quite different concepts of God. The Saducean concept involved ritual service of a mighty but capricious force, that was to be feared and kept under control, and suffered from 'qualities' such as jealousy and desire for vengeance; whereas the Pharisaic God was a spiritual fount of love and compassion.

Sadducaism was almost a magical attempt to harness and control primaeval energy and use it to the Sadducees' advantage and for their benefit; Pharisaism, like the Islam that was to come later, was an attempt to elevate humanity into a life of moral and ethical adherence to spiritual guidance.

The two opposing views crystallized in the attitude of the two Jewish parties to the Torah. According to the Sadducees, whatever they might happen to think of it, the Law had been brought upon them by the oath of allegiance sworn by their forefathers. That oath was binding for all future generations, and built into it was a curse on anyone who strayed from the terms it laid down. This curse did not only apply to the generation that had sworn the oath of allegiance, but to all of their descendants as well. They were duly bound to keep it, or they would suffer dire consequences. Therefore it was a matter of utmost importance that the Law was accurately defined, for to break it out of ignorance was no excuse, any more than ignorance of fire would prevent a person from being burnt.

As far as the Sadducees were concerned, the limits of their obedience were encapsulated in the *written word of the Torah alone*, and that was clear enough. They strenuously resisted all Pharisaic attempts to extend the interpretations of those laws beyond the literal meaning for two reasons: it made life highly dangerous, in that an individual could easily misinterpret a law and bring the curse unwittingly on to oneself or the nation; and it made service to the Law a very onerous business, since the Pharisees were introducing their detailed regulations into every walk of life.

The Sadducees did not resist this out of laziness, because they considered that they had enough to do attending to the ritual aspects of Temple worship, but they thought the Pharisaic innovations quite unnecessary.

The Sadducees knew exactly where they were. They had no intention whatsoever of giving any other burden to themselves except that of performing the correct rituals. In any case, they argued that only written laws were binding under the terms of any contract-oath; any additions, or interpretations (*ijtihad*) suggested by the Pharisees were not in writing, and therefore not legal and binding under those terms. And since they were not laid down by Almighty God and therefore did not carry the curse if they were broken, there was no need whatsoever to keep them!

4 · The Letter or the Spirit?

The Pharisees found the Sadducaic concept of God quite intolerable. They maintained that God, the dispenser of justice and mercy, the searcher of human hearts, bore no resemblance to the kind of primitive despotism of those old priestly notions. They accused the Sadducees of trying to fossilize the Torah, turning it into a museum piece venerated as much for its antiquity as for its content. Learning the laws verbatim, without any attempt to bring them up to date, simply meant that the teachings had decreasing relevance to the religious needs of the time.

Like the Muslim *ulemah* exercising *ijma* and *ijtihad*, the Pharisees saw it as their key role to save the religious life of those who submitted to God from stagnation, from 'bull-headed' blind obedience to an archaic set of commands. God's revelation, once given, was not supposed to be a dead thing, but was a living Law, a set of guidelines and principles relevant to everyday experience.

They could point out that sometimes even the written laws of God revealed progress of thought, a concession for the developing awareness of humanity. Apart from the Torah itself, there was a constant developing path of understanding about God throughout the other writings of the Old Testament, writings that were composed over hundreds of years. Muslim scholars are aware that occasionally even in the revelation given to Muhammad, that spanned a mere twenty-three years, there were a few verses revealed later that contradicted verses given earlier. This was not a problem for Muhammad – God could do and say exactly as he wished.

Whenever He suppresses a verse, or causes it to be forgotten, we bring a fresh revelation which is better or similar. Do you not know that God can do anything? (surah 2.106).

Any scholar of any holy text who tries to prove that every single word must be taken *literally* finds the way strewn with boulders at every point. Literalist Christian scholars, the Fundamentalists, tried this argument – but then ran up against many passages where more than one version of a particular event was given, with differing details: for an example taken from the first couple of pages of the Bible see the two versions of the creation in Genesis 1 and Genesis 2! The examples are far too numerous to catalogue.

This fact never bothered the Pharisees, any more than it bothers modern biblical scholars. It does not detract in any way from their faith in 'revealed principles'. The Muslim holy text, the Qur'an, is particularly resistant to literal translations, because of the very nature of the unique linguistic style in which it was revealed. This is precisely why Muslims insist that it should really only be studied in its own language – no translation is adequate at all; and even the best of Arabic scholars know well that there are many verses where the words break off, or take on several levels of meaning which are untranslatable.

The holy texts, whether Torah or Qur'an, were not intended to 'harden' like concrete, but to be flexible, adaptable to each situation as it arose; in other words, the commands should be capable of fresh interpretation according to the moral enlightenment of new religious teachers and thinkers in each new generation. The point the Pharisees were trying to make was that the intention or *niyyah* of God for his people was far greater, higher and holier than any limits that the written word of the Torah indicated.

And this Pharisaic academic analysis outraged the Sadducees. They were infuriated by what they considered to be an insulting attitude to the Torah on the one hand, and a dangerous tampering with the commands of the Divine Being on the other. That spirit of Sadducaism is still highly active today in some Islamic adherents. Exactly the same issues that rent the eminent Jewish scholars, and later the Christian ones, still raise the blood pressure of Muslim ones for the very same reasons. As the prophet Solomon astutely observed, 'There is nothing new under the sun' (Eccles. 1.9).

The Sadducees would tolerate no 'interpretation' of any word of Torah. What right did any human being think they possessed to suggest alternative meanings to the plain words given by God? As we have seen, they considered that God could be temperamental, exacting retribution when he felt it was called for. The Pharisaic interpretation of the laws was subjective and therefore might invoke the divine curse if it unwittingly contravened a command.

Likewise, some eminent Muslim gentlemen who have spent a lifetime in scholarly pursuits and self-control, perhaps even maintaining the equality of women in Islam, and certainly extolling the praises of the Supremely Merciful One, the Compassionate, ignore the obvious fact that no human brain can encompass the truth about our state in the next life, for Allah is above all human understanding, and they will brook no 'spiritual interpretation' of passages that describe the pleasures of Paradise, or the constantly renewed skins that will be burnt off in Hell! It is not enough to state – 'the Book *says this*'. One has to also ask, '*What does it mean?*'

Muhammad, who had been taken during the Lailat ul-Miraj through the ranges of heavens to glimpse the glory of God's presence, himself declared God's words in unmistakable clarity: 'In Paradise, I prepare for the righteous believers who no eye has ever seen, no ear has ever heard, and what the deepest mind could *never imagine*' (Hadith). The Qur'an itself gives us: 'At this point of time *no person knows* what delights of the eye are kept unrevealed for them, as a reward for their good deeds' (surah 32.17).

Oh dear! 'The value of this world in comparison to the Hereafter is like a droplet in the ocean' (Hadith). The blinkered sages who try to equate a simple reading of a text with the depths that are there for all those who have eyes to see, would perhaps do well to learn from Qoheleth, the Preacher, who said:

He has made everything beautiful in its time; He has put eternity into the human mind, but no human can find out what God has done from beginning to end . . . whatever God does endures for ever; nothing can be added to it or taken from it . . . No person knows how it is to be, for who can tell how it will be? No person has power to retain the spirit, or authority over the day of death . . . As you do not know how the spirit comes to the bones in the womb of a woman with child, so you do not know the work of God Who makes everything . . . However much a man may toil in seeking, he will not find it out; even though a wise man claims to know, he cannot find it out (Eccles 2.11, 14; 8.7–8; 11.5; 8.17).

The Pharisees refused to share the superstitious belief and fear of the Sadducees. They saw it as being primitive and unworthy. They scoffed at it. The Torah was of course authoritative, but this was *because* it was divine and not because they were bound to it by a curse! God was not in need of any of the services outlined in it; God was in need of nothing from any of his creations. As the Qur'an taught later, God was not dependent on any human prayer or service – it is only out of God's mercy that God desires our good.

To God belong all things in heaven and earth; truly God is free of all wants, and worthy of all praise (surah 31.26).

O humanity! It is you that have need of God; but God is the One free of all needs (surah 35.15).

What is humanity, that God should care or instruct or send special messengers to warn of danger or harm? Humanity depends on God and has need of God every moment of life. God certainly has no need of humanity, but bestows grace out of unbounded mercy and loving-kindness. If it were God's will, God could snuff out the whole universe in a moment and create all things new. Any race or people to whom God gives chances should understand that its failure does not affect God. God can create others in their place, as he did in times past, and still does to this day.

Thy Lord is Self-sufficient, full of mercy; if it were His will He could destroy you and in your place appoint whom He will as your successors, even as He raised you up from the posterity of other people (surah 6.133).

The Torah, like the Qur'an and the other holy books, had been given for the benefit of humanity, and not in any way for the benefit of God, as if God had an ego that needed satisfying by slavish service! It was a gift of God's kindness to show all humans the path for living a good life that would not only be pleasing to God but also beneficial to themselves. How could Sadducees imagine that *any* honest efforts to search out the deep meanings of these laws, and take them to their honest conclusions, could bring a curse upon anybody? That was nonsense. If a mistake was made, well – God who knew everything would judge the heart and the motive.

God's guidance for humanity was not just to be circumscribed by details of agricultural practice that befitted a primitive agricultural or nomadic community. It was eternal Law, for all humankind. Therefore it should speak to the modern city-dweller – the accountant or the nurse, the factory-worker or the secretary – as much as to the valley-farmer and the wandering shepherd. A Law intended for all times and for all conditions would have to be newly interpreted, perhaps many times, by the exercise of reason and the religious awareness of the leading exponents in each generation. Their part would be to trust in God to guide them aright, so that they might know the correct things to do.

They might not be able to see very far ahead into the distance, but they should take the next step on the path in faith, or, as the Qur'an put it, hold fast to the Rope and not let it go.

> Hold fast, all of you, to the Rope which Allah stretches out for you; be not divided amongst yourselves; remember with gratitude Allah's favour towards you. For you were enemies, and He joined your hearts in love, so that by His grace you became brothers. You were on the brink of the pit of fire, and He saved you from it (surah 3.103).

The Pharisees were, of course, perfectly well aware of the dangers of misinterpretation of the Law, not that they feared a primitive retaliation from their dear Father, the God they were seriously concerned to serve properly, but that the opinion of any one individual influential scholar might gain pride of place simply because of his personal eminence rather than for his depth and holiness of thought. They did not want to create a class of religious tyrants to take the place of the class of bigoted priests. It therefore became axiomatic that no individual teacher might *ever* have the absolute right to determine the Torah according to his own private judgment. The ruling was always to be arrived at after consultation among the whole body of teachers – just as, in Islam, the *fatwa* of no one individual *'alam* should ever be accepted as authoritative unless it was referred back to the Qur'an, hadith and sunna, and was acceptable in the opinion of the majority.

Many Muslims, of course, are not the least bit concerned with *any* Jewish (or Christian) studies, maintaining one simple line of argument and refusing to entertain any other – that the Torah is not the *Tawrat* revealed to Moses, and therefore they need not even bother to read it. They do their early 'muslim' brothers a great injustice. They need to know that matters are a very great deal more complicated than they have perhaps been led to believe, and that to take such a simplistic line over the researches and disciplines of the 'people of the Book' only invites contempt, if not ridicule, for deliberate – and lazy! – head-burial in the sand! Let us all accept that *Tawrat* (and *Injil*) no longer still exist. Torah certainly does. Pharisaic studies of it gradually evolved into well-defined areas, which have grown into a vast corpus of material.

A statement of a rule of right conduct was known as Halachah. This area covered the whole of the practical life of individuals and of the community. Haggadah was an interpretation of scripture in general for the purpose of edification, and not specifically for the regulation of one's personal conduct. Nevertheless, the Haggadah, or 'drawing-forth' of the content of Torah, was intended to reveal the moral content from which one could deduce lessons. It included such things as the inner meanings of revelations, and numerous philosophical discussions. These discussions certainly touched frequently on the fields of psychology and ethics, both personal and national in scope.

Basically, what the Haggadah was intended to do was to make explicit what was only implicit in the Torah, to unfold any hidden meanings that might be overlooked by the faithful, or conveniently ignored by the less devout if they were not specific.

The Mishnah was the authoritative statement of the Halachoth, a classification of rulings initiated in the time of Hillel and Shammai, possibly by those very men. This classification was continued principally by Rabbi Akiba, then Rabbi Meir, and ultimately by Rabbi Judah the Prince.

The scholars from c.20–200 CE were called Tannaim, and the scholars that came after them and completed the Mishnah were known as Amoraim. The Tannaim were mentioned by name in the Mishnaic collections, and virtually held the same kind of honour afforded in Islam to the first four khalifas. The Amoraim were not permitted to dispute any of their statements, not even a baraita or blessing. If their opinions conflicted, they were simply rejected. Only for those scholars living in the transitional period was a doubt allowed. In an exactly similar way the Sunna of the first four khalifas (Caliphs) after Muhammad is accepted as binding, whereas the teachings of those who came later are open to discussion and debate.

Once put into a written form, the Mishnah itself then became a prime object of study, the main objective being to verify the rulings given by establishing their connections with the written Torah, to elucidate their meanings, and – most important, exactly as in the Muslim exercise of *fiqh* – constantly to bring them up to date by showing how they could be applied to the circumstances of the time. Thus the law could be regarded as truly universal and valid.

The results of such a study of the Mishnah were called Gemara. The Talmud, a massive work stretching over numerous volumes, was the compilation of the Mishnah plus the Gemara, the commentaries on the various passages and statements. There are two Talmuds, one compiled towards the end of the fourth century in Palestine and one in Babylon a century later, but both of these are based on the same Mishnah. By the third century CE there were considered to be 613 regulations, covering such minutiae as whether or not it was allowed to wear a false tooth on the sabbath, or eat an egg laid on the sabbath!

Two subjects I found quite fascinating were the controversies surrounding Erub and Nizzok. Nizzok involved the purity or otherwise of a substance passing from a 'clean' container to an 'unclean' one. Did a stream of water flowing from one vessel into another not unite the two vessels, so that to pour it into an impure vessel would be to defile the lot? Sadducees insisted that this was so, but the Pharisees declared that the flow of water was *not* unifying (Mish. Maksharim 5.9). However, the Temple priests ruled that the flow of water made it and its two vessels one continuous body – which may have been feasible for priests in the Temple, but was hardly practicable for city traders. It would have virtually forbidden all the customary dealing of the market-place! In Mark 7.4–23 we have an absolutely typical Pharisaic statement in disguise as an attack on Pharisees: 'There is nothing outside a man which by going into him can defile him.' Jesus extended his theme to point out that what really defiled people was the evil, malice, pride and lust that come from within.

Erub was a similar law – the 'merging' of households. On the sabbath day the extent that one could travel was strictly limited, but the Sadducees permitted the concept of a network of dwellings within a common courtyard as being 'merged' into one (like the liquid in the vessels), and therefore one could move about freely within those confines and not begin to measure one's 'sabbath day's journey' until one got beyond the artificially extended bounds. The Sadducees then went further, and extended these courts by erecting a rope or some such thing from house to house, so that all that was joined was 'merged' and counted as one. (Finkelstein, in his monumental work on Pharisees, at the turn of this century mentions a whole network of wires, which he at first mistook for an electricity supply. It turned out to be the old Erub law still in action – the network had virtually made the whole city 'one courtyard'!) The Pharisees, for their part, heartily disapproved of these Sadducaic interpretations.

The importance of debate and discussion before any ruling could be given was illustrated by a passage in the Babylonian Talmud (B. Erub 13b), where the schools of Shammai and Hillel were arguing as to the true meaning and implication of one particular *halachah*. Apparently they kept up a debate for no less than *three years* on whether or not it would have been better for the natural world if humanity had never been created, and only came to a decision on the intervention of a *Bath Qol*. A Bath Qol was a psychic manifestation, examples of which can be found throughout the pages of the Old and New Testaments, experiences of a direct guiding voice heard either by an individual or by all those assembled, that was taken by the hearers to be the voice of God (e.g. Abraham, Gen. 12.1, 7; 15.1; 22.1; Isaac, Gen. 26.24; Samuel, I Sam. 3.3f.; John the Baptist, Matt. 3.17; Jesus and his disciples, Mark 9.7 etc.).

In this rabbinical case, the Bath Qol intervened with the judgment that although both scholars had the word of the Living God, the ruling this time was to be according to the statement of Hillel. Shammai was not best pleased! Similarly, an occasion was reported where they debated another issue for two years. A Bath Qol was not normally to be expected for problems confronting the ordinary person in the street. It was a rare and treasured event – in these cases a sign of God's exasperation? – and on these two occasions the decisions given by the 'voice' were accepted as authoritative.

But this was not automatically the case! In a later rabbinic debate, a famous controversy between Rabbis Joshua and Eliezer, even the evidence of a Bath Qol in Eliezer's favour was not enough to sway the opinion of the majority of the Sanhedrin to his side of the argument, and he was over-ruled – a matter he never forgot nor forgave.

The point was a vital one: *no* teacher, no matter how eminent or saintly or scholarly or blessed with mystic intuitions, and *no* 'voice', ever had the right to impose *any* opinion by the sheer weight of authority. Indeed, even after a Halachah was accepted and fixed by the whole assembly, it could *still* be altered and replaced by the findings of later assemblies. That is why it was so alarming for the Pharisees to observe of Jesus that when he spoke, he 'taught with authority and not as the scribes' (Matt. 7.29). If this was the case, then we can see straight away how his mode of speaking and teaching would have been regarded with extreme caution, if not suspicion, or even downright opposition, by Pharisaic scholars. Even if they had been most impressed by what Jesus had to say, and were making allowances for his youthful enthusiasm or prophetic exuberance, they would certainly have wished any pronouncement of his to be debated further. It was not that Jesus had made the pronouncements that would have been their objection; Jesus had as much right to debate theological issues as any person. It was the authoritative and partisan line taken by his followers that would have given them cause for offence. Jesus was apparently claiming to speak on a higher authority than that of a normal human man, as if he were aware of *constant* Bath Qol support for what he said – and whether this awareness were true or false, they were not yet in a position to decide. Jesus demanded that this decision be made, instantly, by all those with whom he came in contact.

According to our Gospels, Jesus *was* aware in a peculiarly intense and intimate way, that God was his Father. He simply assumed without question that what he said and thought expressed fully and with authority the will of God himself. The Synoptic Gospels record a saying: 'If I by the finger (or spirit) of God cast out devils, then the Kingdom of God is come upon you' (Matt. 12.28; Luke 11.20); the Fourth Gospel develops this theme:

> I do not speak on my own authority; the Father who sent me has himself given me commandment what to say and what to speak. And I know that his commandment is eternal life. What I say, therefore, I say as the Father has bidden me (John 12.49–50).

Jesus acted and taught with a style which he apparently did not ground or explain in any official position, but which equally he refused to renounce. Pharisees probably felt that occasionally in his preaching there was an egotism that was out of step with good Jewish piety. For example, in Mark 10.21 Jesus addressed himself to a man who had been obedient to the whole law since his childhood. 'You are still lacking in one thing,' he said. 'Come, follow me.'

Jesus possessed a belief in his mission and relationship with God that could be interpreted in several ways. Either, as Christians later asserted, it *did* prove he was the Son of God; or, as his enemies claimed, he verged on the extremes of self-veneration. So strong was Jesus' belief in himself that he came to rely upon his own insight more than upon that of any of Israel's great ones, even Moses himself!

The third possibility, and the one accepted by Muslims, rests in the nature of prophecy itself. A prophet, when possessed by the divine guidance, does not speak 'of himself'. The words are not his own, but he is simply being used as the instrument through which matters from the sphere and realm of the divine Absolute can be diffused to humanity, which would not otherwise be able to receive them. To use the image of a radio: the waves are there all the time, but the 'box' has to be available for humans to pick them up.

All prophets therefore get accused of grandiose self-veneration, of 'speaking with authority'; they cannot help it. If they are gripped by the divine voice, they have no choice in the matter. Quite often, they are not at all pleased to be the chosen vessels, and object like mad. It makes no difference – what God wills, happens.

And Moses said: 'O my Lord, I am not eloquent . . . but I am slow of speech and of tongue.' Then the Lord said: 'Who has made man's mouth? Who makes him dumb or deaf, or seeing or blind? Now therefore go, and I will be with your mouth and teach you what you shall speak' (Exod. 4.10–12).

I am no prophet, nor a prophet's son, but I am a herdsman and a dresser of sycamore trees; and the Lord took me from following the flock, and said to me to go and prophesy to Israel (Amos 7.14–15).

I said: 'O Lord God! Behold, I do not know how to speak! I am too young!' But the Lord said to me: 'Do not say "I am too young"; for to all whom I send you, you shall go, and whatever I command you, you shall speak!' (Jer. 1.6–7).

'Do not be anxious beforehand what you are to say; but say whatever is given you in that hour, for it is not you who speak but the Holy Spirit (Mark 13.11).

All prophets are usually insultingly accused of being possessed by some madness, some 'demon' – generally because they are upsetting the hierarchy. It was certainly said of Jesus:

'Are we not right in saying that you are a Samaritan and have a demon?' Jesus answered: 'I have not a demon; but I honour my Father, and you dishonour me . . . Truly I say to you, if anyone keeps my word, he will never see death.' The Jews said to him: 'Now we know that you have a demon!' (John 8.48–54).

The same kind of thing was also said of Muhammad, many times, but God sent him personal revelations in the Qur'an to reassure him:

You are not mad or possessed. Your character is above the standard that can be slandered. Soon everyone will see which of you is really mad . . . take no notice of despicable slanderers (surah 68.2–6, 10).

Unbelievers might well stare at you and abuse you, and call you mad – but you have nothing less than a message to the world (surah 68.52).

One can see immediately how this 'fits' the case of Jesus. How is it possible for Jesus ever be thought of as egotistical, he who came to seek and save the lost, who was beloved by children and outcasts and all manner of people the rest of society had rejected? And who taught his disciples to recognize humility and service as the only marks of true greatness:

'Whoever would be great amongst you must be your servant, and whoever would be first among you must be slave of all. For the Son of Man also came not to be served but to serve, and to give his life as a ransom for many (Mark 10.43–44).

When he had washed their feet he resumed his place, and said to them: 'So you know what I have done to you? You call me Teacher and Lord, and you are right, for so I am. If I then, your lord and teacher, have washed your feet, you ought also to wash one another's feet. For I have given you an example . . . truly I say to you, a servant is not greater than his master, nor is he who is sent greater than he who sent him (John 13.12–16).

Jesus' intense awareness of God's presence and God's will is one of the main factors to take into account when coming to a personal decision as to his significance, who he actually was. Recognition of

Jesus as the Son of God is heavily dependent on the prior recognition of who God is, and God's nature, and God's will.

Jesus, the great teacher of Galilee, did not regard equality with God as a matter to be grasped (Phil. 2.6f.), but was always the most devout submitted person. The Christian, taking trinitarian doctrine for granted, sees many passages in the Gospels from a perspective overlaid with atonement theology. However, for those who have eyes to see, the true nature and 'Islam' of Jesus is plain enough in so many places:'Why do you call me Good? No man is good, only God alone' (Mark 10.18); 'Call no man your "father" on earth, for you have one Father, who is in heaven' (Matt. 23.9). When asked what was the most important commandment, Jesus replied without hesitation: 'This is the most important commandment: "The Lord our God, the Lord is One. Love him with all your heart, soul, mind and strength"' (Mark 12.29–30). When he was tempted to think of himself as being the Son of God, he replied stoutly: 'Begone, Satan! You shall worship the Lord your God, and him alone shall you serve' (Matt. 4.8). In countless passages, he prayed to God and confided in him, asked his advice, begged for his help. As the Qur'an later stated of him:

> Jesus said: I have come to you with wisdom, in order to make clear some of the points about which you are in doubt. Fear God, and obey me – for God is my Lord and your Lord. Worship Him. That is the straight path' (surah 43.63–64).

5 · The Hedge

As King Herod's friend Nicolaus of Damascus put it, 'the Pharisees were a body of Jews who professed to be more religious than others, and to explain the laws more accurately', based on 'regulations handed down by former generations which were not recorded in the Law of Moses' (Josephus, *Jewish War*, 5.2.110).

The Gospels suggest that Jesus differed drastically from the Pharisees in his attitude to the Torah. Matthew 23, for example, mounts a stern attack on the 'scribes and Pharisees, hypocrites' whose life under the Law had become a trap. These bigoted sticklers for meaningless minutiae found it vitally important to be meticulous about tithing even 'mint, anise and cummin', but really important issues of true service to God just passed them by (23.23).

The main point of disagreement between those Pharisees and Jesus was apparently not the Torah itself, but the oral tradition with which Pharisees interpreted it. This tradition they referred to as the 'Hedge' (Aboth 1.1). The accusation was that scholars who 'constructed the hedge' had become obsessed with minutiae.

In fact, the Pharisees did not regard the contents of this tradition as being in any way innovatory material, but claimed that these practical rules by which the Torah was actually to be implemented had also been handed down since primaeval times.

To a strict Pharisee, the tradition was a 'hedge' because it gave the 'muslim' or 'separated' person a safety-barrier between living according to the divine statutes and ordinary life that was not submitted to the will of God. To take a trivial example, if the Law stated that one's food crops had to be tithed (a tenth given to God in some way), then there arose debate as to what exactly the nature of a 'food crop' was. The Law in Leviticus 27.30 said merely that 'all the tithe of the land, whether of the seed of the land or of the fruit of the trees, is the Lord's; it is holy to the Lord'. So, did the Law simply refer to corn in the field, or the grapes from one's vineyard, things one might regard as one's commercial crop – or did it include literally everything that grew and was edible? The 'hedge' advised that even one's small patch of herbs intended for culinary use consisted of things that were cropped, so to be on the safe side, one should even tithe one's few leaves of mint, anise and cummin.

To a Western mind this may appear meticulous to the point of being ridiculous. However, those who have lived in the Middle East and seen the little pots of herbs growing by the door will appreciate immediately the difference between the kind of person who would deliberately cultivate and unhesitatingly share even these few leaves with someone who had need, and the person who would not. No Easterner would have any doubt which of the two ways was 'submitted'. The attitude of hospitality is paramount, and this is surely what the Pharisees had in mind. It *was* precisely what Jesus had in mind when he praised the poor widow in the Temple for sharing her few little coins; her unstinting gift was worth more than the huge doles of the wealthy who would hardly miss what they gave! (Mark 12.42).

Another example relevant to the New Testament was the question of plucking ears of corn on the sabbath. As it happens, the third of the thirty-nine articles forbidden on the sabbath in Shabbat 7.2 was reaping. The insinuation in the Gospel is that Jesus' disciples who plucked a few ears of corn were reaping, and they were therefore accused by the Pharisees of breaking the Law. Jesus – if he had been a genuine man of God – should have stopped them (Mark 2.23–28; Matt. 12.1–8; Luke 6.1–5). However, this is grossly inaccurate. The Pharisees had actually ruled that the plucking and eating of a few heads of standing corn was perfectly permissible if done to assuage the hunger of the passer-by, so long as it was only done by hand and not 'plucked' in large quantities by the use of some instrument (Deut. 23.24–25). In the same way, a passer-by could help himself to a handful of grapes, but not fill any receptacle. The farmer who owned the field or vineyard would have had every right to have regarded that not as gleaning, or what modern youngsters might call 'scrumping', but as theft! Galilean Pharisees (where Jesus was supposedly accused!) not only allowed the grain to be plucked and rubbed between the fingers, but in the hand as well. A strict Pharisee *might* have advised the 'hedge' that not even the act of plucking an ear of corn should be allowed on the sabbath, lest the original command should be inadvertently broken – but there is *no* rabbinical reference to this, and the Gospel accounts are wrong.

The purpose of the 'hedge' was to halt a person by cautionary rules long before they were within breaking distance of the Law itself. Not all examples were so trivial as these appear to be. The illustrations given by Jesus in the Sermon on the Mount (Matt. 5–7) indicate that at least in so far as moral conduct was concerned, Jesus made the most sublime use of this principle – *mental* adultery and malice were forbidden, so that there would be no danger of *actual* adultery or murder.

Critics will notice immediately that whereas Pharisaic practice was intended to be kind and loving in reasonable and practicable terms, the high example set by Jesus took those who were able to follow his dicta out of the category of ordinary humans into the realms of sainthood.

'Legalism' became the main criticism of Pharisaism. This accusation was that the Pharisees had reduced true service of God – humility, compassion, and a 'clean and upright heart' – to a knowledge of trifling rules and regulations which could not possibly be of any importance to Almighty God – though by what standards any person dares to declare certain knowledge of what is important to God is not clear.

Many modern followers of Islam feel a similar irritation when faced with the dogmatic prejudice of some of their own number, particularly when the cultural norms of any individual society are interpreted as 'being' Islam, when they patently are not! One could challenge, for example, the very restrictive seclusion of women in certain parts of the Islamic world; the virtual impossibility for some Muslim women to claim for themselves the equality promised by Allah through the Qur'an; the misinterpretation of all sorts of surahs and sunnah practices.

Any legalistic religion is bound to be unsatisfactory in the end, since it involves the impossible search for a system of rules that covers all possible eventualities, in conjunction with the belief that perfect obedience to it is fully adequate as regards God's rights. Legal regulations, always being finite, are limited, and tend to foster the notion that there is a limit to one's duty, at which point obligation ceases. Thus, it was possible for a scribe to ask of Jesus quite seriously 'Who is my neighbour?' in response to the command to love his neighbour as himself (Luke 10.29).

The Gospels tell us that Jesus was opposed by the Pharisees not because he was a bad man, but because he did such things as healing on the sabbath. He was castigated for allowing his disciples to pluck those ears of corn on the sabbath, for eating with unwashed hands, and expecting a cured paralytic to pick up his stretcher and remove it from the public highway on the sabbath – a day when one was not allowed to carry more than the weight of one dried fig!

As we have noted already, in the Christian Gospels there is a curious mixture of accuracy and inaccuracy. Occasionally those Pharisees were supposed to have taken a standpoint *in direct opposition* to what their position would actually have been! For example, in Mark 7 and Matthew 15 it was alleged that the Pharisees taught that a man might legally prevent his parents from benefitting from certain goods to which they had a right (under the law of honouring one's parents) by the device of making them *corban*, or dedicated to the Temple.

Thus unforgiving people who had fallen out with their parents could evade their responsibility and the fifth commandment, that of honouring one's father and mother. In exactly the same way, some unscrupulous and rather unpleasant 'muslims' could work the same device, declaring money or provisions due to their parents as *zakah*, and therefore by the pious fiction of 'giving it to God' depriving those to whom they owed their very existence, by God's grace.

It was implied that this sort of evasion was a fairly common Pharisaic practice, and one good reason why the Pharisees should be despised for hypocrisy! Yet so far as we can tell from the Mishnah, this particular example would have been *completely at variance with Pharisaic practice*, which laid stress on the right care and honour of one's parents. Nedarim 3.2 represents the real Pharisaic spirit, that one should put respect for one's parents even before the Temple, which was just a building.

One can find the same attitude to the 'sanctuary of bricks and mortar' as opposed to the real sanctuary of God's spirit in the human heart well represented in Sufic mysticism:

I see only bricks, and a house of stone.
It is only You, O God, that I desire (Rabia al-Adawiyya).

There are many roads to the Ka'aba . . . but lovers know that the true Holy Mosque is Union with God (Mevlana Jalal ud-din Rumi).

The Sadducees, however, who had an exaggerated respect for the Temple building as the 'house of God', and who could never have regarded it as *just* a building, might well have had the very practise of misusing *corban* that Jesus described. In other words, Jesus was here urging a Pharisaic viewpoint against a Sadducaic one, and yet the Gospels present him as speaking *against* the Pharisees. Strange indeed.

There is another, far more serious, wrongful criticism. One of the main criticisms of the Pharisees throughout the Gospels is that they objected to Jesus' kindness and compassion in working miracles of healing on the sabbath days, because this counted as work, and no healing should have been done on that day! The case of the Bent Woman was an obvious one – this wretched woman had suffered from her bent spine for no less than eighteen years! Surely it would not have hurt if she had waited one more day? Although it seems to have been the normal practice of Jesus to wait until sunset on sabbath days before he began healing (Mark 1.32), this was not his attitude in this instance.

> The ruler of the synagogue, indignant because Jesus had healed on the sabbath, said to the people: 'There are six days on which work ought to be done; come on those days and be healed, and not on the sabbath day!' Then the Lord answered him, 'You hypocrites! Does not each of you on the sabbath untie his ox or his ass from the manger, and lead it away to water it? And ought not this woman, a daughter of Abraham, whom Satan bound for eighteen years, to be loosed from this bond on the sabbath day?' As he said this, all his adversaries were put to shame (Luke 13.10–17).

Take also the case of the man with dropsy, also healed on a sabbath (Luke 14.1–6). Jesus asked the Pharisees:

> 'Is it lawful to heal on the sabbath or not?' And they were silent. Then he took him and healed him, and let him go. And he said to them: 'Which of you, having a son or an ass that has fallen into a well, will not immediately pull him out on a sabbath day?' And they could not reply to this.

The point was that the child or animal was legally too heavy to lift on the sabbath, and yet no one in his right mind would hesitate to break the 'hedge' in such a case.

In fact, once again the details as given are wrong – Jesus was *well within the Pharisaic code of practice*! The only Pharisaic objection would have been to the actual compounding of medicines by such means as pestle and mortar, or to the gathering of herbs, which might reasonably have been done the previous day. There was no stricture whatsoever against the taking of a medicine, or Jesus' methods of prayer or laying-on of hands on the sabbath. In fact, the opposite was the case. All healings were allowed, even of trivial things – because the Pharisees ruled that no human being could possibly know whether even a simple thing, such as a spot or boil, might not lead on to something far more serious, something that could even eventually prove fatal. Therefore *all* medical attention was permissible, even the gathering of herbs if the need had arisen suddenly. Once again, Jesus was acting *as* a Pharisee, but the Gospels present the stories as criticisms of him *by* Pharisees!

A Pharisaic legal detail that was picked up accurately in the Fourth Gospel was when Jesus used the fact that Pharisees allowed the rule of circumcision on the eighth day, if a baby was born on a Friday, to overrule the sabbath law (John 2.22–24). If that small part of a man's anatomy can be 'made well' on the sabbath, how much more a man's whole body? This discussion was presumably referring back to Jesus' sabbath-day cure of a man who had been paralysed for thirty-eight years (John 5.1–18)! This healing particularly raised the temperature of 'the Jews' because Jesus claimed the right to do his healing work on that day for the simple reason that '"My Father is working still, so I am working". This was why the Jews sought all the more to kill him, because he not only broke the sabbath but also called God his Father, making himself equal with God' (John 5.17–18). In fact, the passage that follows has traditionally been interpreted as a trinitarian passage, but a careful reading can reveal quite a different interpretation. Jesus maintained that his testimony *was* greater than that of John the Baptist (v.36); he had come in his Father's name, but they would not believe him. 'How can you believe, who receive glory from one another and do not seek the glory that comes from *the only true God*? Do you think that I shall accuse you to the Father? It is Moses who accuses you, on whom you set your hope' (John 5.44–46).

Later Pharisees certainly took the 'hedge' very seriously. 'Retribution comes in the end to everyone who pulls down the hedge of the wise; for it is written: a serpent will bite him who breaks through a wall', is a saying in the name of Rabbi Ishmael on Eccl. 10.8 (Tos. Hullin 2.22). Nevertheless, they were concerned that the hedge should not become too much of a burden. 'Do not make the hedge about the garden too high, lest it should fall in and crush the flowers' (Gen. Rabba 19 on 3.2), an apt metaphor when one remembers that actual hedges in the Middle East are usually hefty and impenetrable ramparts of prickly-pear cactus!

Once again, we can see the same problem in Islam; obsession with literal obedience to minutiae can take over a person's life and create what Jesus called 'blind guides'. The 'obsessed' Muslim can become intolerant, 'superior', instead of loving and attracting people to God. It is perfectly possible to engender a sense of guilt and inadequacy in lesser mortals who simply cannot remember and put into practice such regulations as always entering the toilet left foot first, saying all the appropriate formulae on waking, washing, dressing, sneezing, going in and out, seeing an unfortunate person, etc., etc. Any Muslim bookshop will provide you with long lists of appropriate actions and phrases to say; there are whole books on etiquette and Muslim social living. Having read them and tried hard to do the right thing, as a new Muslim I made countless errors (and still do!).

The irritant, for a new Muslim, is to feel admiration and respect for all the polite actions and responses, but to resent being 'looked down on' when failing to observe all the details. Here's an example. I lived in a house where there were several other Muslims, some of whom did not actually keep the Ramadan fast at all. One lodger was meticulous and devout, and a stickler for 'doing the right thing'. I kept my fast from daylight to daylight, as laid down in the Qur'an, but discovered that I was accused of being 'at fault' and my efforts 'rendered invalid' because certain scholars had agreed on set times for starting and finishing the self-denial – and in fact those times bore no relation to the actual rising and setting of the light in my part of the UK! Cantankerous and outraged (and had I not been a rebel in the first place, I would never have become a Muslim), I refused to reject my good *niyyah* as invalid, and invited God to be the judge!

The prime concern of Jesus seems not to have been the pointing-out of people's faults, but the much more important restoration to God's grace of the *Amme ha-Aretz*, the common folk who had 'fallen short' and were like sheep without a shepherd. It was not those who were well who needed the doctor, but those who were sick (Mark 2.17). Where Torah had seemingly failed to create a relationship between humanity and God, Jesus' heart went out even to the despised outcasts, and by his exercise of forgiveness made them 'new'.

It is hard for the 'superior' person to remember that God is the Judge, always, and that no human has the right to decide for God what he might or might not like to see or hear, or count as true worship.

The ordinary person was certainly marked off from the Pharisee by refusal or inability to live within the 'hedge', which added so many restrictions on to a person's conduct of their normal business. If people did try to keep even the basic principles, they became involved in a vast network of decisions as to what things were clean and what unclean, and how to keep the two apart; the collection of interpretations of the word of God were indeed becoming so enormous and cumbersome that even the rabbis themselves were beginning to divide up their study and expertise into sections of the whole. Hence, life under their branch of the law was virtually regarded as an impossibility for the ordinary person.

This led to something God would surely never have desired: the Pharisees' drawing ever further apart from the non-Pharisees. A dangerous tendency grew for certain of their number to pride themselves not on being shepherds to their people, but simply on their ability to know the Law and live according to it. We have the parable of the Pharisee and the publican, in which the Pharisee thanked God that he was not like other men, for he carried out all the imposed commandments accurately and devoutly, whereas the publican – beyond any hope of success or salvation – could only be aware of the mess he was in, and beat his breast in despair crying 'God be merciful to me, a sinner' (Luke 18.9–14). According to Jesus, *that publican* was the man who had drawn closest to God, and not the Pharisee. The Pharisee had indeed lived a 'perfect' life according to his principle, but according to Jesus he had missed the point. And the Pharisee's prayer was only self-praise and not communion with God, as was the prayer of the despised tax-collector. The Pharisee's legalistic view of what was righteous and what was not had in effect cut him off from the real truth.

Herein lies the most vital and important caution for some of today's Muslim extremists: they must search and examine their hearts, and be absolutely certain that they have not also slipped into the same kind of blindness from which Jesus' message was intended to set people free.

People can only hope to approach God in humility, penitence and faith, and not on the basis of their complete observance of laws. In the blinding light of God's perfect righteousness, all come under judgment. None are righteous as God is righteous, and therefore the only possible approach lies in an appeal to God's mercy. This theme is to be found in all strands of the Gospels, and may therefore be assumed to be genuinely what Jesus believed.

Was it true that Pharisaism had descended to the level of legalism, an invisible prison in which they spent their lives and in which they, in their turn, tried to impound other people? It was said that the Pharisee would 'traverse sea and land to make a single proselyte (convert)', like a vast and hungry spider luring the unwary into its web. Instead of devotion and worship of God, the individual had become committed to an impossible burden of ritual behaviour. People weighed down by striving to carry out all the hundreds of regulations would have had little time to give to the worship of God that really mattered. St Paul, it seems, certainly regarded the Law as a burden, even though he had been raised as a Pharisee himself, and claimed no less a celebrity than the great Gamaliel as his teacher (Acts 22.3).

This point of view has been taken by all critics of Pharisaism. Certainly the Pharisees could be charged with hypocrisy if after all their efforts and talk they were not, in fact, *more* charitable and compassionate than their non-Pharisaic fellows. Any slip from their self-imposed standards would be immediately noticed, and harsh criticism would ensue. The very membership of such a separated body carried with it the implication that the members *should* be 'better' and 'holier' than the non-members, persons indeed to whom non-members could go for help and spiritual advice, and to have prayers said for them. Non-members could be expected to react with outraged righteous indignation when this was seen not to be the case.

I well remember becoming a member of the Salvation Army in my youth (another act of rebellion), and being appalled to discover that certain 'weaker brethren' who had publicly 'signed the pledge' never to drink alcohol, nevertheless still sneakily drank it. Today's Muslims are ashamed by the slipshod standards of the many who give them a bad name. Take another example: the West finds it hard enough to understand the 'virtues and benefits' of polygamy, and the fact that a Muslim man is allowed to have four wives (although in practice these days very few avail themselves of more than one!). How on earth do they react when they read about certain so-called Muslims, some in positions of great authority and wealth, who have dozens of wives, or who use their legal system in order simply to abuse it, and have as many women as they want – simply elevating them to the rank of 'temporary wife', to be jettisoned again at the man's convenience? So much for Islamic rights of women!

Yet the Pharisees themselves, like the Muslims of today, certainly did not regard the *Halachoth* as a burden but as a joy. According to Josephus, it was an instinct 'with every Jew from the day of his birth, to regard Torah as the decrees of God, to abide by them, and if need be, cheerfully to die for them' (*Against Apion* 1.8.42). So far as the Pharisees were concerned, God had given them the Torah in order to provide them with the means to earn for themselves a just personal salvation. It gave them the opportunity to earn merit or reward. In simple terms, a legalistic system was quite logical, and many Pharisees found it acceptable to envisage the standard of their lives as a series of transactions, rather like a bank balance. A fulfilment of a law earned a 'merit' (what Muslims call *hasanat*), and a transgression of it earned a 'demerit'. Every individual was in a position to consult and discover what was the correct course of action, and perfectly free to choose whether or not to follow it. There was little ambiguity over whether a person was righteous or not. If their merits outnumbered their demerits, then they were righteous, and God would be pleased. If they had gained more demerits than merits, then they were obviously antisocial, if not wicked, and deserved punishment. How would God deal with the person who was exactly in the middle – who had earned exactly the same number of merits and demerits? Why, in his mercy, he would allow one transgression to be taken away from the scale so that it would tip in the person's favour.

It was therefore said to be the whole aim of a Pharisees's existence to make sure that his merits outweighed his demerits, and that this was a blind, dogmatic legalism. But in reality all it implied was a certain attitude of mind. There were numerous ways in which people 'earned merit', or 'became more godlike', apart from simply fulfilling the Law. One very important aspect was that of doing good works. If one could perform an act of kindness or charity over and above what was specifically required by Law, then God's justice would see that it was credited to one's account. You could also earn merit by helping others to understand, or by intercession for those whose 'foolishness' was a hindrance to their progress.

God does not look upon your bodies and appearances; He looks upon your hearts and your deeds (Hadith).

Who shall teach you what the steep highway is? It is to ransom the captive, to feed the orphan, or the poor man who lies in the dust (surah 90.12–16).

On the other side of the spiritual 'bank balance', if one could by some means make up for one's transgressions, put right the things one had done wrong, then the sins would be blotted out, as if they had never been.

Behold, angels are appointed over you to protect you; they are kind and honourable, and write down your deeds. They know and understand all that you do (surah 82.10–12).

Behold, two guardians appointed to learn your doings, one sitting on your right and one on the left. Not a word do you utter but there is a sentinel by you, ready to note it (surah 50.17–18).

Every person's judgment is fastened round his neck; on the Day We will bring forth your book which shall be shown wide open. Read your book; you have no need of anyone but yourself to work out your account! (surah 17.13–14).

It was a system in which humans had dignity and honour, in which they could work out their redemption for themselves, by the sweat of their own brows, or the loving care of their own hands, and the warmth of their own hearts. It goes without saying, of course, that this view was completely contrary to that of trinitarian Christian theology, which taught that no matter how good a person managed to be, the cards were still stacked against them because of the 'original sin' of Adam; and therefore the help of a saviour, a God-man who was not subject to that sin, a redeemer who lived the perfect life and died as an atoning sacrifice for the sins of others, became necessary.

Whether Jesus himself ever thought in those terms is a very debatable question.

However, to view the Pharisaic legalistic system, or the Islamic system of *hasanat*, in the terms given above is far too simplistic a view. Such a view makes the zeal of the devout a perverted and trivial thing. If legalism were a true criticism, then the Pharisaic life under the Law would either cripple people with anxious worrying over whether or not they had done enough to ensure their place in the heavenly kingdom (and thus whittle away the very trust in God which had engendered the wish to live this kind of life in the first place!), or would make them overbearing and arrogant snobs if they thought that they had!

Are we seriously to suppose that the great Pharisaic rabbis of the first century were so blind, so unethical, so lacking in understanding of their Father? God claims believers wholly and utterly, demanding their whole will, their whole heart – and therefore there is no such thing as an action that can earn 'extra merit'.

Believers cannot make any claims, but are like slaves who have only their duty to do, and can do no good deed that is not their duty. 'Does the master thank the servant because he did what was commanded? So you also, when you have done all that is commanded of you, say: "We are unworthy servants: we have only done what was our duty"' (Luke 17.1–10). As Antigonus of Socoh put it, in words that suggested very strongly that the Pharisees would have agreed with the point of view just quoted: 'Be not like servants who serve their Lord on condition of receiving reward; but rather like servants who serve their Lord under no condition of receiving reward' (Pirke Aboth 1.3).

The true Pharisee did not regard *any* commandments as irksome requirements that had to be fulfilled, while one's real will was directed at something else. Rather, believers had to become like children before their Father, not appealing to any rights or merits, but simply willing to love, and to be given a gift in return.

6 · The Great Kelal

Those who patiently persevere and seek God with regular prayers, and give generously – these overcome Evil with Good (surah 13.22).

The estimate of Pharisaic religious experience as anxiety coupled with arrogant self-righteousness rests on three theories about their theology, all wrong. They are firstly the view that for salvation a person *must* do more good deeds than commit transgressions, secondly that God is inaccessible, and thirdly that the individual feels lost, with no access to a remote God (E. P. Sanders, *Paul and Palestinian Judaism*, p. 277).

E. P. Sanders, in his monumental work, was alarmed to note that in spite of the study done by a multitude of scholars such as Herford, Moore, Schechter, Montefiore, Buchler, Marmorstein, Finkelstein, and many many others, the view of rabbinic Judaism as a religion of legalistic self-righteousness has continued to flourish and be propounded with enthusiasm, to this day. Yet the traditional trinitarian view that the way of salvation in rabbinic (and later Islamic) systems consisted of weighing deeds, is wrong: it is not supported by the texts taken to support it, and it is contradicted by another, all-pervasive view.

The biblical view that God's justice should be seen to be done in one's present life was a very tenacious one, and it never completely disappeared in Judaism. However, in the first century CE there was a strong combination of the Pharisaic belief in personal resurrection with the observation that the righteous very often *did* suffer 'unmerited' adverse conditions in this world; hence, a belief in reward or punishment in a world to come became a logical part of belief in God's justice. This belief was particularly prominent in rabbinical writings after Akiba, but it had its roots in very ancient material.

In Islamic thought, the significance of this earthly life as a preparatory test for the much more important life to come became a matter of faith, and not just speculation. During earthly life we all have different sets of experiences. Some people are fortunate, others are not, but whatever the individual set of circumstances, life is not just a purposeless wandering towards death, or a game. It is a test, in deadly earnest. Humans are all *born* equal, but because their real beings are not mechanical bodies but souls equipped with freewill, they have the ability to love and be kind, or to hate and be destructive. *Therefore they do not remain equal.*

The spiritual faculties of human beings raise them above the animal kingdom and make them responsible for it. But some behave so badly that they actually sink below the level of animals. God does not control anyone's mind by force, but has allowed freewill, and given the ability to reason. Nothing can happen without the will and knowledge of Allah. He knows the present, past and future of all created beings. Our destiny is already known, and whether we will obey or disobey Allah is also known to him – but that does not affect our freedom of will. Humans do not know what their destiny is, and may choose whatever course they will take. If people choose to act deliberately against their consciences, and do evil instead of good, then it is their own fault if one day they have to pay the penalty.

If people wander aimlessly through this life they are wasting it. We have no control over our circumstances – we could be wealthy or poor, healthy or sick, strong or weak, beautiful or ugly; it is a complete waste of time moaning about these circumstances. We know neither the reasons for them, nor what we are intended to learn from them. We can be bitter and resentful, or we can accept. To a Muslim, as to the Pharisee, it was all God's will, and one should every day do one's best with patience, having trust in the words of consolation that 'On no soul does God place a burden greater than it can bear' (surah 2.286; 23.62).

If God lay the touch of trouble on you, no-one can deliver you from it save God Alone; and if He wills good for you, no one can prevent His blessing. He confers them on His servants as He chooses (surah 10.107).

What is it that is being tested? First, our characters: are we greedy, selfish, lacking in sympathy, mean, spiteful, cowardly? Secondly, our reaction to misfortune. If anyone thinks they are going to sail through life without being touched by misfortune, that is real 'wishful thinking'. No one escapes – the wheel turns for every living soul. So, when our tragedies strike, are we frightened, full of complaint, a burden to others, depressed? How do we react to good fortune? Are we selfish, conceited, arrogant, proud, miserly? What about our way of life in general? Are we dishonest, lazy, disrespectful, hurtful, unforgiving?

It is all too human for any believer in God to sit down under adversity and beg for help, for an easing of the terrible conditions, for an escape – but when the loved one *still* dies of cancer, the son *still* goes bad despite all our prayers, the husband *still* runs off or becomes brutal despite the patience of a long-suffering wife, what then? Do we turn in fury and wave our helpless fists at an unfair, capricious, malicious God, sitting 'up there' laughing at our wretched struggles? Or simply assume that all this misery merely proves that there is no God?

By no means. The prophet Job (Ayub) went through all this doubt and agony of mind centuries before Jesus. Why had *he* been singled out for such awful suffering and misfortune, when he had always been a good and devout man, and had done no terrible sins to earn this punishment? He demanded an interview with God, and in the end – when he saw a vision of the incomprehensible splendour of the universe and its vastness, the whole scheme of things which was far beyond all human understanding – he accepted that everything he personally suffered was trivial, nothing, of no consequence at all besides that Ineffable All. It was his duty simply to bear his tests, and accept, trusting only in his knowledge that his Redeemer did exist and did see and did care (Job 19.25).

God sees the tiniest of sparrows fall to the earth; it is noted. But the sparrow is not spared the fall. God knows the number of hairs on our heads, but our heads are not immune from testing (Matt. 10.29–30).

Don't be anxious, saying: What shall we eat? or What shall we drink? or What shall we wear? Your Heavenly Father knows that you need all these things. Seek first his kingdom and his righteousness, and all these shall be yours as well (Matt. 6.31–32).

How often do we all pray, like Jesus, 'O Father, let this cup (the test, or suffering) pass from me!' If we are submitted, as he was, we should end our prayer as he did: 'Nevertheless, not my will but thine be done' (Matt. 14.36).

Of utmost importance was the question whether one's place in the next world was earned by personal performance or was a gift of grace. The Pharisees were totally convinced that God was just: God was not to be thought of as arbitrary or capricious, or open to bribery like some oriental potentate. Yet it was axiomatic to the Pharisees that God's justice was full of mercy, and the very fact that there would be any future places at all was in itself an extension of his justice and mercy.

Christian scholars seized on three basic passages to support the notion of weighing merits and demerits. These were Kiddushin 1.10a and its surrounding material in the Tosephta and Talmuds; Aboth 3.15, imputed to Akiba; and Aboth 4.22, in the name of Eleazar. The passages from Aboth are both late, but the material in Kiddushin is believed to contain very ancient Mishnaic material. But here, the phraseology about the weighing is ambiguous.

> Everyone who fulfils one commandment, God benefits and lengthens his days, and he inherits the land. And everyone who does not fulfil one commandment, God does not benefit . . .

This passage led to speculation as to two possible interpretations. Did it mean that a believer had to perform at least one more merit than demerit in order to be saved? This seems to be implied by Aboth 3.15 and 4.22. 'The world is judged by grace, but everything is according to the majority of works.'

Or, did it mean that despite the mediocre quality of a believer's life, so long as *at least one commandment had been fulfilled*, God would be merciful? 'God will incline the scale in the favour of one who performs one commandment' (P. Kiddushin 61d). Would the fulfilment of only one *mitsvah* be sufficient to permit God to tip the scale to the side of innocence, for the simple reason that it meant a child of God had repented, and was seeking after reconciliation?

That was what really counted. 'If 999 angels declare a man guilty, and one declares him innocent, then the Holy One inclines the scale to innocence' (P. Kidd. 61d.). 'If a man is wicked all his life and repents at the end, he shall be saved' (P. Kidd 1.15). No matter how virtuous a person manages to be, they should nevertheless not attempt to claim merit, but only appeal for mercy:

> If Moses and David, who were able to suspend the world by their good deeds, only besought God that he should give them mercy, how much more should one who is no more than one of a thousand of the thousands of thousands' (Sifre Deut. 26).

A penitent sinner might even be deemed *superior* to a righteous person, simply because a weakness had been overcome to which the latter may not have been susceptible. The charming Muslim story of Harut and Marut illustrates this.

> The morning star, az-Zuhra, was once a woman . . . There were two angels, Harut and Marut, who forgot to be humble and boasted of their invincible purity. 'We are above all sin and desire, unlike the weak sons of men!' But they forgot that their purity had not come from their own strength, but only because they had never known desire or been called upon to resist it. They were sent down to earth. On the very first night they saw az-Zuhra, the Shining One, and the desire to possess her immmediately arose in them. She agreed to belong to them if they would kill the man who owned her. So they killed him, and with his blood still on their hands, satisfied their lust with the woman – all this on their first night on earth! (Legend given in Muhammad Asad, *The Road to Mecca*, Dar al-Andalus 1981, p.146).

The whole point of the weighing passages was simply to encourage obedience to the covenant and discourage disobedience. No person could *earn* salvation, but the wilful intent to disobey would remove one from the covenant and its promises.

A third area of speculation considered whether the one commandment that would save referred to a particular *specific* commandment, or any one of them picked at random. Was there a single command, or *kelal*, that summed up the whole? Many Rabbis considered this last theory to be highly possible. Rabbi Simlai's famous third-century homily on the Law was based on earlier traditions that followed this tendency to reduce the bulk of the Torah to one *kelal*. He said:

613 commands were given to Moses on Sinai: David reduced them to eleven (Psalm 15.2–5); Isaiah reduced them to six (Isaiah 33.15); Micah to three (Micah 6.8); Isaiah again to two, as it is said: Thus saith the Lord, 'Keep my commandments and do justice' (Isaiah 56.1); then Amos came and reduced them to one, as it is said: 'Seek the Lord, and live!' (Amos 5.6). Habbakuk also reduced them to one, as it is said: 'But the just shall live by faith' (Hab. 2.4).

Conversely, was there a single kelal which, if broken, was unforgivable, and would exclude a person from the place of bliss? Was it to say that there was no resurrection? Or that the Law was not from heaven? To pronounce the Name of God with its proper letters (Sanh. 10.1; P. Peah 16b)? Two more frivolous suggestions were that it was to pay for a woman (Baraita Erub 18b) or to employ verses from the Song of Songs in a vulgar fashion (T. Sanh 12.10). Rabbi Eleazar of Modiim was more fulsome: it was to profane the holy things, despise the feasts, shame one's fellows publicly, obliterate circumcision, and pervert the Law (Aboth 3.12).

It is interesting to notice that in the words attributed to Jesus in the Sermon on the Mount, we have the stern Pharisaic disapproval of the one who shames his brother, who calls his brother a fool (Matt. 5.22). Also, of course, we have a controversial passage in all three Synoptic Gospels about the negative *kelal*: the one unforgiveable sin. Jesus stated specifically that it was blasphemy against the Holy Spirit (Mark 3.28–29; Matt. 12:31–32; Luke 12.10), a sentiment that was quite in keeping with rabbinic speculations. According to Mekilta Pesha 5, exclusion comes for 'those who sin with the intention of denying God'; and Sifre Deut. 54 states bluntly that 'everyone who confesses to idolatry denies the entire Torah; and everyone who denies idolatry confesses to the entire Torah'.

On the positive side, the rabbis' attempts to sum up the good commandment are best represented by the statement of Hillel, based on Leviticus 19:18: 'What is hateful to you, do not do to your neighbour' (Shabb. 31a). The emphasis was on love and compassion, and there are many more examples of positive injunctions in the early Christian writings than the negative.

Apart from the use of Hillel's *kelal* in Mark 12.31, Matthew 22.34 and Luke 10.27, we have the same thing emphasized in the letter of James, as in 2.8: 'If you fulfil the royal Law according to the

scriptures, "Thou shalt love thy neighbour as thyself", you do well.'
This letter, however, does go on to the more negative side: 'For
whosoever shall keep the whole Law, and yet offends in one point,
he is guilty of all' (James 2.10). Yet the author concludes that
although 'judgment is without mercy to him who has shown no
mercy, yet mercy triumphs over judgment' (James 2.12).

The Fourth Gospel gives the New Commandment quite specifically: 'Love one another' (15.9–13). The theme is pursued in the First
Letter of John: 'He who does not love, does not know God; for God
is love' (4.7–12). Again, 'If anyone says "I love God" and hates his
brother, he is a liar; for if he does not love his brother whom he has
seen, how can he love God, whom he has not seen? And this
commandment we have from him, that he who loves God should
love his brother also' (4.19–21). 'If anyone has the world's goods,
and sees his brother in need, yet closes his heart against him, how
does God's love abide in him?' (3.17).

The Qur'an expresses exactly the same sentiments.

They of God's right hand shall ask of the wretched: 'What has cast
you into hell fire?' They will say, 'We were not of those who
prayed, or those who fed the poor, and we wasted our time with
empty arguments . . .' (surah 74.40f.).

Likewise, the hadith:

How can you call yourself a believer if your neighbour is hungry?

God does not accept beliefs if they are not expressed in deeds;
and your deeds are worthless if they do not back up your beliefs.

According to Origen's commentary on Matthew, on 19.16
onwards, the Nazarean Gospel put an interesting addition after the
Rich Young Ruler's declaration that he has observed all the Law
from his youth. Jesus replied:

How can you say 'I have fulfilled the Law and the prophets?' For
behold it stands written in the Law: Love your neighbour as
yourself; and behold, many of your brothers, sons of Abraham,
are covered with filth and dying of hunger, and your house is full
of many good things, and yet nothing at all comes forth from it to
help them (Hennecke, *New Testament Apocrypha*, Vol. 1, p. 49).

St Paul was also in accord with the Bet Hillel on this issue, that all
the commandments are comprehended in the word of love for one's
neighbour. 'For he that loves another has fulfilled the Law' (Rom.
13.8). 'For the Law is fulfilled in one word, "You shall love your
neighbour as yourself"' (Gal. 5.14). 'Love is the soul of perfection'
(Col. 3.14). This doctrine of love was movingly expounded in the
famous thirteenth chapter of 1 Corinthians.

> If I speak in the tongues of men and of angels but have not love, I
> am just a loud noise; if I have prophetic powers, and understand
> all mysteries and all knowledge, and have all faith so as to remove
> mountains, but have not love, I am nothing. If I give away all that
> I have, and deliver my body to be burned, but have not love – I
> gain nothing (13.1–4).

So, the true 'righteous believer' might not be a saint, but was any
person who was faithful to the covenant and doing their best to keep
it. The intention (or *niyyah*) was of vital importance, and a bad
intention was considered to be rebellion.

> If a man were righteous all his days, but rebelled at the end, he
> would destroy everything. But if a man were wicked all his days,
> but repented at the end, God would accept him (T. Kidd 1.15).

Jesus' parable of the Labourers in the Vineyard illustrates exactly
this attitude. Men were hired at different hours throughout the day,
and at the end those who had only worked one hour received the
same wages as those who had toiled all day (Matt. 20.1–16). This
may have caused the full-time workers to grumble, but the point of
the parable was to illustrate God's generosity.

What mattered ultimately was being included in the covenant,
and God's grace would enable even the eleventh-hour penitent to
be received back. As Jesus expressed it, there would be more joy in
heaven over one sinner that repented than over 99 just people that
had no need to repent (Luke 15.7, 10). Trade-union shop stewards
might find this unjust repayment, but anyone whose heart was full
of God's love would find it utterly reasonable.

Unjust? There is no question of penitent sinners *earning* their
place in God's kingdom; this was the gift of God's mercy and grace.
Indeed, no person could ever be accounted good enough really to
have earned such a reward.

If God punished people according to what they deserved, He would not leave on earth a single living thing! (surah 16.61).

Any rejection of God's commands with conscious intent excludes one from the covenant.

You should worship Allah as if you are seeing Him; for He sees you even if you do not see Him (Hadith).

People should really conduct themselves as if they were to meet God and give account of themselves at any moment, since the condition of the heart *at that moment* would govern the relationship they could then expect with God. If they had given up and rejected God, no matter how saintly their past, that rejection would put them outside the covenant bond. God would not force them back into it. But God always has mercy on those who turn again to him, no matter how wicked their past; therefore the situation of being outside the covenant bond was entirely dependent on the person's being willing to turn again to God in hope and confidence that God would forgive, and love.

The idea of Jesus telling the parable of the Prodigal Son in order to *discomfit the Pharisees*, who were supposed only to accept a weighing sort of judgment, is thus seen to be ludicrous. The parable was squarely in the Pharisaic tradition that God *would* accept the penitent, no matter what his past deeds, once he had undergone the necessary change of heart and re-established his intention to rejoin the covenant relationship (Luke 15.11–32).

One late source expressed very succinctly the true Rabbinic humility: 'Even when we consider our pious deeds, we are ashamed of their pettiness as compared to the greatness of God's mercy towards us' (Pesiqta Rabbathi 98b). Luke's sentiment in 17.7–10, that when people had tried with all their might and done absolutely all that they could, they had simply done no more than their duty, was echoed in a saying attributed to Rabbi Johanan ben Zakkai: 'If you have done much within the Law, do not claim merit for yourself, for to this end you were created' (Aboth 2.8). There is a famous story of this particular rabbi weeping on his deathbed that was supposed by some critics to indicate the nightmare of legalism. Even after he had spent his entire lifetime doing his best, this good rabbi still could not be sure that he had done enough to earn a place in heaven! However, interpreting the story a different way, one could equally well argue that far from indicating that here was a man whose last hours were ruined by a dreadful anxiety, rather he felt close to God, and was conscious – as all such close people are – of his own unworthiness.

Salvation, in rabbinic religion, came through election and repentance. The point of any of the sayings about damnation or salvation for one good deed or a majority of good deeds was in both cases to urge the people to do their utmost to keep the command-ments to the best of their abilities. They should always be prepared for God's command to lay down their lives and return to Him (Amr Allah), for they did not know the day nor the hour. Therefore, it was their duty to live every day, every moment, as if it might be their last – then there would be no cause for regret.

People who live on this level live quite differently from others. Their lives are crammed with good deeds and deep thoughts, and they do not waste them in bitter and helpless regrets.

It is therefore patently untrue to maintain that Pharisaic soterio-logy consisted of a system of balancing merits and demerits. The rabbis certainly did believe that in his perfect justice God would punish transgression and reward obedience, but God's mercy was far beyond that of any human judge

> How can I give you up, O Ephraim! . . . My heart recoils within me, My compassion grows warm and tender. I will not execute my fierce anger . . . for I am God and not man, the Holy One in your midst' (Hos. 11.8).

God alone knows the full story of our inner motives, trials and tribulations. He alone understands fully how little the violent, ignorant thug is responsible for the unhappiness he causes, and how great is the fall of the saint who allows a fleeting malicious thought.

It was not rabbinic (nor is it Muslim) doctrine that one's place in the world to come is determined by counting or weighing. The point was that people were urged always to do their best. A man should behave at all times *as if* his deeds were evenly balanced and the next would determine his fate, or, if that was too difficult, as if he would be judged by the majority of his deeds.

The teachings of Jesus were full of this same sense of urgency: the importance of being awake, being prepared, being watchful, for no one knew when the kingdom of God would come. The 'crisis' parables exhort people to live *as if* every day was their last, to make use of every opportunity of service, to treat all people as if they were God in disguise, so that when the kingdom came at an hour no one expected – like a thief in the night (Luke 12.39), or an inconsiderate bridegroom (Matt. 25.1–13) – the faithful would not be caught napping.

If anyone can ask whether it is fair for God to welcome back with open arms the thoroughly despicable young waster, and yet shut out those silly girls who had waited faithfully for ages for the bridegroom, he has completely missed the point.

The possibility cannot be excluded that there *were* some Pharisees accurately hit by the polemic of Matt. 23, who attended only to trivia and left undone the weightier matters. Human nature being what it is, one supposes there were some such. One must say, however, that the surviving Jewish literature does not reveal them . . . Therefore we must say that the Judaism of before 70 CE kept grace and works in the right perspective, did not trivialize the commandments of God, and was not especially marked by hypocrisy. The frequent Christian charge against Jews, it must be recalled, is not that some individual Jews misunderstood, misapplied and abused their religion, but that Judaism *necessarily* tends towards petty legalism, self-serving, and self-deceiving casuistry, and a mixture of arrogance and lack of confidence in God. But the surviving Jewish literature is as free of those characteristics as any I have ever read (E. P. Sanders, *Paul and Palestinian Judaism*, p. 427).

How easy misunderstandings are! Here is an extract from a Jewish observer of Christian behaviour at the holy places at Jerusalem, showing how he managed to avoid a misunderstanding that has raised contempt in many other such observers.

Last Easter I was in Jerusalem, and along the façades of the Church of the Holy Sepulchre I saw the stalls of the vendors of the second relics, of painted beads and inscribed ribbons, of coloured candles, gilded crucifixes and bottles of Jordan water. There these Christians babbled and swayed and bargained, a crowd of buyers and sellers in front of the church sacred to the memory of Jesus. But . . . I did not think that this was the sole motive which brought thousands of pilgrims to Jerusalem; . . . Nay, as I turned away, I thought that perhaps if I had the insight to track a dealer

in relics to this inmost soul, I might after all find there a heart
warm with the love of Christ' (I. Abrahams, *Studies in Pharisaism
and the Gospels*, p. 88).

What was vital to true 'separated life' was the 'directing of the
heart', the motivation and intention, what Muslims call *niyyah*. The
Pharisees would certainly have agreed with Jesus over the offering
of the widow's mite (Mark 12.41–44): it was not the size of the
offering that was important, but the intention. Leviticus Rabba 111
states that the poor man's offering of two doves was more
preferable to God than King Agrippa's thousand sacrifices. The
passage goes on to mention a priest who was scornful of a woman
who had offered only a handful of flour. This priest was pulled up
sharp by a Bath Qol warning: 'Despise her not; it is as though she
offered her life.' Similarly, Exodus Rabba 30 gives: 'He who robs
the widow and orphans is as though he robbed God Himself.'

Such passages prove, incidentally, that to accept such offerings
from the poor was not thought of as 'devouring widows' houses', a
criticism made in Mark 12.43. Their sacrifices were not dragged out
of them by grasping priestly hands, eager to squeeze money from
those who could not afford it, but were treated with great honour
and respect. Jesus, if the words in that phrase are his, must have
been referring to some other practice: maybe of some individual
known to him. According to Rabbi Meir, 'the value of the words
depends on the intention' (Berakoth 3–4). 'The one who prays must
direct his heart to God' (Berakoth 17a). 'The scholar who studies is
not superior to his fellow the common man, provided that the latter
directs his heart to Heaven.'
Rosh HaShanah 3–7 gives an interesting example.

If a man was passing behind a synagogue, or if his house was near
a synagogue, and he heard the sound of the shofar or the reading
of the Megillah, and he directed his heart to it – he has fulfilled his
obligation; but if he did not, then he has not fulfilled his
obligation.

Though two persons may have heard the same summons to worship,
one may have directed his heart and the other not – only the
former's intentions are valid and acceptable, even if the latter
directed his feet! The person who did *not* go, but who prayed, is

closer to God than the person who went but did it like an automaton, without directing the heart.

A man had two sons; and he went to the first and said 'Son, go and work in the vineyard today.' And he answered 'I will not,' but afterward he repented and went. And he went to the second and said the same; and he answered, 'I go, sir,' but did not go. Which of the two did the will of the Father? (Matt. 21.28–30).

One can imagine a modern-day Pharisee making the same point about those perhaps not in church on a Sunday, but involved in thoughts of God or actions for him, comparing the directing of their hearts to those of the faithful slumbering peacefully through the sermon in a pew. Or the Muslims who hear the call and stop for a moment to draw close, even though they may not actually be at the mosque, compared to the devout who are there punctually at every opportunity – leaving their 'support teams' to do all the supporting.

According to one Muslim story, Jesus came across a holy-looking man and asked him what he was doing. He replied that he was serving God. Jesus then asked him who was taking care of him. 'My brother,' he said. 'Then,' replied Jesus, 'your brother is serving God better then you.'

The Pharisees extended this principle to a situation in which a person would have dearly loved to have given alms, but his personal circumstances were such as would not permit it – for example, if he had only heard about a case of need too late to do anything about it, or he had nothing to give on that occasion. In a case like this, the intention would be credited to that person as if they had acted (Sifre Deut. 117), since God would know whether or not the intention of the heart was genuine. This was a way of saying that a good thought was almost as good as a good deed. One Muslim story tells of a man who, after a lifetime saving to go on the *hajj* did not go because he used his money to help someone who had fallen on hard times. Friends who did go insisted that they had seen him at every place on the pilgrimage.

In God's mercy, a bad thought was not counted as a bad deed. One had actually to fulfil the evil intention for it to be punishable (Peah 1.4). God always put his weight on the side of mercy and understanding, and was always ready to welcome and forgive the penitent. People's past lives were not seen as fair cause to remove them beyond all hope of salvation. Repentance created a new situation, in which previous disobedience was no longer counted against them. Penitence was the means of restoring the relationship that had been spoiled.

The Pharisees were so aware of God's love that they argued that sins against God were much more easily forgiven than sins against one's fellows, since the latter required proper restitution in human terms, and that could be much harder. God was ever waiting with open arms to receive the lost sheep or the prodigal son. The beautiful mediaeval poem of Jehuda Halevi expressed it in these words:

> Longing, I sought Thy presence,
> Lord, with my whole heart did I call and pray;
> And going out towards Thee,
> I found Thee coming to me on the way.

But God can only accept the repentance of one who has offended another human once that human has been appeased (Sifre Ahare pereq 8.1). As Jesus said:

> If you are actually standing before the altar of God and even there you remember that you have offended someone, leave your gift and go. First be reconciled to that person, then come and make your gift to God (Matt. 5.24).

Forgiveness was not conditional on the repentance of a sinner (that is God's business alone), but it *cannot be received by the sinner* without turning to God with a repentant and receiving heart. In other words, God is always willing to forgive, but humans put up the blockades. It is repentance alone that makes the recipient capable of receiving the forgiveness offered. This is the principle that lies behind such New Testament passages as Luke 7.36f., the sinful woman who loved before being forgiven; Matthew 18.22f, the ungrateful servant whose heart was certainly not in the right condition for forgiveness; Matthew 6.14f., the comment in the Lord's Prayer that forgiveness cannot come to you if you are unprepared to forgive your brother; and Matthew 11.25, where the attitude of bearing a grievance against anyone would stand in the way of God being able to forgive you the wrongs you had done yourself.

One's repentance does not mean that one has deserved or earned forgiveness, but simply that one's new attitude towards God and one's fellow humans has provided the capacity for receiving it. It follows, therefore, that Jesus' statement about the one unforgiveable sin was quite correct. Blasphemy against the Holy Spirit surely means a refusal to recognize the loving influence and rightness of this forgiving activity of God, when it is offered.

One cannot help but believe that Jesus was directly in this Pharisaic line in his teachings. Sifre on Deut. 13.18 reads: 'Whenever you have mercy on other creatures, they in Heaven have mercy on you.' Jesus said: 'Forgive us our trespasses, as we forgive them that trespass against us. For if you do not forgive people their sins, then neither will God forgive your sins (Matt. 6.12, 14–15). Midrash Tannaim 15.11 reads: 'As you withhold mercy, so they will withhold mercy from you.'

> The recompense for an injury is an injury equal thereto; but if a person forgives and makes reconciliation, his reward is due from God' (surah 42.40).

The Pharisees and later the Muslims considered that the whole of human life ought to be capable of holiness, not just one's activities at certain times and in certain places. Nothing in human life was considered too trivial to be beneath the divine concern, so no action of God's servants was too unimportant to be carefully examined for its merits. Some commandments seemed easier to keep or more trivial than others, but it was not the place of any human to judge between them, since what might seem very unimportant to an individual might have extreme significance when seen through God's eyes.

> Behave towards an easy command exactly as towards a difficult one; for you do not know what reward will be given for the commandments (Aboth 2.16).

> The scriptures make the easiest among the easy commandments equal to the hardest among the hard (P. Kidd. 1.61b).

The Sadducees sought to limit holiness to the Temple and its appurtenances, and criticized the Pharisees for confusing the people. The Pharisees acknowledged openly that in their search for truth it was quite possible that their human and finite minds might sometimes find two different courses of action equally correct, a concept the Sadducees branded inconsistent and nonsensical. Pharisaism, on the contrary, regarded active debate on difficult issues as vital and fundamental, and not a cause for embarrassment. Disagreements among the sages simply reflected the determination of the group as a whole to serve God with as much discernment and dedication to truth as possible. Differences of opinion were nothing to be ashamed of or unduly worried about – on the contrary, they were the 'glory' of the whole movement.

The Pharisees were well aware of the weakness of human nature, and were kind in the allowances they made. 'Many an old camel is laden with the hides of younger ones' (a saying often claimed to be Islamic, but actually found in Sanh. 52a). They looked for ways of giving people the opportunity for repentance and readjustment in their relationships with God. They may well have seen the idealistic stance taken by the Jesus of the Gospels as being hopelessly high and beyond the reach of ordinary people, an opinion often expressed by struggling Christians.

Jesus disregarded the social edifice and based his teachings on the individual conscience, seeking a fundamental reconstruction of human nature. There was an urgent, all-or-nothing quality to much that he said. This is not the place to argue out the nature of his special knowledge or awareness, but we must accept that there was a strong eschatological element to his thoughts. It seems he believed in the immanence of a divine intervention, soon to disrupt the present social order of things, therefore he had to be drastic in his reforms.

The time was short, and soon the kingdom of God would come, at an hour no one would expect. Therefore, if your eye offended you, you should pluck it out (Mark 9.47). It was better to go through life maimed than with two eyes to be thrown into hell. Or, as both Jesus and the Qur'an taught, if your hand offended you (by stealing), you should cut it off (Mark 9.43; surah 5.38, 39). Jesus expected his call to be obeyed instantly, leaving 'the dead to bury the dead'. A contrasting saying of Johanan ben Zakkai illustrated a shrewd common sense.' If, while engaged in planting a tree, you hear that the Messiah has come, finish your work and then follow him' (Aboth 11.31, 34a). If the call was genuine, the meticulous worker would in no way be rejected.

The Pharisees approached the same problems as Jesus, but in

terms of this world, of social realities. After all, they bore the responsibility for the peace and welfare of society and the state, and had to interpret the Pentateuchal Law by which their society was governed. Jesus was not in that position. He was appealing to their consciences, in order to change their very natures, so that ultimately there would be no need for judgment and punishment at all. Punishments had been decreed in the Pentateuch because human nature was weak; thus, by changing human nature, the need for punishments would be removed.

Yet one may not conclude that the motivation of Jesus was purely apocalyptic, or based on the old craving for 'pie in the sky'. Jesus would surely have agreed with the dictum of Rabbi Eleazer ben Zadok:

> In serving God you must not think, 'I shall study Torah so that I may be rich, or so that I may be called Rabbi, or so that I may receive a reward in the world to come.' The scripture says 'Thou shalt love the Lord thy God.' All that you do, do only from love (Sifre Deut. 41).

These sentiments are exactly in accord with those of the Sufi mystic Rubia al-Adawiyya (who died in 801 CE).

> 'O God, if I have worshipped you for fear of hell, burn me in hell; if I have worshipped you for hope of paradise, exclude me from it; but if I worship you for your own sake, then do not keep me from your everlasting beauty.'

7 · Legends of the Famous Pharisees

The period that produced the great Pharisaic celebrities began with the creation of the Great Sanhedrin, and great teachers such as Simeon the Just and Antigonus of Socoh. After them came a series of Zugoth or 'pairs' – such rabbis as Jose ben Joezer and Jose ben Johanan; Joshua ben Perahiah and Nittai the Arbelite; Judah ben Tabbai and Simeon ben Shetah; Shemaiah and Abtalion, friends of Herod the Great; the cantankerous Shammai and the gentle Hillel. Later notable Pharisees were Johanan ben Zakkai and his disciples; Gameliel and Simeon ben Gamaliel, Akiba, Meir and Judah the Prince.

Very little is known with certainty of the history of these men, but legends abound and are often as amusing as they are enlightening. In this chapter some of the sayings and happenings attributed to them are simply retold for the reader's interest, without any pretence at historical criticism.

Simeon the Just (second century BCE) was famous for the psychic phenomena associated with him. He actually ruled as high priest, and on one occasion heard a Bath Qol whilst on duty in the Holy of Holies on the Day of Atonement. He took note that the heavenly voice spoke in the colloquial Aramaic dialect – which caused him great surprise!

Simeon was notable for two much-talked-of phenomena, both happening regularly and both concerned with the effect he had on fire. It was said that the Western Lamp in the Temple – a huge lantern – never once needed refuelling the entire time he was in office. It just carried on burning until the day he died, when all of a sudden it went out. After his death the priests began fully to appreciate their loss of his unusual blessing, for to their great annoyance the lamp started fizzling out frequently, and they had to put a lamp-watchman back on to the duty rota.

Also, in Simeon's time, it was said that the fire of the wood-offering used to burn strongly all day long once it had been arranged on the altar, and only needed the laying-in of two logs in the evening to keep it going for the night. But after Simeon's death, the priests had to go back to piling on wood all day long.

Two sayings of Simeon were, 'On three things the world stands – Torah, the cult, and deeds of loving-kindness' (P. Taanit 4.2 repr. Gilead 21a), and, referring to the false pride felt by someone who shaved his head in accordance with the Nazirite vow: 'You take pride in what is not yours. It belongs to the dust, the worm and the maggot. Lo, I shave you off for the sake of Heaven' (Sifre Num. 22, ed. Friedman 7a–b).

Simeon, like other clairvoyants, predicted his own death. Every year, as he entered the Holy of Holies on the Day of Atonement, he had been aware of the figure of a ghostly double, an old man dressed in white, who entered and departed alongside him. In Simeon's last year the mysterious 'double' appeared dressed in black. It entered with him as usual, but this time it did not depart (P. Yoma 5.2; B. Yoma 39b and B. Men 109b). His namesake, Simeon ben Shetah, was a leading Pharisee who, with his sister Shelomzion, enjoyed enormous political influence in the first century BCE. Shelomzion married two kings. Her first husband was the Hasmonaean king Aristobulus. She survived his fierce reign and death, ordered the release of his three rival brothers who had been incarcerated for years, married the eldest of them, Alexander Jannaeus, and took the name Queen Alexandra Salome. As we saw, Jannaeus' reign was notable for a fierce persecution of the Pharisaic sect, but Salome managed to survive him also, and finally ruled in her own right.

The legends about her fiery and uncompromising brother Simeon suggest that he was not in the least afraid of Jannaeus. On one occasion Jannaeus had been summoned by the Sanhedrin in connection with the case of a slave who had killed a man. Simeon, who objected bitterly to the fact that Jannaeus had taken the office of high priest as well as being the king, observed Jannaeus pompously sitting on his throne and demanded bluntly that he should stand up like the other assembled men, on the grounds that 'it is not before us that you attend, but before him who spoke and the world came into being, as it is written: "*both* the men between whom is the controversy shall stand" (Deut. 19.17).' Jannaeus, however, refused to stand unless Simeon's colleagues all agreed with him. The cowardly rogues bowed their heads and kept silence. But Simeon was vindicated, for the angel Gabriel 'descended and smote them, and they died' (Sanh. 19 a-b and 2.1).

Simeon was reported as having had a very stern nature. On one occasion he was responsible for attempting to stamp out witchcraft in Ashkelon, and ended up by killing eighty women in a single mass execution (B. Sanh 64; P. Sanh 6.9.23c). However, he tempered his justice with a move towards more humane sentences, for he allowed these women to be stoned and not burnt – which was considered to be a more merciful form of death (P. Sanh 7.4).

A group of 'false witnesses' plotted to get revenge for this execution by bringing about the destruction of that he loved most, his son. The youth was 'framed', tried, found guilty and condemned to death. While he was actually being led out to execution, the schemers repented, and confessed to their perjury, but the son refused to accept an illegal reprieve, saying, 'Father, if you wish salvation to come through you, you must let the Law take its course' (P. San. 6.3.23b).

Such dedication to the Law must have been unique. The event undoubtedly shook Simeon. It is not surprising that one of his recorded dicta was, 'Be very searching in the examination of witnesses!'

In future, he insisted that a court should only judge capital cases on the evidence of at least two witnesses, and not just on circumstantial evidence. This was illustrated on one occasion when he actually pursued personally an armed man who was chasing a villain into a ruin. He arrived in time to see the unfortunate victim expire on the ground. To Simeon's exasperation, although he had caught the murderer in the act he could not bring him to justice, since he was the only witness to what had taken place. He did declare that 'He who knows man's thoughts will exact payment for that victim'. Before he left the ruin, he had the satisfaction of seeing a snake bite the murderer, and kill him (Tos. Sanh 8.3).

Simeon was also famed for his honesty and integrity. Once he purchased as ass from a bedouin, and when he got it home he found that it had a precious stone tied round its neck. He at once sought out the vendor saying, 'I bought an ass, and not a jewel' (Deut, Rabba 3.3). Another version of the story added that when Simeon was gently laughed at for handing it over, he said: 'Do you think

Simeon is a barbarian? No, he would prefer to hear the Arab say "Blessed be the God of the Jews" than to possess all the riches of the world' (P. Baba Metzin 2.5.8c).

One of his moves that may or may not have been popular was that he pioneered education for the young, and introduced compulsory school attendance for children, obliging parents to send their offspring to establishments he set up in each district instead of relying on their own ability to teach them (P. Ket. 8.11.32c). Another charitable act was the insistence on a written contract with witnesses for a marriage, and not just a verbal contract which could be broken all too easily.

One of Simeon's contemporaries was a most fascinating eccentric, Honi ha-Me'aggel, the 'Circle-Drawer'. Honi was a holy man of the old charismatic tradition, a renowned miracle worker with the special gift for being able to 'persuade God' to make it rain – a gift shared by his eminent forebear Elijah. A saying in the Midrash Rabbah states: 'No man has existed comparable to Elijah and Honi the Circle-Drawer, causing mankind to serve God' (Gen. Rabba 13.7). Apparently it was to Honi that people resorted in times of drought, to get him to appeal for rain. If no answer was given to his 'normal' prayers, Honi would then draw a circle around himself, stand within it, and say: 'Lord of the World, your children have turned to me because I am as a son of the house before you. I swear by your great Name that I will not move from this spot until you are merciful to your children' (P. Ta'an 3.8). Sure enough, after a few moments rain would commence.

If they got a useless drizzle that dried up before it sank in, or a cloudburst that would sweep their soil away, Honi would pray again until the rain became acceptable. Simeon ben Shetah disapproved of this importunity, and did not know what to do with this unconventional character. He would have placed him 'under the ban' for troubling God as he did, but he gave up. 'What can I do to you who importune God and he accedes to your request, as a son importunes his father and he accedes to him?' (Pla'an 3.8).

This gift of producing rainfall was apparently maintained in Honi's family for several generations, passing first to Hanan ha-Nebha (the Modest), his daughter's son, and then to Abba Hilkaiah, his son's son (B. Taan 23ab). It was reported of this Hilkaiah that once messengers came to ask him to pray for rain whilst he was hoeing a field, but he refused to take time off at his employer's expense to do so, and made them wait until he had finished his duties. The same reference also gave credit to his wife, stating that they used to pray together and he considered her to be more worthy than himself (B. Taan 23ab).

Apart from making it rain, Honi was highly revered for his great piety. It was said that he always walked barefoot with his shoes slung round his neck, so that he could put them on if he needed to wade through water. The reason for this apparently odd behaviour was quite logical. When he entered water he was not able to see what he was treading on, and might have made himself unclean.

His death was tragic and unjustly caused. When civil war broke out between Hyrcanus II and Aristobulus II, he was sought out by Hyrcanus, who was besieging Aristobulus in Jerusalem. Hyrcanus ordered him to place a curse on his brother's army. This Honi refused to do, and prayed instead: 'O God, King of the Universe, these men are thy people and those who are besieged are thy people; therefore I beseech thee *not* to do as they ask . . .' (Josephus, *Antiquities* 14.22–24). For this refusal to co-operate, he was stoned to death.

An Amoraic haggadah mentions a legend that he lay beneath a carob tree and slept for seventy years, and when he woke up nobody recognized him or believed who he was; so he prayed for death, and died. However, this is a frequently recurring legend, repeated of several other celebrities.

Shemaiah and Abtalion were the fourth of the Zugoth. Shemaiah was the Nasi and Abtalion the Ab-Beth-Din. Both were said to have been descendants of Sennacherib, their ancestors having become proselytes (Gittin 57b). Some scholars have identified Shemaiah with the Samaias who stood up against Herod, and was so admired by him. Abtalion is believed by many to be the scholar Pollio, the beloved tutor of Herod's children. A variant manuscript of Josephus, *Antiquities* 4.172, makes it Abtalion who was the one to denounce Herod, and who prophesied the bitter fate in store for the Jewish people. He persuaded them that they might as well open the gates and accept Herod, since he had foreseen by clairvoyance that Herod would be king.

The study of the relationship between Herod and the Pharisees in general is too complicated to find a place here. However, one should note that Herod was not the monstrous villain that centuries of Christian press would have us believe. Both Herod the Great and his son Antipas (the governor of Galilee who put Jesus on trial, Luke 22.6–12) were pious men, well educated, who seem to have favoured the Pharisaic party over the Sadducees. Herod always admired courage and loyalty, and those who spoke their minds openly. Typically, one of Shemiah's most famous dicta was 'Love work, hate lordship, seek no intimacy with the ruling power.' Herod would not have been in the least offended.

Both these two men were so beloved by the people that when the crowd escorting the high priest on the Day of Atonement heard that they were approaching, they actually deserted the pontiff's procession, and flocked to welcome their favourite rabbis (B. Yom 71b)!

The next Zugoth were the famous Hillel and Shammai. Hillel had spent his early life in the company of Shemaiah and Abtalion, and his first colleague was not Shammai but the seer Menahem the Essene, another saintly man much revered by King Herod. This Menahem's son became a foster-brother of Herod Antipas, and may have been the Manaen mentioned as a member of Herod's court and a friend of Paul's great colleague Barnabas in Antioch. It is interesting to notice that this Manaen was also a friend of Simon of Cyrene; he may have been converted to Christianity by the man who actually carried the cross for Jesus (Acts 13.1).

When Menahem retired and Shammai was appointed, Hillel very soon himself retired, but not before he had established a dynasty that was destined to guide Jewish religious life for over 400 years. Hillel was said to have been a scion of the House of David (Ket. 62b; P. Ta'an. 4.2); Gamaliel I was his grandson, and the line of descent went from Gamaliel to Simeon, to Gamaliel II, to Simeon II, to Judah the Prince.

Shammai was a builder by trade, known for his stringent approach to the Torah. On one occasion, when he was asked by a proselyte to teach him the whole Law in the time that he could balance on one foot, he was so annoyed that he hit the proselyte with the builder's cubit-measure he was holding. It was said later that one should be as 'meek as Hillel, and not as quick-tempered as Shammai' (Shabb 30b), although perhaps one can understand his desperation with that foolish proselyte.

Despite his irascible nature, the best-known dictum of Shammai was to 'make your study of the Torah a matter of established regularity; say little and do much; receive all people with a friendly countenance' (Aboth 1.15). One assumes that he must therefore have worn a friendly countenance himself on at least a few occasions!

One of his main contributions in criminal procedure was to establish that people who hired killers to commit murder on their behalf were themselves guilty of that murder and liable to judgment (Kid.43a).

Shammai and his school were a very strong force with a large following, but they were completely overshadowed by the magnetism of the saintly Hillel. Shammai was respected, but Hillel was loved. A legend in Yoma 35 told of an occasion when Hillel, who in his youth was extremely poor and could not afford the fee to hear a particular lecture, sat at an open window adjacent to the room in which the talk was taking place. It happened to be bitterly cold, and as Hillel sat entranced by the rabbi's words, he was gradually covered in snow. When the lecture reached its conclusion, Hillel was too stiff from exposure to move, and it was not until the following morning that his frozen person was discovered, still sitting in the window. This caused great consternation, because it was the sabbath day, and the Pharisees had ruled that the kindling of fire of that day was to be counted as work, and was therefore forbidden. However, to save the unfortunate Hillel, the rabbis did not hesitate, and declared that 'this man deserves that the sabbath laws be suspended on his behalf'. The sabbath was broken, a fire lit, and Hillel saved.

Although his finances improved later, Hillel remained the very soul of kindness and humility. It was said of him that on one occasion he supplied an impoverished man who had known better times with a horse to ride on and a servant to run before him. One day the servant failed to appear, and to prevent shaming him, Hillel himself took the servant's place and ran before him, for three miles (Ket. 67b).

Hillel was fond of taking a daily bath, which amused his students so that they good-naturedly forced him to justify himself.

When he took leave of his students, he used to say he was going for a walk. His students asked him, 'Where are you walking to?' He replied, 'To perform a meritorious deed.' They said, 'And what is this deed?' He said, 'To take a bath in the bath-house.' They said, 'And is this a meritorious deed?' He said, 'It is; if statues erected to kings in the theatres are scrubbed by those in charge of them, how much more should we, who have been created in God's image and likeness, take care of our bodies.'

A variant version of the same story has:

'Rabbi, where are you going?' He said, 'To do a charitable deed for a guest in my house.' They said, 'Does this guest stay with you every day?' He said, 'This poor soul – is it not a guest in the body, here today and gone tomorrow?' (Lev. Rabba 24.3).

Hillel was also noted for his great patience, and his careful avoidance of irritation and anger. He was never too busy to be kind and considerate, or to listen to the problems of others and try to help them. He was prepared to receive all comers, and replied to all questions courteously, even if they were deliberately designed to irritate him. When the same wretched proselyte who had been so rudely repulsed by Shammai came to him with the same question, he gave the famous reply:

What is hateful to you, do not do to your neighbour. That is the whole Torah, while the rest is commentary. Go and learn it (Shabb 31a).

Incidentally, there is a similar story in Islamic folklore, which is interesting to compare.

Once an illiterate man met Hazrat Ali (the Prophet Muhammad's adopted son) and asked him to explain how far a man is free in doing whatever he pleased. It was an intricate and philosophical problem. Hazrat Ali advised the man to stand on one of his legs. The man stood on one leg. Thereupon Hazrat Ali asked the man to lift his other leg as well. The man said he would fall if he lifted his other leg also. Hazrat Ali said: 'One is free to do what one pleases as long as one stands on one leg'; i.e. he is neither absolutely free in his action, nor absolutely constrained' (Naha-jul-Blagha).

A story is told of a man who wagered 400 zuzim that he could provoke Hillel to anger. He kept on making a noise outside Hillel's house and asking foolish questions that the sage continued to answer politely. Finally he cried out, 'Are you really Hillel? May there be few such among our people!' 'Why, my son?' the scholar

asked. 'Because you have just cost me 400 zuz!' came the rueful
reply (Shabb. 31a).

Rabbi Jonathan ben Uzziel, one of his disciples, reported that
such was his mystic power that 'when he was sitting and labouring at
the Torah, every bird that flew over him immediately burnt up'
(Sukk. 28a).

His practical benevolence was revealed in such matters as the
marriage rights of young women, the redemption of property, and
the closure of debts in sabbatical years. If a man gave his daughter in
marriage when she was more than twelve years old, would that
marriage be held valid? A man's rights over his daughter were as
those of property; but Hillel ruled that after twelve years she should
be free to marry whom she wished, therefore at that age a father's
action against her wishes would be void.

The rule about houses in a walled city was that they should be able
to be redeemed for a year after their sale, if the original owner
raised the money to buy them back. This led to the custom of
purchasers hiding themselves away as the year drew to its close, so
that the sellers could not find them and return the purchase money.
Hillel ordered that the seller (who had presumably been forced to
sell his inheritance because of hard times) need not hand the money
over to the purchaser directly if he could not find him, but could
leave it in a specially appointed place, thus thwarting their attempts
to keep the property (Lev. 25.29; Acts 9.4). Also, the purchasers
were not to sell the houses back at a profit but at the price they had
paid. Usury against those who borrowed out of their need was
forbidden.

This is in keeping with the teachings of the Qur'an, which
stipulates: 'God will deprive usury of all blessing, but will give
increase for deeds of charity' (surah 2.276); 'If the debtor is in a
difficulty, grant him time till it is easy to repay. But if you remit it
altogether that is the best thing to do' (surah 2.280); 'That which
you lay out for increase through the property of others will have no
increase with God' (surah 30.39).

The cancellation of all debts in a sabbatical year was imperilling
the whole economy based on the credit and loan system – and Hillel
saw to it that the Law was adjusted so that debts could still be
claimed and people not be ruined by others taking out debts that
they had no intention of reimbursing, and thus using the relief of the
sabbatical year given to them to defraud others.

Hillel's grandson was Rabbi Gammaliel I, who was apparently tolerant towards the first Christians (Acts 5.34–39), and is said in the New Testament to have been the teacher of St Paul (Acts 22.3). He followed the practical rulings of his grandfather in that he permitted women to remarry on the evidence of only a single witness to the death of their husband (Yer 16.7).

Gamaliel's son Simeon was the Nasi at the time of the destruction of the Temple. He had been a bitter opponent of the governor-historian Josephus, yet even Josephus praised him: 'a man highly gifted with intelligence and judgment; he could by sheer genius retrieve an unfortunate situation in affairs of state' (*Life*, 191). Perhaps his 'gift' lay in his ability of knowing when to speak and when to say nothing, for one of his most famous sayings was: 'All my days I have grown up among the wise, and I have found nothing of better service than silence; not learning but doing is the chief thing; he who is profuse of words causes sin' (Aboth 1.17). True to his family interests he was a practical man, concerned in the affairs of women, and his contribution was to order the price of birds used by the women as sacrifices after childbirth to be kept at a minimum (Ker. 1.7). The controlled price of doves had risen to an exorbitant height, and Simeon ordered that in future only one bird need be sacrificed for every five demanded by tradition. At once the price fell to a quarter of a denarius, instead of a gold denarius per pair!

Simeon was a lively character, rather disdained by some of the more sedate priests, because he had a somewhat unusual and light-hearted attitude to the feastings. Sukkoth was a celebration which appealed to the people in particular, and it ended with a torchlight procession round the altar carrying willow-branches which were beaten to shreds against the altar. Forgetting his dignity, Simeon would leap about and juggle with eight burning torches, 'throwing them into the air and catching each as it came down, before it fell to the ground' (Tos. Sukk. 4.4). His flexibility and agility was also remarked upon when he prostrated himself. Apparently, he 'placed his finger upon the pavement, bowed, kissed the ground, and immediately stood upright' (Sukk. 53a).

His son, Gamaliel II, became Nasi in c.80 CE. It was his role to strengthen the new centre at Yabneh, which had been founded by Hillel's pupil Rabbi Johanan ben Zakkai. At Yebneh, Gamaliel II worked hard, and made himself rather unpopular in so doing, to raise the status and honour of the Nasi. He did insist that this was not to glorify himself, but because the nation after the crisis of 70 CE needed reunification under firm leadership. Since they had lost the priesthood, the spokesman for Judaism should now be the Nasi alone. Gamaliel II seems to have been rather a sober-sided fellow when compared to his father. Nevertheless, he was a keen and enlightened scholar, and permitted the study of Greek wisdom and science (Sot. 49b). He actually bathed in the bath-house of Aphrodite at Acre, ruling that the statue of the goddess there was nothing but a decoration (Ab. Zar. 3.4). One wonders what Shammai would have made of that!

His son was Simeon II, one of the few survivors after the Romans destroyed the House of the Nasi in revenge for Bar Kokhba's revolt in 132, and his grandson was the brilliant Judah the Prince (Sot. 49b).

However, following this line of Hillel has taken us well out of our period. Let us retrace our steps.

Of Hillel's eighty students, the one who claimed to have been the 'least' was Johanan ben Zakkai (Sukk 28a), and yet he became the next great scholar and was a man of extraordinary qualities, spending much of his time in meditation. One of his practical contributions was to have the ancient ordeal of bitter water for a suspected adulteress done away with (Sot. 9.9).

One of his legends concerned his prediction that the Temple was soon to be destroyed. He was walking in its precincts, deep in thought, when suddenly the great gate of richly ornamented Corinthian bronze with massive double doors which took the full strength of twenty men to open and close, began to swing silently open of its own accord, as if by invisible hands. Johanan chuckled to himself. 'Temple,' he chided softly, 'why are you trying to frighten me? Do you not know that your own destruction is at hand?' (Ber. 34). The mischievous force was rebuked, and stopped.

When Jerusalem was under seige, despite his foreknowledge that the Temple and the city would soon be destroyed, he decided to try to meet the Roman general Vespasian and plead with him. Knowing that the Zealots would never allow this, he had asked his devoted pupils Joshua and Eliezer to give out the news that he had suddenly died, and have him carried beyond the walls in a coffin (Git. 56a). The meeting availed the city nothing, but Vespasian was said to have been so impressed by the rabbi's courage and saintliness that he offered him the chance to choose a favour for himself. He was even more impressed when all Johanan requested was for permission to be allowed to carry on with his work of teaching in another city, and that a doctor might be allowed to find his sick friend, Rabbi Zadok, and treat him. Vespasian granted both requests, and Johanan was allowed to go to Yabneh and establish the centre of rabbinic learning there.

As he left Jerusalem with his disciples, Rabbi Joshua looked behind him and saw the Temple in flames, and broke down in despair. Johanan replied gently:

> No, my son, do not weep. Do you not know that we have the means of making atonement that is its equal? And what is it? It is deeds of love, as it is said, 'For I desire kindness and not sacrifice' (Hos. 6.6) (Aboth 4.21).

In Nedarim the speech is given thus:

> My sons, weep not and dry your tears; the enemy has destroyed the sanctuary of stone and mortar, but the true altar of the Lord, the place of forgiveness, is still with us. Do you not know where? Behold, in the houses of the poor, there is the altar; love, charity, mercy and justice are the offerings, the sweet incense which pleases the Lord. Love one another, and you shall find mercy and forgiveness . . . Wherever the people of the Lord may go, there the Holy Presence goes with them.

Johanan was said to have been a merchant businessman before his call to rabbinic studies, and was noted for his quiet and urbane dignity. A speech was recorded from his deathbed which some have suggested showed the terrible effects of legalism, that even after a lifetime of goodness, a Pharisee would still be selfishly anxious as to whether or not he had fulfilled all that he ought to have done. Others argue that the speech indicates rather his humility and his total lack of arrogant pride. He lay weeping, with his disciples at his bedside, remembering how he had been taken to Vespasian and had faced him not knowing what sort of reception he might have got from him. Now he was

> being taken before the throne of the King of Kings, who lives and endures for ever, whose anger is an everlasting anger, who if he imprisons me imprisons me for ever; and whom I cannot persuade with words or bribe with money. Nay, more, I can see

two ways before me, one leading to Paradise and the other to Gehenna, and I do not know by which I shall be taken (Ber. 28b).

One feels sure that the insights by which he had lived stood him in far greater stead than the confidence of the Pharisee of the parable who 'thanked God that he was not like other men'.

The most famous Pharisee of the Gospels has to be Nicodemus, who is mentioned in John 3.1, 7.50 and 19.39, but not in the Synoptics. Sadly nothing is known of him from other sources, unless he can be identified with the very eminent Naqdimon ben Gurion, one of the richest and most distinguished citizens of Jerusalem at that time (Ta'an. 20a; Kethub. 66b; Git. 56a; Aboth 6; Ber. R.42). Ta'anit 20a reveals that Naqdimon's real name was Bunni ben Gurion, and the Talmud has a fascinating reference to *five* disciples of Jesus: Mattai, Naqai, Netzer, Todah and Bunai. One wonders if there could be a genuine tradition buried here, especially as the Fourth Gospel seems to imply that Jesus did have only five disciples, at least in the early stages of the ministry. Josephus identifies this same person as Gorion ben Nicodemus, reversing the name order (*Jewish War* 2.17.10). The Talmud praised his generosity, love of peace and service to the nation. It told that he was a Pharisee born into the class of chief rulers, and had inherited the monopoly for fetching the lustral water for Temple use, and was also overseer of the reservoirs in Jerusalem. During the main festivals he provided water for pilgrims by the hundred thousand. The Temple monopolies were a leading bone of contention between Sadducees and Pharisees. The House of Nicodemus may have had a very long history, since an overseer in the Temple shortly after the Exile had been a Bunni (cf. Neh. 9.4; 11.15).

During the drought, Naqdimon went to the Roman general, who had reservoirs of water laid by for his troops, and paid twelve talents of silver to 'borrow' twelve wells. On the last day of his pledge, when he should have redeemed the wells, they were empty. He prayed, and the rain came flooding down (Ta'an. 19b–20a).

His fortunes inevitably crumbled when the revolt broke out. He and two other wealthy men had the means of keeping the city in food for several years, but the Zealots burned down their storehouses to force the people to break out and fight. None other than Johanan ben Zakkai had officiated at the marriage of his daughter, and her marriage-portion was no less than a million gold pieces.

During the siege Naqdimon was killed and the daughter left destitute. It was recorded that Ben Zakkai saw her picking grain out of the dung of Roman horses, until finally she appealed to the Romans for help (Keth. 66b).

Ben Zakkai had very nearly been killed himself by his fiery Zealot nephew Ben Battiah, who heard him exclaim 'Woe' and thought that he had cursed them. Ben Zakkai hastily explained that he had only said 'Wah!', an expression of disapproval; so the nephew let him live.

Ben Zakkai's pupils included several great and famous scholars: Rabbi Tarfon, Eliezer ben Hyrcanus, Joshua ben Hananiah, Simeon ben Nathanel, and the mystic Hanina ben Dosa.

Simeon ben Nathanel was a priest, married to a daughter of Gamaliel I (Tos. Ab. Zar. 3.19), and was known as 'Simeon the sin-fearing', probably having been influenced by the attitude of Johanan. His best known saying was:

When you pray, regard not your prayer as a mechanical task, but as an appeal for grace and mercy before the All-Present . . .; and do be not wicked in your own esteem (Aboth 2.13).

Hanina ben Dosa was one of the most interesting charismatic figures of the first century. He lived in the Sepphoris district, not ten miles from Nazareth (P. Ber. 7c), and Jesus must have known of him, if not actually been an acquaintance. He appears to have been a man of extraordinary devotion and miraculous healing talents. It was said of him that he used to spend a whole hour 'directing his heart' towards God before commencing his proper prayers, and that once he sank into communion, nothing would distract him.

Though the king salute him, he shall not return his greeting. Though a snake wind itself around his ankle, he shall not interrupt his prayer (P. Ber. 5.1).

This unfortunate snake crops up in several references:

When Rabbi Hanina prayed, a poisonous reptile bit him, but he did not interrupt his prayer. The onlookers departed, and later found the same snake dead at the opening of its hole. 'Woe to the man,' they exclaimed, 'bitten by a snake; but woe to the snake which has bitten Hanina ben Dosa! (P. Ber 9a; P. Ber 2.20; B. Ber 33a).

When told of the bite, Hanina stated that he had not even been aware of it.

He frequently prayed for the sick and those in trouble, and knew in advance what the outcome of their illnesses would be.

> He used to say: This one will live; this one will die. They said to him: How do you know? He replied: If my prayer is fluent in my mouth, I know that the sick one is favoured; if not, I know that his disease is fatal (P. Ber 5.5).

The words of the prayer he did not consider to be his own, but placed in his mouth by God; and when this phenomena occurred, he knew that his prayer would be efficacious. If no inspiration was present, he knew no cure would follow.

He cured the son of Rabban Gamaliel (B. Ber. 34b; P.Ber 9d):

> It happened that Rabban Gamaliel's son fell ill, and he sent two disciples to Hanina ben Dosa in his town. He said: Wait until I go into the upper room. He went into the upper room, and then came down. He said to them: I am assured that Rabban Gamaliel's son has now recovered from his illness. They noted the time. In that hour he asked for food.

This healing has interesting similarities with that of the official's servant or son in John's Gospel (4.46–54).

He was also reported to have cured the son of his master Johanan ben Zakkai.

> He said to him: Hanina, my son, pray for him that he may live. Hanina put his head between his knees and prayed, and he lived. Johnanan ben Zakkai said: Even if Ben Zakkai had squeezed his head between his knees all day long, no attention would have been paid to him. His wife chided him: Is Hanina greater than you? He said to her: 'No, but he is like a servant before the King (Ber. 34b).

> On one occasion his daughter was very sad because she had mistaken the vinegar for the oil jar, and had filled the sabbath lamp with vinegar. He said: 'My daughter, why should this trouble you? He who has commanded the oil to burn will also command vinegar to burn.' And so it did (Ta'an. 25a).

Many other miracles were recorded of him, but few sayings. His most famous was: 'He whose deeds exceed his wisdom, his wisdom shall endure, but he whose wisdom exceeds his deeds, his wisdom will not endure' (Aboth 3.9). It was reported that his wife resembled him in his piety (Baba Bathra 74b) and was 'accustomed to his miracles (Ta'an. 25a).

The rabbis Tarfon and Eliezer ben Hyrcanus were a pair both known for their fiery tempers, although they were both much loved. Tarfon was a priest of considerable wealth, and one of the leading scholars at Yabneh, and he had the unfortunate rural habit of cursing his children. He would frequently cry such abominations as 'May I curse my children to hell' or 'May I bury my children if . . .' (B. Shabb. 17a; 116a). Many years later, when the rabbi Judah visited his city, he was said to have inquired humorously whether there were 'any descendents left of that saint who used to curse his children' (Baba Mezia 85a). Tarfon was actually extremely fond of them, as he was also of his mother. In his mother's old age, he used to kneel on the floor at the side of her bed so that she could use his back as a step up (P. Kid 1.7; 31b).

He was known for other idiomatic phrases, such as the notorious curse 'May I ruin my son if . . .'; the phrase 'My son shall not go down with thee' to indicate disapproval; 'knob and flower' from Exod. 25.33 for approval; and when he was in distress he used to be heard muttering 'Tarfon, Tarfon, your ass has gone!'

His kindness extended beyond his family. Once he saw a poor bride pass his house, and immediately insisted on taking her into his home and having her properly groomed, anointed and adorned. In a year of drought, he once betrothed himself to 300 women at once, so that they might be cared for, as wives of a priest (Tos. Ket. 5.1).

Once he went to eat some figs on his own property, but having been absent for a long time, he was arrested and beaten by his own servants, who did not recognize him. They were appalled and terrified when they found out what they had done, but he was delighted at the way they had protected his property, and replied, 'As each stick came down on me, I pardoned you' (P. Sher 4.2).

His dictum was: 'The day is short, the work is great, and the labourers are sluggish; but the reward is much and the Master is urgent' (Aboth 2.15). Also, 'God did not cause his Divine Presence to rest upon Israel until they had worked.' According to legend, he was one of the ten martyrs put to death by the Romans. Another suggestion is that he was the eminent Jew Trypho who featured in the famous *Dialogue* by the Christian apologist Justin Martyr – or at least that the character of Trypho may have been based on him.

Eliezer ben Hyrcanus was a fierce and quick-tongued rabbi, who was nevertheless much loved. However, his refusal to give an inch over his principles caused him great distress in his later life. He had a phenomenal memory, a 'cemented cistern that never lost a drop' (Aboth 2.8), and spent practically all his time studying. He was the chief pupil of Johanan ben Zakkai, and became the teacher of Akiba. He was married to Imma Shalom, the sister of Gamaliel.

His legends recount that he was a man who, despite his memory, had grown up with no learning at all. It was not until he was twenty-eight that he decided to leave his father's farm and find Ben Zakkai, to persuade him to accept him as a pupil. Ben Zakkai's initial response to this somewhat retarded and over-age student was one of scepticism. He was not at all eager to take him on, but gave him one lesson to learn and told him to come back a week later, thinking that would probably be the last he would see of him. To his surprise, at the end of the week Eliezer presented himself again, with the lesson learnt completely by heart. Ben Zakkai bent to kiss him, but Eliezer's breath was so foul that before he had time to realize how hurtful his action would be, Ben Zakkai involuntarily turned his head away. Eliezer burst into tears, and it was revealed that he had been so eager to learn that he had not eaten all week – hence his bad breath. Ben Zakkai laughed when he heard this, and said, 'My son, if your learning may rise to heaven as forcibly as your breath reached my nostrils just now, you will surely be great among the doctors of the Law,' a prediction that was soon fulfilled.

The legends also record how his father, angry that he had not returned to his work, went to Jerusalem to find him and fetch him home, but became involved in a meal at which the guests were expecting two great celebrities, Rabbi Johanan and his eminent pupil Rabbi Eliezer. The father was amazed and humbled to discover that this was none other than his own 'ignorant' son.

Despite his learning, for which he became a byword amongst the rabbis, he retained his fiery peasant temper. Once, when Simeon the Pious assumed that he had been near the altar with unwashed hands and remarked upon it, Eliezer leapt up in a fury shouting, 'Are you not ashamed to admit that the high priest's dog is better than you? I swear that even if the high priest himself were to come near the altar with his hands unwashed, his head would be split with a log!' (Tos. Kelim. 1.6).

Rabbi Akiba, his favourite pupil, once bested him in an argument. He screeched at him, 'From the laws of slaughter you have refuted me; by the slaughter may you find death!' (Pesah 69a). This was recalled when Akiba was indeed martyred in 135 CE.

Yet it was possible to love him. He had a niece who had grown up in his household and who wished to marry him. He kept on refusing, because she was so much younger than himself, and introduced her to a constant stream of suitable bridegrooms. She finally cornered him by actually making advances to him herself, whereupon he gave in, and took her to wife (P. Yebamot 13a).

He was once arrested for heretical opinions, but could only think of one occasion that could possibly fit, when he had listened with sympathy to Jacob of Kefar Sekhania, the pupil of Jesus ben Pandira. This name was sometimes given in the apocalytic writings to Jesus of Nazareth.

His colleague, Joshua ben Hananiah, was the third of Ben Zakkai's inner circle of five disciples. Unlike Eliezer, who had a brilliant retentive memory but reasoned rather mechanically and clung to the ancient traditions, Joshua was noted for his worldly wisdom, and the subtlety and flexibility of his reasoning. His mother used to take him as an infant to the synagogue 'so that his ears might become accustomed to the word of Torah' (P. Yeb 1.6.3a). He was a Levite by birth, and as these commenced their Temple duties at the age of thirty (Num. 4.3), we know that he must therefore have been at least thirty years old at the time of the destruction of Jerusalem. The description of the joyful ceremony of the water-drawing in Sukkah 53a was attributed to him. He was said to have studied Latin, Greek, mathematics, geography, physics and astronomy – the Sanhedrin was responsible for the fixing and intercalation of the calendar – and computed the appearance of a comet, which duly appeared in 89 CE (B. Ber 584; Hor. 10a).

At one stage Joshua ben Hananiah fell in love with the daughter of a priest, but her father regarded his Levitical status as beneath this match and married her instead to a priest of full rank. There is no evidence that Joshua ever married after this heartbreak. Instead, legends remark on his careless, even unkempt appearance, and the development of a sparkling wit and biting sarcasm that may perhaps have been the results of this romantic disappointment.

He and Eliezer were two of the trusted disciples who had carried
Ben Zakkai to Vespasian in the coffin (Git. 56a), and it was Joshua
who subsequently returned to Jerusalem to bring out Rabbi Zadok,
who had been ill (Lam. Rabba 115.31). After the fall of Jerusalem
B. Ber 28a indicates that he earned his living as a blacksmith, and
P. Ber. 4.17d adds that he was a maker of needles.

Gamaliel II, the great-great-grandson of Hillel, whose sister was
married to Eliezer, was the ruler of the school at Yabneh, and
Joshua discovered that he could not get on easily with him,
particularly as they disagreed over so fundamental a matter as the
date of the Day of Atonement. Gamaliel, unfortunately, was
intolerant of criticism and dispute, and twice embarrassed Joshua
publicly on points of law. On one occasion when Joshua had stood
up to raise an issue, and been ruled to be in the wrong, Gamaliel
turned his attention to other matters without giving Joshua the
required permission to sit down. Joshua was no 'rebellious elder'
and accepted the rebuke, but he did not quietly slink away either.
He remained standing throughout the rest of the long proceedings.
Various people kept trying to draw Gamaliel into facing him again,
but he bluntly and deliberately refused to acknowledge him. The
Sanhedrin became so outraged at this cavalier treatment of one of
its favourites that the session ended in uproar, with Gamaliel being
dismissed from the presidency. Shortly afterwards the two men
were reconciled, and Joshua was among the number of those who
insisted that Gamaliel be reinstated. Gamaliel, however, was
obliged thereafter to share the office with Eleazer ben Azariah, who
had been appointed in the interregnum (B. Ber. 26a).

One of the most amusing legends about Joshua concerns his
discomfiture in a bath-house. A sorcerer recognized him and cast a
spell upon him, striking him with total paralysis so that he could not
get out of the tub. Joshua guessed what had happened, and located
his adversary, who happened to be standing just beside the
entrance. He proceeded to retaliate by devising his own spell
against the sorcerer, so that he too was rooted to the spot. Joshua
then extended his influence on the man's right hand and left foot, so
that every time a person came in, the sorcerer's arm fell and hit him,
and he kicked all those leaving. The bath-keepers, in consternation,
tried to eject the nuisance, but found that they could not move him.
The spell was only broken when he agreed to release Joshua, and let
him emerge from his chilly tub.

Joshua's story became tragically entwined with that of his old colleague Eliezer ben Hyrcanus, in the notorious case of the oven of Akhnai. Akhnai was one of Eliezer's pupils, and he had made an oven for Temple use, the ritual purity of which came under dispute. Eliezer took up the case for his pupil, appealing to ancient traditions. Joshua, however, realized that the crucial elements in the debate were two-fold: the inflexible refusal of Eliezer to consider innovations, whereas Joshua thought that the Law should always be reinterpreted to suit the prevalent conditions; and the upholding of the rule of the Sanhedrin by the wishes of the majority and not by the authoritty of one great scholar alone – even if he happened to be in the 'right' and the majority were 'wrong'. The offending oven faded into the background, and the battle raged over the principle that the religious leadership of the nation 'could only grow in strength when they sustained the will of the majority'.

Eliezer was obstinate; Joshua was shrewd and calm. Ben Zakkai had once described him as being like 'a three-ply cord which does not break'. Eliezer held the traditional interpretation as being so sacred that he refused to bow to the wish of the majority, which had sided with Joshua against him. Feelings ran extremely high as Eliezer stood alone. In this tense atmosphere Eliezer was suddenly comforted and confirmed in his stance by a Bath Qol that pronounced in his favour. Joshua, however, insisted that even this divine intervention be set aside, on the grounds that 'the Torah was not in Heaven (Deut. 30.12) but in the will of the majority' (B. Baba Metzin 59b). Heavenly voices were very impressive, but who was to prove that the voice was truly from God? Rabbi Jeremiah backed him: 'The Law was given on Sinai. We pay no attention to a heavenly voice. For already from Sinai the Law said: By a majority you are to decide' (Exod. 23.2). Eliezer was helpless to do more – but he would never give in.

Joshua was just as inflexible. He saw that despite Eliezer's just case, the danger was that the Sanhedrin would accept the principle of remaining servile to the will of one man. His maxims would then prove disruptive, and the Sanhedrin would lose the power of independent action. The indictment of a 'rebellious elder' was a vital procedure which insured that even in controversial matters the opinion of the majority would prevail, and thus that there would never be private dictatorship in the matter of the Torah. Eliezer realized his predicament, and appealed to let the 'people' decide whether his authority should stand or not. Joshua saw that this move threatened the very existence of the Sanhedrin, and appealed that 'the people should be guided by the decisions of the Sanhedrin' and not vice versa. Gamaliel ruled that this was correct, and that anyone who could not accept this should be excommunicated.

Eliezer then left the chamber defeated, never really believing that his own brother-in-law would do such a thing to him. Sadly, the issue was too vital, and Eliezer was condemned and removed from the Council. Akiba was sent to break the news to him as gently as he could, but the blow nearly killed him. The hardest point was that his pupils, whom he loved dearly, were no longer to associate with him. The old man never gave way, and was still under excommunication when he went to his deathbed. As he lay helpless, at last Akiba and the others were released from the ban on his presence, and hurried to be with him. His son and his wife were also there, and his son took his phylacteries from him at a tactless moment. At once the famous temper flared up, and Eliezer scolded him violently for being so premature. The embarrassed son apologized to the visitors, excusing his father's bad manners on the grounds of his delirium, whereupon the enraged rabbi shouted at him, 'You and your mother are delirious, not me!' (B. Sanh. 68a).

Finally, he delivered his thoughts on the subject of those scholars who had withdrawn from him. 'I shall be surprised if they die a natural death, because they did not come to study under me. Woe for my two arms, that are like scrolls of the Law and are about to depart from the world' – as he folded his arms in readiness across his dying chest – 'For were all men writers, and all the seas ink, and all the reeds quills, and all heaven and earth for parchment, they would not suffice to write all that I know of the Law.' His last words came softly: 'Yet I know of the Law only as much as a man might take of water from the ocean upon a needle-point.'

A similar passage occurs twice in the Qur'an: 'If the ocean were ink wherewith to write out the words of my Lord, sooner would the ocean be exhausted than would the words of my Lord, even if we added another ocean like it, for its aid' (surah 18.103).

As soon as he died, the excommunication was annulled, and for this cantankerous old man his famous disciples broke out in wild grief. Akiba rent his clothes, and tore his hair until blood flowed (P. Shabb. 2.6.51). Joshua defended and conserved all his literary works, as if there had never been a day's controversy between them.

When some of the Sanhedrin tried to repeal certain sections of his laws and decisions, Joshua would have none of it, declaring 'It is not seemly to fight a dead lion!' (B. Sanh. 68b).

Joshua later participated in missions to Rome with Gamaliel and Eleazar ben Azariah to strengthen the bonds between the Jewish Disapora and the motherland. He debated with eminent non-Jews, and was received favourably in the courts of Domitian, Nerva, Trajan and Hadrian. Domitian's daughter once commented rudely upon Joshua's somewhat disreputable appearance:

'Rabbi, how is it that such a great mind as yours dwells in so homely a body?' 'Tell me, princess,' he replied, not in the least abashed, 'in what kind of vessels your father keeps his best wines' (B. Taanith 7).

After the death of Gamaliel, he became the next leader of the Sanhedrin. His last public service was to avert the wrath of the people from bursting into open revolt against Rome when Hadrian rescinded the permission to go and rebuild the Temple in Jerusalem.

'A lion had swallowed a bone which stuck in its throat,' he said. 'He promised a great reward to anyone who could extract it. A Nile stork came along and took the bone from the lion's throat. When the stork asked for the promised reward, the lion said, 'Go home, and tell the people that you have been in the mouth of a lion, and have come away unharmed' (Midrash Gen. Rabba 64.10).

Joshua died just before Bar Kokhba's revolt broke out.

The leading rabbi at the time of the Revolt was Akiba. In his early life he had actually been a member of the *Am ha-Aretz*, and a bitter enemy of scholars. 'Had I a scholar in my power I would maul him like an ass,' he is reported to have said (Peah 49b). 'Like a dog,' his disciples corrected him. But he relied, 'An ass's bite breaks the bone; a dog's does not.' He was a shepherd to a wealthy Jerusalem man, and fell in love with his daughter Rachel. Rachel was a woman of extraordinary perception, and agreed to marry him on the condition that he studied the Torah, which he agreed to do. Her father was furious, and cut her off without a penny, forcing the couple into poverty. She even once sold her hair to buy food.

However, Akiba sat down with his own son to master the alphabet. Soon he had progressed enough to go away to study, which he did for many years, under Eliezer and later under Tarfon. One legend says that when he returned to Rachel after being away from her for no less than twelve years, he was just entering the courtyard when he heard her say that she would willingly wait another twelve years for him if it would increase his learning twofold – whereupon he turned about and went off for another twelve years!

A funny story was told of Akiba that both illustrated his reputation for learning, and gave an insight into the later rabbinic affectionate attitude to the 'Hedge'.

When Moses left the earth and ascended to Heaven, he found the Almighty scribbling flourishes and ornamental lines upon every letter of the Torah. Moses asked God what he was doing, and God replied: 'In generations to come there will be a man, Akiba ben Joseph, who will deduce heaps of rules from each little stroke of the pen.' Moses expressed a wish to see that man. God granted his request. When Akiba's time came, Moses descended to earth and visited Akiba's school-house where he took a seat in the back row amongst the freshmen. There he listened to learned discussions, overcome and bewildered, because he was unable to follow the scholarly argumentation. When, finally, a difficult problem arose and one of the more advanced disciples was bold enough to ask Rabbi Akiba whence he derived his authority to lay down a ruling that would settle the matter, Akiba replied: 'It is a ruling that was given to Moses on Mount Sinai.' Whereupon Moses felt much elated, and his confidence was restored (B. Menhoth 29b).

It was Akiba who had to break the sad news to Rabbi Eliezer of his excommunication. When Bar Kokhba revolted against Rome in 132, in contrast to the conciliatory line taken by his teachers, Akiba the passionate encouraged it with enthusiasm. When Rome issued an edict forbidding the teaching of the Torah, he redoubled his efforts in defiance of them (Sanh. 12) and was arrested. He still refused to give way to the Romans, and was finally tortured to death by having his skin torn off with iron 'combs'.

Yet it was his teaching that whatever God sent was for the best. He said that to love God with all one's heart, soul, mind and strength, meant that a person should be grateful to God, and trust him and love him, whatever the measure meted out to him. 'A person must bless God for evil no less than for good' (Sifre Deut. 32). Akiba lived by those principles to the last.

Even as he was being tortured to death, when the hour to recite the Shema came, he forced his cracked lips to form the words. When he got to the phrase 'Thou shalt love the Lord thy God with all thy soul,' he stopped and smiled. Someone asked him how he could possibly be able to smile in his pitiful circumstances. He said that he had repeated the same words every day of his life without ever knowing for certain whether or not he truly loved God with all his soul, that is, his life. Now, he knew.

Now that the day of my death has come, and the hour for repeating the Shema has returned, and I have loved the Lord my God with all my heart and with all my life, why should I not smile?

8 · In Support of the Pharisees

Some of our earliest descriptions of Pharisees are found in the writings of the Jewish historian Josephus who had himself once been a member of the sect (*Antiquities*, 18.1). He describes them as people who

> live simply, and despise the delicacies of life; they lived according to reason, and if reason indicates that something is good for them, they do it . . . they pay respect to the wisdom of age; and while they maintain that all things are in the grip of fate, they also believe that people have the freedom to act as they think fit; since their philosophy is that it has pleased God to make a temperament whereby what He wills is done, but at the same time so that the will of man can allow him to act virtuously or viciously.

Earlier he had stated:

> There was a certain sect of the Jews, who valued themselves highly in the exact skill they had in the Law of their fathers, and made people believe that they were highly favoured of God (*Antiquities*, 18.2.4).

It is this second statement that seems to accord most closely with the strange distorted picture of the Pharisees that we glean from the Gospels, because it can be interpreted ambiguously – either that the Pharisees were so exemplary in their conduct and skills that people could not help but believe that they were 'highly favoured of God', or that they were very proud of themselves, and were often self-righteous hypocrites.

The very word 'Pharisee' sets off a whole train of ideas; they were the chief of Jesus' enemies; they opposed him at every turn in his teaching: they instigated and caused his death. In short, they represented all the least pleasing features of Judaism, and were responsible for its decline. Yet Jesus and his teaching stood closer to Pharisaism than to any other school of thought, and I believe that Pharisaism is the branch of Judaism closest to Islam. In most matters arising out of the Law, Jesus taught and acted exactly as a Pharisee would have done; but our sources represent Jesus as engaged in controversy with them so often that we are not entitled just to dismiss these conflict-narratives as mere imaginary constructions based on conflicts which took place in the church after 70 CE.

According to our Gospels, Jesus condemned the Pharisees for seven key reasons: spiritual blindness (Mark 3.5; 4.12; 8.11–12; Matt. 9.13; 13.13–17; 15.12–20; 16.1–4; Luke 5.39; 8.10; 11.37–54; John 3.1–14; 6.44, 64f.; 9:40f.); formalism (Matt. 5.17–6.18; Luke 2.37–54; 18.1–14); prejudice (Matt. 11.16–19; Luke 7.29–35; John 5.40); traditionalism (Mark 7.1–23; Luke 15.1–20); hypocrisy (Mark 7.6–7; 8.4–21; Matt. 5.15–23; 6.2–7; 15.7–9; 16.5–12; 23.3–29; Luke 6.37–42; 12.1–2; 13.15–17); blasphemy against the Holy Spirit (Mark 3.28–30; Matt. 12.3–33; Luke 12.10); and rejection of God in that they rejected himself as God's Son (Matt. 17.12; John 5.42f; 6.52; 7.48; 8.2–52; 10.25–38). We must examine these charges, and see how far they were justified.

For a start, Jesus preached a message of 'loving one's enemies' and 'doing good to them that hate you'. In the Gospels, the Pharisees are supposed to be far more than any other group the enemies of Jesus, and it is implied that they were spiritually blind and deaf, if not dead! If that were indeed the case, where was Christ's mission to heal them? Did he have no pity on these lost souls? Surely they were worthwhile people and worthy to be saved? Surely as much so as the prostitutes and cheating tax-collectors with whom Jesus consorted? The point could be made that the more the emphasis is put on the alleged spiritual depravity of the Pharisees, as opposed to the simplicity of the 'lost' denizens of the seamier side of city life, the more noticeable becomes the absence of any attempt of Jesus to reconcile them, and lead them into a better way.

The keynotes throughout the Gospels are hostility, denunciation and defiance on the part of Jesus, and the Pharisaic retaliation in anger, fear and hatred towards him. If the Pharisees really did exist as an identifiable sect during Jesus' lifetime, then either we have a situation in which any account of attempts at reconciliation by Jesus are deliberately omitted, or there *is* surely a charge of hypocrisy that can be levelled: not so much at the Pharisees as at Jesus. Of all people, surely he ought to have practised the love and forgiveness to his enemies about which he preached?

However, close scrutiny of the Gospels reveals the embarrassing fact (for the opponents of the Pharisees) that Jesus was *not* always at loggerheads with the rabbis. He was frequently invited to preach in the synagogues (Mark 1.21; Luke 4.31; Mark 1.39; Matt. 4.23; Luke 4.44; Mark 6.2; Matt. 13.5; Luke 4.16 [where it says 'as his *custom* was', surely indicating regular practice?]; and Luke 13.10). Jesus was often in Pharisaic company, being entertained to meals and treated with honour; Pharisees were to be found amongst his adherents and supporters (Luke 19.39), sometimes warning him of danger. Jesus found himself able to be outspoken about certain individuals and their shortcomings quite freely, not behind their backs, but in their company (Luke 14.7–11), in true Pharisaic manner.

Jesus a Pharisee? He apparently prayed before taking meals (Mark 6.41; 8.6; 14.22) and gave blessing over the wine at table (Mark 14.23) in true Pharisaic manner (Tos. Ber. 4.1; Pes. 10.7) He sang the hymn at the Passover feast (Mark 14.26). He wore the *kraspeda*, or fringes, on his garment (Matt 9.20; 14.36). He agreed to the payment of the half-shekel offered to the Tabernacle according to the prescription of Exodus 30.11–16 (Matt. 17.24–27).

This last detail is interesting, because at the time of Christ there was actually a raging controversy between the religious authorities as to the compulsory nature of this obligation. The Sadducees took exception to it as a *halachah* of recent origin, namely from the Hasmonaean period; the members of the Qumran community apparently considered it necessary to pay it only once in a lifetime and not every year. In the Gospel instance, whether or not the story is legendary material, it is concluded that Jesus took the Pharisaic line.

Other seemingly Pharisaic activities included Jesus' disapproval of vessels being carried through the Temple enclosure (Mark 11.16; Ber. 9.5), and he postponed the healing of invalids after the sunset on the sabbath, at least on one occasion (Mark 1.32; Luke 4.40), but the passage implies that this was his normal practice.

If you look closely at the passages in which the Gospels mention the opposition to Jesus, you can see that the writers are not always consistent as to the source of this opposition, even within individual stories. For example, in the Beelzebul controversy, Mark 3.22

specifies that it was the 'scribes who came down from Jerusalem' who accused Jesus; Luke 11.15 says the accusation was made by some of the people standing around; and Matt. 9.34 alone states that it was 'the Pharisees'. Those three expressions are neither mutually exclusive nor inclusive!

Assuming that Mark's was the earliest version, it is interesting to note that he deliberately differentiated between the scribes of Jerusalem and other, presumably Galilean, scribes. It is possible that he may have intended the implication that the Jerusalem ones were actually *Sadducaic* scribes, although it must be admitted that the title *darshan* or rabbi fits more snugly on a Pharisaic head.

Form critics do not usually bother to take these differences seriously, since they maintain that it is impossible to rely on any of the narrative framework as being historical. They argue that although the saying of Jesus at the heart of the narrative *might* be genuine, the framework in which it was set was probably only the creation of the church tradition. For example, the German theologian Rudolf Bultmann stated categorically:

The controversy dialogues are all of them imaginary scenes. Therefore we must keep away at first from the question of whether Jesus sometimes healed on the sabbath day, or whether he used a certain saying which we find in a controversy dialogue in a discussion with his opponents. Of course, it is quite possible that he did; indeed, very probable; but the first question to be asked, methodologically speaking, must be about the literary form of the controversy dialogue, and its origin as a literary device (*The History of the Synoptic Tradition*, p. 39).

To argue that the hostility of the Jewish authorities had already been revealed 'as early as' Mark 3.6f. is to ignore the standpoint of form critics, who would maintain that the passage is no 'earlier' chronologically than Mark 14.64; the order is that of the evangelist, and owes nothing to history or chronology. Paul Winter declared that 'all the Marcan controversy stories, without exception, reflect dialogues between the Apostolic Church and its social environment, and are devoid of roots in the circumstances of the life of Jesus (*On the Trial of Jesus*, p. 125). Redaction criticism, the study of the evangelists' approach to writing their Gospels, has taught us that where Matthew and Luke alter the wording of a Marcan pericope, it may not necessarily be because they were trying to be more accurate in the historical sense, but simply in order to further their own aims. Luke, for example, might drop specifically Jewish references because he was writing for a Gentile church for whom they were no longer relevant; M. D. Goulder suggested that 'Matthew' was a converted scribe, and therefore altered the wording in order to favour scribes to the detriment of the Pharisees (*Midrash and Lection in Matthew*).

It is possible that the Gospel writers had assumed that the authorities against whom Jesus was preaching, and whom they made him strongly condemn, were of the same class and type as the opponents of their own time, but this cannot be proved. One could argue alternatively that they *did* have before them genuine material about Jesus' controversies with various authorities, but since after 70 CE the Sadducean and high priestly families hardly continued to exist, the Gospel writers may well have made the Pharisees into Jesus' opponents, as the other parties were no longer relevant. The evangelists might have been a great deal nearer the mark had they substituted the word 'Sadducee' in many of the places where they put 'Pharisee', as it was basically the Sadducean hierarchy, along with certain others with vested interests in maintaining the *status quo*, who persecuted Jesus for mainly political reasons.

Are the Gospels really that inaccurate? Well, a good example of wrongful accusation against the Pharisees is that of the *corban* controversy. In Matthew 15.3–6 Jesus accuses the Pharisees and scribes who had 'come from Jerusalem' of transgressing the tradition of honouring their parents by devoting their substance to God. So far as we can ascertain from rabbinical writings, such an action *would have been totally against the Pharisaic tradition*. However, the accusation *could* have been laid at the door of certain Sadducees. If any Pharisee had acted in such a manner, he would certainly have been roundly taken to task by his fellows, and a suitable way out of his *corban* vow would have been suggested to him.

The *corban* procedure was rather interesting, and was the subject of much mental gymnastics at the time of Jesus. It could literally mean the gift of some particular thing to the Temple, or it could be quite a secular pronouncement, simply a pledge not to do something normally permitted. If a person declared that any object was *corban*, it meant that it could not be used for anything other than as a Temple offering, or be used except in the service of the Temple.

But if he said a thing was to 'like a *corban*', that merely meant that it was not to be used by him or by the people he specified. For example, a harsh father might decide to beat his son no more, and declare that the rod he had previously used would become in his household 'like a *corban*'. It was hardly dedicated to the Temple, but it could no longer be used. To take a modern example: if he wanted to give up smoking, he could declare that his cigarettes were 'like a *corban* to him', and that would mean he would no longer be able to smoke them, although this ban would not apply to anyone else. If he declared an object to be 'like a *corban*' to any other specified person, then that person might not have use of it. A husband could even declare himself to be 'like a *corban*' as far as his wife was concerned – and that would effectively prohibit their marital association. (The Muslim equivalent is to declare one's wife to be like the back of one's mother.)

At the time of Christ, the notion that *corban* vows could have been 'made in error', and could therefore be declared invalid, was illustrated by Nedarim 111.2, where a man caught a crowd of people cheerfully helping themselves to his figs. He furiously declared that they were *corban* to them, only to discover that members of his own family were tucked away among the eaters. Obviously, he could not deny the produce to his own family, so advice was sought to find a loophole in the vow. The school of Shammai ruled that here was a vow that was not binding on his own family, since they were not included in the *intention* of the prohibition, but it remained binding on the others. The school of Hillel, however, declared that the whole vow should be declared invalid on the principle that a vow could not be nullified in part only.

There are two cases in the Talmud of *corban* being legitimately uttered in order to prevent people taking what was not their own. In both, the mere formula 'May this be *corban* to you!' was not sufficient, and the goods had to be physically handed over to the Temple treasury.

The skins of sacrificial victims used to be placed in the Chamber of Beth ha'Parwah. Every evening these were divided among the men of the paternal division. But the men of violence would seize them by force. It was then enacted that the skins should be divided on the sabbath eve, and that all the wards should gather to receive their share at this time. Yet the (servants of) the chief priests still seized the skins by force. Thereupon the owners arose and consecrated them to Heaven (Pesahim 57a).

There was a store of sycamore trunks in Jericho, and the men of violence seized them by force, whereupon their owners arose and consecrated them to Heaven.

In both these examples, incidentally, the 'men of violence' mentioned seem not to have been miscellaneous thugs, but the armed servants of the Temple hierarchy, who had come along to do the humbler priests out of what was rightfully their due. By the use of this procedure, the money was guaranteed to go into the Temple treasury (where it was intended to go) and not into the private pockets of the high priest's family. This manoeuvre could be repeated whenever these high-ranking 'men of violence' re-appeared.

The specific example quoted in the Gospels, of offspring defrauding their parents, was legally vetoed shortly after the destruction of the Temple. It became possible at that time for undutiful sons to defraud their parents easily by declaring that possessions the latter had expected to be reserved for the support of their old age had become *corban*. Since the Temple treasury could no longer benefit, the property remained in their hands. 'Jesus' had indicated that this was a normal Pharisaic practice, but when Rabbi Eliezer found out what was going on, he declared that any vow against the interests of one's parents *must* be annulled at once; and Rabbi Meir taught the same principle forty years later (Ned. 9.1). The fifth commandment took precedence over the vow. Naturally, the rabbis were not in a position to force an individual into behaving correctly, and no doubt many parents continued to be defrauded, but it can hardly be a fair criticism of the Pharisees for the Gospel writers to claim that they encouraged this blatant disregard of the intention of the fifth commandment!

The real Pharisaic attitude is presented more realistically in their debates over the 'loosing' of vows. People often made pronouncements rashly, and then regretted having done so. When that happened, they could seek advice from a rabbi to see if there was any way in which they could negate such a vow. The rabbi would 'seek an opening' for them. Jesus, or at least the author of Matthew 18.18, suggested that the system of binding and loosing was still maintained within the church, and that such was the trust God had in the judgment of the Christians, that whatever they bound or loosed would be valid.

Truly I say to you, whatever you bind on earth shall be bound in heaven, and whatever you loose on earth shall be loosed in heaven (Matt. 18.18; 16.19)

If you forgive the sins of any, they are forgiven; if you retain the sins of any, they are retained (John 20.23).

On one occasion a man vowed that he would not marry his young niece to whom he had been betrothed, so her relatives took her to a certain Rabbi Ishmael. He felt sorry for her, and noticed that she was indeed rather a plain and pinched-looking creature who would not delight any ardent young husband. The rabbi reckoned that a major cause of her sad appearance was the fact that she was underfed, so he immediately took her into his house and cared for her, and gave her plenty of good things to eat until she blossomed – as he had hoped she would. Then the young man was called back to have another look at her, and, amazed at the transformation (and hopefully ashamed of his callousness), regretted having made her *corban* to him. Rabbi Ishmael pointed out that she had only been *corban* in her previous condition. Since that condition was now quite altered, the ban no longer applied. Thus the couple were able to marry after all (Nedarim 9.10).

This little illustration goes towards the suggestion that the Pharisees not only opposed the use of the *corban* procedure to deny one's parents upkeep, but also disapproved of *any corban* promises that were unkind or unsympathetic or excused a person from obligations.

Another example of probable wrongful criticism of the Pharisees is the suggestion that they would have opposed Jesus for healing on the sabbath. This criticism is presented time and again in the Gospels, and has usually been accepted without question by Christians. However, passages in the later rabbinic writings indicate quite clearly that the Pharisees themselves would have acted exactly as Jesus did on those occasions!

For a start, the tradition demanded that 'when there is the least danger to life, the sabbath laws are to be suspended' (Yoma 83a; Deut. Rabba 10.1). Before the time of Jesus, according to his legends, Hillel owed his life to this very principle. In fact, anyone who attempted to observe the sabbath at the risk of another's life was denounced as a sinner – it was his positive duty to disobey the Law in such a situation (B. Ber. 19b; B. Meg. 3b; B. Shabb. 81b). Any danger to life overrode the sabbath Law: for example, in cases of fire, or the collapse of buildings, the laws against digging or the carrying of water were automatically suspended for the duration of the crisis, and any person who attempted to avoid offering the help required on the grounds that it might break the sabbath would have seemed not only ridiculous but also a murderer. As Jesus declared – a true Pharisaic sentiment –, the sabbath was made for man's benefit, and not man for the benefit of the sabbath.

The incident of the man with the withered hand in Mark 3.1–6 is a typical case in point.

> They watched him, to see whether he would heal him on the sabbath, so that they might accuse him. And he said to the man with the withered hand, 'Come here.' And he said to them, 'Is it lawful on the sabbath to do good or to do harm, to save life or to kill?' But they were silent. And he looked around at them with anger, grieved at their hardness of heart, and said to the man, 'Stretch out your hand.' He stretched it out, and his hand was restored. The Pharisees went out and immediately held counsel with the Herodians against him, how to destroy him.

In this narrative the Pharisees are roundly criticized and made to look villainous, and yet in fact their line of thought should have been exactly the same as that of Jesus, that the basic principle was *always to do good*, and that it was *never right to do evil*. Saving life was obviously good, and killing was obviously evil. The observance of the sabbath was also good, and this should have been maintained as far as possible. Christians usually present the Pharisaic reasoning as being that since the man was in no great danger, he could easily have waited until the next day. Jesus is made to ask whether it was right on the sabbath to save life or to kill. The Gospel story implies that 'they were silent' when asked this question out of their shame, since they knew that Jesus was right. In what, then, consisted their attempt to catch Jesus out? It is implied that the man with the withered hand had been 'planted' in the congregation, simply because they knew that Jesus would not be able to resist healing him, and this would constitute an offence against the sabbath and give them some grounds for accusing him of breaking the Law.

In actual fact, the Pharisaic rabbis themselves had long since argued that the condition of risk to life could be stretched to apply to almost *every* illness, no matter how trivial, since it might conceivably be fatal to neglect even a slight swelling or rash. What human being was in a position to know whether or not they might be committing the evil of taking a life by such neglect? To give just one example, the Mishnah specifically permitted the treatment of a sore throat on the sabbath (Yoma 8.6).

Incidentally, according to Jerome's commentary on Matthew 12.13, the Nazarean Gospel had offered the details that this man had not been 'planted' at all, but was in fact a mason who earned his livelihood with his hands, and who pleaded for help that he might 'not with ignomiy have to beg' for his bread (*New Testament Apocrypha*, Vol. 1, p. 148).

In any case, if Jesus had merely commanded the man to 'stretch forth his arm', the Pharisees would have had no grounds for complaint whatsoever. A command or a prayer did not break the sabbath. The most literal-minded of sticklers could have objected only if Jesus had carried out such things as the preparation of plasters or ointments or bandages, or used mud-plasters or given a massage. The collecting-up of herbs, pounding of ingredients, stripping of cloth and the like *were* activities of work that might reasonably have been done before the commencement of a sabbath. There are a couple of accounts of Jesus mixing his saliva with clay to form a kind of mud-plaster, and it was apparently this that the Pharisees objected to in John 9.

> Now it was a sabbath day when Jesus made the clay and opened his eyes. The Pharisees again asked him how he had received his sight. And he said to them, 'He put clay on my eyes, and I washed, and I see.' Some of the Pharisees said, 'This man is not from God, for he does not keep the sabbath'.

It was the making of clay that was objected to, and not the healing, but the purpose of healing and doing good would have overruled this small act.

One passage makes the Pharisaic position crystal clear: 'A man may break one sabbath so that another may keep many' (Yoma 85b). In other words, Jesus could have healed on the sabbath with impunity had he argued that this would have enabled the invalid to perform his own sabbath duties better in the future. It was also duly noted that sometimes injuries sustained on a Friday were better by the Sunday, so 'God himself, though he keeps the sabbath, performs cures on the sabbath' (Exodus Rabba 30.9). This reminds one of Jesus' statement, 'My Father is working still, and I am working' (John 5.19).

One can, of course, challenge the use of rabbinic material from a period later than the time of Jesus as an indicator of the standpoint of his contemporaries, but many scholars feel that the tendency of the disciples of rabbis to memorize meticulously and transmit their traditions justifies such a use. The problem of dating individual items of material in rabbinic works is notoriously difficult; any work, even the latest, may be drawing material from the oral tradition, which in origin may go back to the period well before the Fall of Jerusalem; the date of a particular item does not depend on the date of the work in which it is found. (This is also true of the Gospel pericopes, of course.)

It has been held that the first attempts to form a 'midrash' may well have been part of the activities of the rabbis at Yabneh (probably a large part), in which case the first moves towards the present Mishnah would have been a conscious effort to consolidate Judaism immediately after the fall of Jerusalem. This would mean, obviously, that much of the Mishnaic material inevitably *did* go back to the period before that traumatic event.

W. D. Davies thought it was quite 'legitimate to define the Mishnah as a deposit of four centuries of Jewish religion and cultural activity in Palestine, beginning at some uncertain date, possibly the earlier half of the second century BC'. He thought further that 'our Rabbinic sources represent the triumph of the Pharisaic party, and moreover of a party within the party. Pharisaic opinions alone were recorded, and contrary opinions excluded' (*Paul and Rabbinic Judaism*, p. 3). In another work, *The Setting of the Sermon on the Mount*, Davies had stressed that the laws now codified in the Mishnah had long been preserved orally, a point taken up by J. D. M. Derrett:

The jurists and their students were a privileged section of the community, an aristocracy of learning . . . the scholar was a man who *lived* righteousness, and his qualities were open to constant supervision from his neighbours and pupils. The latter often lived with him. A good teacher only taught because pupils wanted to learn from him, and believed in him. He had no public appointment, to be won by intrigue or imposture. His learning was in his head, and although books would certainly be used at various stages in education, the most famous teachers would rely entirely on their memory, or on the memory of assistants who specialized in memorizing traditions. The Asian student to this day despises a teacher who has to refer to books! (*Law in the New Testament*, Introduction).

Several passages in the Talmud even seem to preserve a principle that the oral law should not have been written down at all (Gittin 60; Temurah 14). The life of a rabbi was in itself Torah. It was not enough just to learn a rabbi's words. It was necessary to live with him, absorb his thought, and copy his every gesture.

In the period following the destruction of the Temple, Derrett points out,

A great deal was remembered about the Law obtaining while the Temple still stood, and about the morality and ethics which underlay those highly technical principles. The Talmuds, in essence commentaries on the Mishnah, contain further material additional to Mishnah, and not inferior to it in antiquity. On the whole one can say that the Mishnah give a very fair picture of what the Pharisees believed Jewish law to be in the last years of Jewish self-government, including those when Rome was the political master in fact, but before the rebellions had made Jewish social and political life a nightmare . . . If the actual rules of the Talmud are not in every case to be read back into the time of Jesus, the point of view and outlook can claim a fair continuity with those of his contemporaries.

If, as we have seen in this chapter, a good case can be made in support of the Pharisees, we may well need to conclude that the material in the Gospels tells us more about the concerns of the developing Christian community than about the facts of Jesus' life. So as a next step we need to look at the material available to us in the Gospels, and see if any sort of consistent picture emerges.

9 · The Pharisees in the Synoptic Gospels

In this chapter we shall look at the various references in the Synoptic Gospels – Mark, Matthew and Luke – to the Pharisees as enemies of Jesus. In the next chapter we shall turn to John. In the four canonical Gospels, the Pharisees are supposed to have disliked and attacked Jesus for numerous reasons: blasphemy (Mark 14.64; Matt.26.65; Luke 5.17–26; John 5.18; 10.22–42); claiming messianic authority (John 2.13–22); association with publicans and sinners (Mark 2.15f.; Matt. 9.10; Luke 5.29f.; 7.29; 15.1–32); neglect of fasting (Mark 2.18–22; Matt. 9.14–17; Luke 5.33–39); being in league with Beelzebul (Mark 3.19–30; Matt. 9.34; 12.22–37; Luke 11.14–36); being a regular sabbath-breaker (Mark 2.23; 3.6; Matt. 12.1–4; Luke 6.1–11; 13.10–21; 14.1–24; John 5.9); giving inadequate signs (Mark 8.11; Matt. 12.38–45; Luke 11.16–32); an insolent defiance of tradition (Mark 7.1–23; Matt. 15.1–30; Luke 11.37–54); being an ignorant impostor (Matt. 27.63f.; John 7.14–30); plotting to destroy the Temple (Mark 14.58; 15.29; Matt. 26.61; 27.39f.; John 2.19–22); and treason against Caesar (Mark 15.9–14; Matt. 27.17–25; Luke 23.2; John 18.8–20; 19.15).

However, as I have already indicated, the Synoptic Gospels are not consistent in their identification of the opponents of Jesus. For example, whereas in Luke 3.7 it is the multitudes that came out to be baptized by him whom Jesus called 'offspring of vipers', and demanded that they bore fruit that befitted repentance, in Matthew 3.7 we find that 'the multitude' has become 'the Pharisees and Sadducees', that odd juxtaposition of the two rival factions that seems to be characteristic of the 'M' source of this Gospel (that is, the material peculiar to this Gospel alone).

Can we ever know for certain whether or not the contents of the various individual narratives, or the settings in which they are placed, can be proved to be historically true? A. T. Hanson has commented,

> 'In the present state of Synoptic studies, he who claims that *any* element in the teaching attributed to Jesus in the Gospels is authentic, proves himself thereby willing to rush in where angels fear to tread. But Christology cannot maintain itself for long on the basis of complete agnosticicm about the historical Jesus' (*Grace and Truth*, p.16).

Most scholars generally assume that Mark was the first of the Synoptics to be completed. Some 600 of its 661 verses appear in Matthew more or less exactly, word for word, so it is further assumed that Mark was extensively copied by Matthew and to a lesser extent by Luke – about 350 verses of it. It is also assumed that since Matthew and Luke have about a further 200 verses of material in common that is not to be found in Mark, they must have had access to another early document, as yet unidentified. These passages are usually labelled 'Q' from the German word 'Quelle', meaning simply 'a source'. Alternatively, 'Q' might have been no more than the result of Matthew having read Luke and including some of his material, or vice versa. The document theory seems more likely, on balance, as the alternative solution raises rather more problems than it solves (which does not, of course, put it out of court!). When one subtracts the Mark and Q passages from Luke and Matthew, one is left with material peculiar to those Gospels alone, which are traditionally labelled for convenience as 'M' and 'L'. These are only umbrella titles, and include the possibility of written source materials, collections, eye-witness reports, and traditions of individual local churches, or even the personal contribution of the author.

The motives of the authors of individual units (or pericopes) are of great interest and importance, but it is also important that the completed work should be seen as a whole and the fact acknowledged that there must in the end have been one final pen in one final hand with the motives of the author of that pen and hand, putting on the final gloss, and taking the final responsibility for the whole thing. It was, after all, the *finished* Gospels which were the propaganda material for the church.

We do not know how many stages were gone through, from oral traditions, collections of sayings, private manuscripts, primitive versions of the Gospels (such as the tentative Ur-Markus or Proto-Luke – two theoretical early versions widely accepted by Christian scholars). We do not know that the Gospels as we have them were considered even then to be finished – although the last verses of Mark 16 and the pericope of the woman taken in adultery in John 8 are often given as footnotes – indicating that the text as it stood then *was* considered to be acceptable.

The first hint of opposition, an incident arousing adverse comment, occurs in Mark 1.24–28, where Jesus healed a possessed man in a synagogue, and astounded the onlookers because 'he taught them as one who had authority, and did not teach as the scribes teach'. Presumably this was a comment on the fact that Jesus did not claim to be in the tradition of any particular rabbinic school, or call on the opinions of his theological forebears. Matthew placed this astonished reaction at the end of the Sermon on the mount (Matt. 7.28–29). Luke retained it in the same incident as Mark, but did not contrast Jesus' authority with that of the scribes (Luke 4.31–32). Following this dramatic healing, the fame of Jesus spread throughout the region like wildfire.

The next incident to arouse comment was Mark 2.1–12, the cure of the paralysed man. This took place in Capernaum when Jesus was 'at home' – presumably in the house of Peter that he had accepted as his own dwelling, and where so many of the Gospel stories may have taken place. If the modern archaeologists are correct in their identification, this site is no more than a stone's throw from the synagogue of Capernaum, which, according to the Gospels, had been paid for by the local centurion, a man sympathetic towards Judaism.

This particular healing was witnessed by 'some of the scribes' who 'were sitting there, questioning in their hearts.' When Jesus saw the paralysed man, he told him that his sins were forgiven. The scribes considered this to be blasphemous, taking upon himself the role of God alone. Their criticism was, however, balanced by their acceptance of the very point that Jesus underlined – that if it had been the will of God for the man to have remained paralysed, then Jesus *could not have cured him*. The result of the healing was that all were amazed and glorified God, since Jesus' action had justified his statement. Matthew 9.3 sticks to the phrase 'certain of the scribes', whereas Luke 5.21 alters it to 'the scribes and Pharisees', specifically implicating the Pharisees for the first time. Earlier in v.17, he had stated that Pharisees and doctors of the Law had taken the trouble to come from all the villages in Galilee and Judaea as well as from Jerusalem to observe Jesus' behaviour and hear his teaching.

When Jesus called Levi the tax-collector, and had sat down for a meal with other publicans (Mark 2.15–17),

> 'the scribes of the Pharisees, when they saw that he was eating with sinners, said to his disciples: 'Why does he eat with tax-collectors and sinners?' Then, when Jesus heard it, he said to them: 'Those who are well have no need of a doctor, but those who are sick; I came not to call the righteous, but sinners.'

Naturally, by his action, Jesus had made himself non-Pharisee, or unclean. In the parallel passages, Matt. 9.11 names the Pharisees alone (Matthew has a characteristic of dropping references to scribes from his version), and Luke 5.30 has 'the Pharisees and their scribes' and then 'the disciples of the Pharisees' in v.33. In Mark 2.18–22 the disciples of the Pharisees also expressed surprise that although they fasted, as did the disciples of John the Baptist, Jesus' disciples did not. Apparently they tried to exert their influence over Jesus' disciples, an attempt which Jesus resisted, comparing the Pharisaic movement to an old, tired and stretched wineskin which would burst if it tried to contain the new wine of his own movement.

Yet another controversy pericope follows, this time for plucking ears of corn on the sabbath.

> The Pharisees said to him: 'Why are they doing what is not lawful on the sabbath?' And Jesus said, 'Have you never read what David did when he was in need and hungry . . . how he entered the house of God during the high priesthood of Abiathar, and ate the bread of the presence, which it is not lawful for any but the priests to eat? . . .' And he said to them: 'The sabbath was made for man, not man for the sabbath.'

Matthew 12.2 agrees that the Pharisees did criticize them for this, but Luke 6.2 restricts the censure to 'certain of the Pharisees'. Both Matthew and Luke omit the incorrect reference Jesus supposedly made to Abiathar the high priest (I Sam. 21.1–6 states that the priest was in fact Ahimelech). They also omit the saying about the sabbath being made for man and not man for the sabbath, which is interesting, since the saying *was* a Pharisaic one.

The incident of the man with the withered hand in Mark 3.1–6 presents the Pharisees as plotting with the Herodians to destroy Jesus. There is some debate as to who exactly these Herodians were: some scholars think that they can safely be identified with the Sadducees, and others assume that they were a specific party who supported the descendants of Herod the Great. Certainly it was the Sadducean party who generally supported Herodians, and not Pharisees – and the high-priestly house of Boethus was actually related to the Herods by marriage.

Luke 6.7 amends the opposition to 'scribes and Pharisees'; Matt. 12.10–14 omits the statement that the Pharisees had been deliberately watching the man, as if he had been 'planted' by them in order to catch Jesus out. Both omit the reference to Jesus' anger, and the fact that Herodians were involved in any plotting, although they both agree that plotting against Jesus did follow.

Mark 3.10–20 has the scribes from Jerusalem accusing Jesus of healing by the power of Beelzebul, whereas Matt. 12.24 and 9.34 insist that it was the Pharisees whom Jesus heartily rebuked and ended up calling 'offspring of vipers' in 12.34. Luke however, states that the bystanders or multitudes were the ones in controversy with Jesus on this occasion, and Jesus' reproof is given to the people as a whole and not specifically to the Pharisees.

The incident of the healing of Jairus' daughter in Mark 5.21–43 provides a story in which there seems to be a friendly relationship between Jesus and the rulers of the synagogue at Capernaum. Matthew 9.18–23, however, drops this possible implication of friendly and considerate dealings (omitting the implication elsewhere in the Gospels that Jesus taught regularly in this synagogue). Only Jairus is involved, and he is not named.

One fascinating little detail is that during the healing of the woman with the haemorrhage that interrupts the raising of Jairus' daughter, where Mark's version simply states that the woman reached out and touched Jesus' garments, Matthew and Luke specifically mention that she touched his *kraspeda* or 'fringes'. The instruction to wear these fringes comes from Num. 15.33f and Deut. 22.12: 'You shall make yourself fringes on the four corners of your cloak with which you cover yourself.' The wearing of distinctive fringes was one of the particular distinguishing marks of a Pharisee.

Somehow it looks as if an unconscious memory of Jesus wearing a Pharisaic garment has crept into the tradition!

Why all the fuss? What were these fringes for? Later tradition revealed that the rabbis maintained that the fringes represented the whole summary of the Torah. The Torah was said to contain 613 commandments; the numerical value of the letters of the word *sisith* (fringes) was 600, so that if one added the eight threads and five knots of a correct fringe, one obtained 613. Thus the rabbis suggested, in light-hearted vein, that whoever observed the commandment to wear the fringes was considered by God as if he had observed them all (Sifre on Num. 15.39; Num. Rabba on 13.38, see D. Daube, *The New Testament and Rabbinic Judaism*, p. 251).

At the time of Jesus, the Shammaite school apparently accentuated the length of their fringes by the length of another centimetre or so, thus arousing the contempt of the school of Hillel for being 'showy'. The Shammaites made their fringes the length of four fingers, whereas Hillelites settled for only three. Incidentally, one can here probably pick up Jesus' reference to those who liked to wear their fringes long (Matt. 23.5) and note that this may have been a pointed criticism of the Shammaite school in particular.

This provides us with an interesting thought. If it could be true that the criticism against Jesus only came from *certain* of the Pharisees, may there perhaps have been a group of extremist Shammaites from Jerusalem disrupting the peaceful Hillelite majorities in Galilee, especially perhaps in Capernaum?

The healing of the centurion's servant (Luke 7.1–10; Matt. 8.5–10,13), a miracle not included in Mark, provides another opportunity to mention the Pharisees of Capernaum. Bultmann commented quite bluntly on this pericope that 'the scenes depicted are imaginary, and we must treat them as the products of (the imagination of) the church'. Some have felt that the picture conjured up of this wealthy centurion is quite incredible, and flies in the face of all that is known about centurions. In fact, Bultmann dismissed the scene on quite other grounds, that 'hardly anyone will support the historicity of a telepathic healing' (*The History of the Synoptic Tradition*, p. 39), to my embarrassment and that of many others with healing experience, who would *never* reject the story on those grounds!

The narrative is particularly interesting as an illustration of how Matthew and Luke deal with the same piece of material, shaping it to their own ends. Luke obviously wanted his readers to feel a pleasant sympathy with this good Gentile centurion, and his version stressed that the 'elders of the Jews' were very appreciative of him. This necessitated regarding these elders in an equally favourable light. Luke 7.1–10 therefore mentions that the elders actually went to Jesus in person with the request that he might heal their benefactor's slave. They recommend the centurion in glowing terms, pointing out what a worthy fellow he is, for 'he loves our nation and himself built us our synagogue'. The plea would lose all its point if there were antagonistic relations between Jesus and the synagogue rulers. They seem to expect Jesus also to love their synagogue, and appreciate what the centurion had done for them; and Jesus is obviously in accord.

Matthew 8.5–13, however, has no such friendly converse between Jesus and the elders. It is the centurion himself who approaches Jesus, and all mentions of the synagogue and his relationship with it are omitted. The passage ends with the very anti-Jewish statement peculiar to Matthew that 'the sons of the kingdom shall be cast forth into outer darkness; there shall be weeping and wailing and gnashing of teeth' (8.12). Whether it was Matthew who had deliberately dropped the friendly implication, or Luke who had deliberately invented it, is impossible to judge now.

When Jesus preached at his local synagogue, the one at Nazareth (Mark 6.1–6) where he had grown up and where his family was well known, he was certainly opposed and 'they' were 'astonished', and caused Jesus to marvel at their unbelief. Matthew's version follows Mark closely, but Luke 4.16–30 presents the actual content of Jesus' preaching, and details the very violent reaction from his hearers from which Jesus was extremely lucky to have escaped with his life – they intended to throw him off a cliff!

Luke 4.16–30 highlighted the fact that Jesus was welcome, and regularly attended the synagogue, and had already achieved considerable fame. 'He went into the synagogue, *as his custom was*, on the sabbath day. And he stood up to read; and there was given to him the book of the prophet Isaiah.' He read the lesson and gave the address, claiming that the scripture – which concerned the anointing of the messianic servant of the Lord to preach good news to the poor, release the captives, give the blind back their sight, and set at liberty the oppressed – was being fulfilled by himself before their very eyes. At this, he ran into opposition from the 'attendants' who had known him from childhood and observed him growing up in their midst.

Mark's version at this point is very blunt indeed.

> Where did this man get all this? What is the wisdom given to him? . . . Is not this the carpenter, the son of Mary and brother of James and Joses and Judas and Simon, and are not his sisters here with us? And they took offence at him.

Luke 4.28 is the only version that gives an account of what happened next. It states that 'all in the synagogue were filled with wrath', their outrage being so violent that 'they rose up and put him out of the city, and took him to the brow of the hill on which their city was built in order to throw him down headlong. But he passed through the midst of them and went away (Luke 4.29–30).

Whether or not this was supposed to have been at Pharisaic instigation is not mentioned. It was a golden opportunity to show up Jesus' enemies as being Pharisees – *yet in all three Gospels no mention is actually made of them on this occasion.* In fact, the text even indicates that following this climactic moment, they actually supported him. Mark 6.6 gives us 'Jesus went about among the villages teaching', which is amended in Matt. 9.35 to 'Jesus went about in all their cities and villages, teaching in their synagogues, preaching the gospel of the kingdom, and healing every disease and every infirmity'.

However, Mark's version is full of antagonism. It commences with 'Pharisees and certain of the scribes who had come from Jerusalem' noticing that Jesus and his disciples were not observing their laws of ritual purity. One might, of course, ask why on earth they should have been, if they were not themselves known to have been members of the Pharisaic sect. Jesus stoutly defends what he and his disciples are doing, or rather not doing, and calls his critics hypocrites. He charges them with honouring God with their lips but not with their hearts, and accuses them of neglecting the commandments of God in order to get away with their own wishes, giving the *Corban* practice as his example. He ends with the blunt statement that *nothing* from 'outside a man' can defile him by contact or by being eaten. Evil thoughts and evil actions originating in evil hearts are the real cause of defilement.

The strong implication is that the Pharisees had overlooked or ignored this aspect in their concern for ritualistic legalism. This passage, as we have seen, is fraught with all sorts of difficulties as regards its accurate presentation of the Pharisaic point of view, of which it is quite possible that Matthew and Luke were well aware – for Luke omits it altogether, and Matthew abbreviates it drastically and omits the *corban* question. Luke adds, incidentally, that the Pharisees were scandalized (Matt. 15.12), and that Jesus went on to call them 'blind guides'. If a man who was himself 'blind' through his ignorance expected the Pharisees to lead him on the right path, they would be doomed and 'fall into the pit'. Matthew 15.7 has Jesus calling the Pharisees 'hypocrites' to their faces.

Yet in this vehement passage we find Matthew omitting one very telling verse. Mark 7.19, after the teaching that 'nothing that goes into a man from outside can defile him since it enters not his heart but his stomach, and so passes on', declares in an editorial bracket: 'This he said, making all meats clean.' Matthew drops this verse. This might have been because the author belonged to a community that wished to retain some of the food laws; but might it not have been simply because Jesus had *not* taken this free line over what foods should be eaten? If he had, why on earth do we discover (as Muslims point out) that some considerable time after Jesus' death, Peter was still resisting the idea of eating 'unclean meat' (Acts 10.9–16)? If a genuine declaration of Jesus had been made on that very subject, it would have been a drastic step for a Jew to take, since it went against God's specific Torah commands, and could hardly have passed unnoticed! Such a change would affect the whole of a family's shopping and kitchen arrangements – a basic and fundamental change indeed. The emphasis of Jesus' teaching seems rather to have been that 'from within, out of the human heart, come evil thoughts, fornication, theft, murder, adultery, coveting, wickedness, deceit, licentiousness, envy, slander, pride, foolishness'. These were the things that truly defiled people.

In Mark 8.11–21 we have the Pharisees urging Jesus to perform a sign from heaven.

> The Pharisees came and began to argue with him, seeking from him a sign from heaven, to test him. And he sighed deeply in his spirit, and said: 'Why does this generation seek a sign? Truly I say to you, no sign shall be given.'

Jesus warns his company to beware of their influence, which was 'like leaven'. Leaven, or yeast, suggested a sinister, silently pervasive influence, that could work on a substance and radically alter it. Matthew 16's parallel passage lumps Pharisees and Sadducees together again in the uneasy wedlock of the M source, and seems to show Jesus warning his disciples about the teachings of both groups. Luke has no parallel context, but there are similar phrases elsewhere. In 12.21, for example, he states that the 'leaven of the Pharisees' is hypocrisy, and hypocrisy is mentioned again in vv.54–56.

Another occasion on which a sign was requested occurs in Matthew 12.38, when certain scribes and Pharisees are told that they will only be given the 'sign of Jonah', which is usually taken by Christians to be a veiled reference to the resurrection in three days, but which Muslims would see as a comparison between the people of Nineveh (who repented and thereby escaped the judgment of God) and those Pharisees to whom Jesus had preached who showed no signs of repenting of their ways at all – leading to parallel fates. Luke 11.16 does not say that the questioners are Pharisees, but makes them just miscellaneous persons from the multitude.

In Matthew 8.19 a scribe declares that he will follow Jesus wherever he goes: in Luke 9.57 the scribe has been down-graded to 'a certain man'.

The passion predictions are interesting in that in Mark 8.31 the Pharisees are not specifically named at all.

> And he began to teach them that the Son of man must suffer many things, and be rejected by the elders and the chief priests and the scribes, and be killed, and after three days rise again. And he said this plainly.

Of course, either of the expressions 'elders' or 'scribes' could be applied to Pharisees, particularly the leading ones of Jerusalem; but since the Pharisees are specified quite freely elsewhere, as we have seen, it is odd that they are not so specified here. Matthew 16.21 and Luke 9.22 follow Mark closely here. Mark's second prediction is non-committal, but in the third one Mark 10.33 has the chief priests and scribes. So does Matt. 20.18, but Luke 18.32 drops all mentions of them and simply refers to Jesus' delivery into the hands of the Gentiles.

In Mark 10.2–12 the Pharisees quiz Jesus over his attitude to the divorce law, about which there were frequent contemporary debates and many differing opinions. Jesus seems to have taken a line similar to Rabbi Shammai on this occasion, although modern scholars do argue over interpretation.

> Whoever divorces his wife and marries another, commits adultery against her; and if she divorces her husband and marries another, she commits adultery (Mark 10.11–12).

Matthew 19.1–9 alters the ruling to:

> I say to you, whoever divorces his wife *except for unchastity* and marries another, commits adultery.

According to Gittin 9.10, the Shammaites ruled that a man might not divorce his wife 'unless he has found unchastity in her'. The school of Hillel allowed a much freer attitude – 'even if she spoiled a dish for him.' Luke omits the subject altogether. One might ask why it was suddenly brought up at all. It does seem as if the Pharisees were interested to know what the ruling of Jesus would be on this topic which, like the length of fringes, was currently being hotly debated by the schools of Hillel and Shammai.

Naturally, as the Gospel narratives enter Holy Week, opposition to Jesus mounts. Mark does not mention the Pharisees at all during the triumphal entry, but Luke's version (19.36–40) indicates that there were Pharisees amongst the multitudes of *supporters* who cheered Jesus on his way.

> And some of the Pharisees in the multitude said to him: 'Teacher, rebuke your disciples.' He answered: 'I tell you, if these were silent, the very stones would cry out.'

This does not necessarily mean that they were angry with Jesus, but were warning him of the danger the enthusiasm of his disciples was putting him in; but Jesus was not prepared to stop their shouting or acclamation of him as the Messiah. His hour had come!

One of Jesus' first acts in Jerusalem was the cleansing of the Temple, a dramatic affray which would inevitably bring him into open conflict with the religious authorities. The Booths of Hino, a public poultry market, had previously been situated on the Mount of Olives across the Kidron Valley; but the chief priests, to spare the pilgrims an arduous climb, bought the sacrificial birds wholesale and had them delivered to the outer court of the Temple, where they were sold at a fixed price by salaried Levite Temple servants, as were the drink-offerings also. The routine is described in Shekalim 5.4:

> The devout would approach Johanan, the overseer of the tokens, and pay money in exchange for a token. Johanan would then approach Ahijah, the overseer of the drink offerings, hand him the token, and receive the drink offering. In the evening, when these two consulted together, Johanan would pay Ahijah the value of his tokens.'

Money-changers simply provided 'clean' change, that is, Tyrian coins, which had no emblems or inscriptions on them that could be regarded as blasphemous (like the Roman coins). A surcharge of a half *ma'ah* was levied on every transaction, and this went into the Temple funds – the money-changers made no personal profits (as is implied in the Gospels!).

This token system and the ban on private trading had actually *been introduced by the Pharisees* as part of their reforms, and they had also forbidden pilgrims to enter the Temple precincts carrying sticks, bags, or coins tied in kerchiefs; and, since the Law forbade the wearing of shoes on the Temple Mount, dirty feet were also forbidden. Josephus (*Against Apion 2.8*) added the information that the Temple might not be used as a thoroughfare, a point backed up by Berakoth 9.5 and Tosefta 7.19; 'They shall not use it to shorten a journey.' Mark 11.16 specifically mentioned Jesus taking the Pharisaic line, stopping people from carrying vessels through, and claiming that the house of prayer had become a 'den of thieves'.

It was unfortunately true that despite the Pharisaic reforms, the wholesalers working their monopolies had managed to amass vast fortunes. The ban on competitive trading had in fact encouraged extortion. Simeon ben Gamaliel later managed to force down the price of doves at a stroke, by altering the number that pilgrims would require for sacrifice (Kerithoth 1.7).

Mark 11.18 states that after this act of cleansing, 'the chief priests and scribes heard it and sought a way to destroy him, for they feared him, because all the multitude was astonished at his teaching'. Matthew 21.12–17 agrees that the opposition came from the chief priests and the scribes, and Luke 19.45–48 adds a mention of the 'principal men of the people', which might well refer to the leading Pharisees. Mark 11.27–33 shows that the Temple hierarchy were taking a natural lead in the build-up of opposition to Jesus, and all three Gospels agree that the chief priests, elders of the people and scribes were acting as one in this matter (Matt. 21.33, Luke 20.1).

> As he was walking in the Temple, the chief priests and the scribes and the elders came to him and they said: 'By what authority are you doing these things?'

The parable of the Unfaithful Stewards of the Vineyard was told against the Pharisees specifically in a frontal attack (Mark 12.1–12). Matthew's version mentions the Pharisees being with the chief priests at this point (Matt. 21.45), and they 'tried to arrest him, but feared the multitude, for they perceived that he had told the parable against them'. Luke 20.19 mentions only scribes and priests. Before the parable of the Vineyard, Matt. 21.28–32 interposed the parable of the Two Sons, which we must presume was also intended by this author to have been addressed to the chief priests and elders. This ends with a statement that they would have regarded as highly offensive, that the publicans and harlots would enter the kingdom of heaven before them, because those people had accepted John's message and his identification of Jesus as the Messiah, whereas the hierarchy had not!

On the question of paying tribute to Caesar, Matthew stipulates that the Pharisees asked it (Matt. 22.15–22); Luke only talks of 'they', probably retaining the previous mention of chief priests and scribes in his mind (20.20–26); Mark agrees with Matthew that it was the Pharisees, but as in the incident of the man with the withered hand, he introduced the Herodians into the story as their allies (12.13–17).

The series of questions put to Jesus in Mark ends with that of a scribe, and his recommendation by Jesus for being 'not far from the kingdom of heaven' (Mark 12.26–34). In Mark, this particular scribe is no enemy, and it states that he knew that Jesus had answered well, and commended him. In the view of the opinion Jesus supposedly taken by the other scribes, he must have been a brave man! Sadly, in Matt. 22.34–40, that friendship and mutual approval has characteristically disappeared. Instead, when the Pharisees observe how Jesus had put the Sadducees to silence, they close ranks and one of them puts the question about the 'great commandment' to test him. Jesus' answer was defensive, and the commendation given in Mark is completely omitted. Luke 20.39, however, seems reluctant to take that line, and mentions that 'certain of the scribes' thought Jesus *had* answered well, and said so, but it adds that they did not dare to ask him any more questions after this.

Mark 12.38–40 follows the question session with a reproach to the whole order of scribes in which Jesus vehemently denounces their practices of being ostentatious in their dress and mode of living; their desire for recognition and approval; their long, pretended prayers, and the way in which they sponged off gullible widows who should probably have known better. Matthew and Luke both extend this passage considerably, with relish. Luke's 'woes' are placed in chapter 11, before Holy Week, at a meal in which Jesus is actually the guest in the house of a Pharisee. This incident may well have been the original setting for the material in the *corban* controversy of Mark 7.

You Pharisees cleanse the outside of the cup and the dish, but inside you are full of extortion and wickedness. You fools! Did not he who made the outside make the inside also? But give for alms those things which are within, and behold, everything will be clean for you. But woe to you Pharisees! For you tithe mint and rue and every herb, but neglect justice and the love of God.

The host had apparently criticized Jesus when he noticed that he had not bathed first. He had obviously expected Jesus to behave in the proper Pharisaic manner. Jesus promptly rounded on him, calling Pharisees in general hypocrites, and comparing them to unmarked graves. (It was the usual practice to lime-wash graves before the Feast of Passover so that people might not accidentally tread on them and become defiled and therefore unable to partake in the Feast.)

One of the scribes at the feast had obviously not expected that *his* group would be included in Jesus' attack: 'Teacher, in saying this you reproach us also' (v.45), but Jesus did not spare him. On the contrary, a whole spate of further 'woes' ensues, this time for loading people with burdens, 'building the tombs of the prophets', and 'taking away the key of knowledge; you entered in yourselves, and those who were also entering in you hindered! (v.52).

This attack on the Pharisees, who saw themselves as the successors to the prophets, really rankles with them, and they begin to 'press upon him vehemently, and to provoke him to speak of many things, lying in wait for him, to catch something out of his mouth'.

The bitter polemic in the Matthew 23 version accuses them of shutting the kingdom of heaven; of going to enormous lengths to make proselytes so that even more unfortunate people can become 'sons of hell'; of undermining the severity of oath-taking so that the whole practice becomes farcical; tithing any number of minor and trivial things, but totally neglecting the important matters; cleansing the 'outside of the cup' but not the inside; being like whited sepulchres, very plausible sounding but in fact full of rottenness and corruption; and alleged regret for, but actual participation in, the persecution of truly religious people.

If these words truly represent an actual speech of Jesus, the criticism that these Pharisees liked 'to make their fringes long' may well have implied that it was the school of Shammai in particular to which Jesus was referring. In *The Pharisees and the Teacher of Nazareth*, A. Finkel took precisely that view. He said: 'The polemics with the Pharisees, the harsh woes addressed to their teachers, were in fact directed at the disciples of Shammai's academy' (pp.134f.). He suggested that those who 'shut up the kingdom of heaven' against people (Matt. 23.13) would be a fitting description of the Shammaites, who were much keener to deny the sinner a share in the world to come than the merciful school of Hillel. The Pharisaic approach adopted by the Hillelites – the humility, restraint, clear argumentative reasoning and liberalism – was in fact *very close* in spirit to the teaching of Jesus and not in opposition to it, and it is really inconceivable that Jesus could have had Hillelites in mind if he uttered that most stern of passages of condemnation.

Examples proliferate of Hillelite sayings that compare comfortably with those attributed to Jesus. Aboth 2.4 gives us: 'Do not judge another until you have tried yourself in the same situation.' B. Sotah 15a (in the name of Hillel's descendant Gamaliel II) stresses that the measure you mete will be measured again to you. Aboth 1.12 and Aboth de Rabbi Nathan 12 give Hillel's exhortation to peaceful living: 'Be as the followers of Aaron, loving peace, seeking peace, making peace between man and his wife, loving all creatures.'

The *Kerygmata Petrou* (10.11.28.4), which scholars like Cullmann and Schoeps supposed to offer numerous parallels to the earliest literary pronouncements of the original church, commented that Jesus *did* criticize certain of the Pharisees, but not all of them.

'Our teacher convicted some of the Pharisees and scribes among us, who are separate and as scribes know the Law better than others, and (described) them as being hypocrites because they kept clean only what was visible to men, but neglected purity of the heart, which is visible to God alone' (*New Testament Apocrypha* Vol. 2, p.125).

The Jesus' reference to the killing and scourging of the prophets is interesting. Finkel suggests that there were indeed Pharisees who acted violently towards those who opposed their decisions, and these, as we might guess, were Shammaites. It is a common religious failing, one which Muslims identify as *tughyan* or 'tyranny'. One might think here of the extremist groups of 'pious' men who supported one faction against the more 'lax' of their fellows in such countries as Khomeini's Iran or Cromwell's England, or the fervour of devotees of all new systems, including – in this century – Communism. In many places of the world, where pious extremists hold sway, it does not do to voice one's contrasting opinions too loudly, unless one is ready for martyrdom.

On one occasion, for example, the Shammaites had maintained that 'peace offerings may be brought on a festival day, but hands are not to be laid on them' – these offerings were shared with the owner-presenter – 'but not burnt offerings' (P. Hag 2.10,11). Hillel disagreed, and presented a burnt offering in the Temple, whereupon Shammai's disciples gathered in a raging protest, shouting and waving fists.

On another occasion Hillel disputed the Sanhedrin's decision that the juice of grapes pressed into a vat could make other food susceptible to impurity (B. Shab 17a). The Shammaites were so enraged about this that they actually planted a sword in the Academy's hall as a warning sign, thereby forcing nervous Hillelites into accepting the Shammaite decision.

In other words, it was the Shammaites who showed evidence of a violent attitude. P. Shab 3b indicates that later, in the last years before the destruction of the Temple, when eighteen measures against the heathen were opposed by the Hillelites, numbers of them were actually massacred.

It is not unjustifiable to wonder whether the words of Matthew 23 might not have come from a tradition taking an uncharacteristically exasperated, but understandable, Hillelite stance against the Shammaite extremists.

The 'L' passages, with their special interest in the poor and outcast members of society, include several references to the Pharisees not found elsewhere in the Gospels. In Luke 7.36–50, when a prostitute washed the feet of Jesus with her tears, Jesus was actually being entertained to dinner in the house of a certain Pharisee called Simon. The rather strange thing here was that apparently Simon had not attempted to cleanse Jesus in the normal Pharisaic manner (which *might* be interpreted as extraordinary politeness on his part, not vice versa, if his own principles were being laid aside so as not to embarrass his guest) – and Jesus rounded on him quite smartly for not doing so, once the Pharisee expressed surprise that he had allowed the woman to touch him. (I have often wondered how it was that the Pharisee let the woman into his house; or even how he knew what her trade was – but maybe that was obvious.)

We have already noted the warning, presumably friendly, given to Jesus by the Pharisees at the Triumphal Entry. In Luke 13.31 we have another interesting detail. 'Some Pharisees came and said to him: 'Get away from here, for Herod wants to kill you'; surely a friendly warning that he was in danger from Antipas (the Herodians) and should get away quickly.

Luke 13.10–17 gives the incident of Jesus being rebuked by the ruler of the synagogue, in which he had been the guest speaker, for healing a bent woman on the sabbath, simply by straightening her back. Jesus countered this rebuke with an almost typical Pharisaic answer, the strength and logic of which apparently reassured his 'opponents', and caused the multitude to rejoice.

> 'Does not each of you on the sabbath untie his ox or ass from the manger and lead it away to water it? And ought not this woman, a daughter of Abraham, whom Satan has bound for eighteen years, to be loosed from her bond on the sabbath day?'

Luke 14.1–6 gives another incident concerning sabbath healings, set at yet another dinner in the house of a Pharisee, this time a Pharisaic 'ruler'. Here, Jesus himself raises the question, before healing a dropsical man:

> Is it lawful to heal on the sabbath or not?' And they were silent . . .
> And he said to them: 'Which of you, having an ass [other ancient

authorities read 'son'] or an ox that has fallen into a well, will not immediately pull him out on a sabbath day?' And they could not reply to this.

In fact, *every Pharisee would have thought exactly as Jesus did on this issue.*

In Luke 14.7–11 Jesus launches into a parable about humility when choosing seats at a feast, which seems to have been rather pointed!

He told a parable to those who were invited, when he noticed how they chose the places of honour . . . for everyone who raises himself up will be humbled, but he who humbles himself will be raised up.

In Luke 15.2 the Pharisees and scribes openly 'murmured' against him because he was eating with unclean publicans and sinners. In Luke 16.14 Luke accuses the Pharisees of being 'lovers of money', and says that they scoffed at Jesus' teachings about not being able to serve both God and Mammon (self-interest). It is significant, one feels, that this is an editorial note, and is not given as the actual opinion of Jesus.

Luke 18.9–14 has the famous parable of the Pharisee and the publican, where the two types are deliberately exaggerated by Jesus to make his point.

Two men went up to the Temple to pray, one a Pharisee and the other a tax-collector. The Pharisee stood and prayed to himself in these words: 'God, I am thankful that I am not like other people, extortioners, unjust, adulterers – or even like this tax-collector! I fast twice a week, I give tithes of all that I get.' The tax-collector, standing far off, would not even lift up his eyes to heaven but beat his breast saying: 'God be merciful to me a sinner.' I tell you, this man went back to his house justified, rather than the other; for everyone who exalts himself will be humbled, and he who humbles himself will be exalted.

Finally, Luke 17.20–21 presents the Pharisees questioning Jesus about what truly was dear to their hearts – when would the coming of the kingdom of heaven take place? Jesus answered them along with his disciples: 'The kingdom does not come in any way which can be observed – for behold, it is within you (within your grasp).' It may even be possible that these Pharisees among his hearers were to be considered among the disciples of Jesus.

Moving finally to the events of the trials and death of Jesus, Mark 14.1 indicates that it was the chief priests and scribes and not the Pharisees who sought to kill him. Judas' plot was with the chief priests (Mark 14.10; Matt. 26.14). Luke adds the detail that the 'captains' were also involved (Luke 22.4). These captains may have been the *Seganim*, chiefs of the Temple police, or there may be an indication here, as in the Fourth Gospel, that the Romans were already involved. At the actual arrest, Mark records the arrival of a mob with swords and staves 'from the chief priests, scribes and elders'. Matthew 26.47 simply omits the mention of the scribes, and Luke 22.52 adds the 'captains of the Temple', here surely the *seganim*.

At the trials, Mark 15.1 mentions the chief priests, elders, scribes and the whole council; Matt. 26.57–59 has the scribes and elders gathering at the house of Caiaphas with the chief priests and the whole council; and Luke has the assembly of the elders of the people, both chief priests and scribes (Luke 22.66). As the trials progress, the chief priests and elders are mentioned consistently in Matthew, whereas the scribes are omitted (Matt. 27.1,3,6,12,20). Luke, however, has the scribes still there (Luke 23.10), in particular to do the accusations before Herod Antipas. Luke 23.13 mentions the 'rulers of the people', as does 24.30.

When Jesus has been crucified, Luke 23.35 mentions the 'rulers' scoffing at him along with the mob, Mark 15.29–31 gives chief priests and scribes, and Matt. 27.39–41 has the same groups plus the elders. Matthew alone has the narrative about the chief priests and Pharisees – the first time Pharisees have been mentioned by name for quite some time – going to Pilate with the request that a guard be placed at the tomb of Jesus so that the disciples might not be able to steal his body and pretend that he had risen from the dead. They are allowed to seal the tomb and place their own guard, presumably the Temple guard. After the resurrection, the terrified guards report to the chief priests what had happened, who then call an assembly with the elders and bribe the soldiers to say that the Christians had indeed stolen the body!

When one examines all these passages, one cannot really see any consistent pattern emerging. Sometimes Matthew and Luke feel that Mark's version is in error, and correct it according to what they propose as being nearer the truth, or according to their own motivational interests. Occasionally they make specific what had only been general statements, and sometimes they act in reverse and make an actual identification of a particular group into a general reference. The Pharisees sometimes get the benefit of this rearrangement, and sometimes come out of it less favourably. The main point is that there is *no* consistent development in the handling of the sources, and one has the feeling occasionally that all the Jewish religious bodies were really lumped together and regarded as much of a muchness by the Gospel writers – usually to the great detriment of the Pharisaic sect.

As regards the Marcan narrative, there seems to be all the difference between the opponents in the controversies of Jesus in chapters 2–12 (Pharisees and scribes) and his enemies in chapters 14–15 (chief priests and elders). If this passion narrative contains the oldest strands, then it seems quite possible that the oldest Synoptic tradition *did not include the Pharisees among the real enemies of Jesus at all.*

The historical foundation of the hostility of the priests towards Jesus seems a fairly reasonable assumption, but there may be far less ground for assuming the hostility of the Pharisees. Therefore, the narratives in which hostility towards Jesus is ascribed to the chief priests and those in sympathy with them could have come from a period in church history several decades earlier than that which turned the Pharisees into Jesus' enemies!

10 · The Pharisees in the Fourth Gospel

When we turn to the Gospel of John, we find that it is not so much the Pharisees who are the enemies of Jesus, as an ubiquitous and amorphous group known simply as 'the Jews'. Antisemitism had really taken off. The most popular explanation for this phenomenon is to claim that the Gospel is a very late piece of writing and that by the time it left the hands of its final editor the antagonism between Jews and Christians was quite different from what it had been in the time of Jesus. The expression 'Jews' no longer represented any ethnic group, but the unbelieving world in general, and in the relations of 'the Jews' to Jesus, the relations of all unbelievers to the Christian church and its message were mirrored. Jesus and his disciples now appear as 'non-Jews' (5.16; 8.17; 10.31,34; 18.36)!

The Fourth Gospel is totally unlike the other three. It presents a ministry of Jesus based on long philosophical discourses, as opposed to the short succinct sayings that are a feature of the Synoptic Gospels. Jesus can no longer be recognized as the gentle story-teller of Luke's Gospel. There are, in fact, only six narratives which the Fourth Gospel has in common with the first three: the cleansing of the Temple, the feeding of the five thousand, the walking on the water, the anointing at Bethany, and a variant version of the events of Holy Week and the death and resurrection of Jesus. The rest of the narrative is peculiar to this Gospel alone: the seven signs, the discourses, the controversies.

Controversy has raged over the dating and authorship of the Fourth Gospel, and these two topics must inevitably play a part in any consideration of it. Traditionally, it was believed to be the last of the Gospels to have been written, but in more recent times focus on many of its distinctive features has led many scholars to believe that an ancient tradition independent of the other Gospels must lie behind it.

Apart from any other factors, there are now known to be so many echoes of the Dead Sea Scrolls in this Gospel that it is no longer necessary to relegate it to a late date simply because of what were once seen as its Gnostic, anti-docetic, or post-Gnostic tendencies. The Dead Sea Scrolls have revealed that a certain brand of Jewish Gnosticism was highly worked out by the time of Christ, and may well have been a major influence.

The Gospel is full of details of places in Palestine, especially of Jerusalem and its environs, that are absent from the Synoptics. Places mentioned with significant topographical details include Sychar (84.5); Jacob's Well (4.6); Gerizim (4.20); Bethany beyond Jordan (1.28); Aenon near Salim (3.28); Bethzatha (5.1); Solomon's Portico (10.23); Kidron (18.1); the Gabbatha (19.13); Cana (2.1; 4.6); Siloam (9.7) and Ephraim (11.54). These place names have no theological significance, and must have come from an old tradition, whence they appear in the Gospel more or less by chance.

Apart from details of places, other significant details, which could even come from eye-witnesses, appear. For example in the Fourth Gospel alone we are told that a lad was present at the feeding of the five thousand, whose loaves were barley bread and fish were *opsaria* – little salted fish like sprats. We are also told that the crowd wanted to make Jesus their king, and later we are told of its attempts to find Jesus.

Pharisaic custom is taken for granted. At Cana, the stone water jars held water 'for purification'; purification is shown to be important in 11.55; 18.28. The rabbinic method of arguing is casually presented as if well understood, and the most natural thing: we are told how they searched their scriptures for isolated texts to support their themes (5.3). This seems a strange and almost dishonest method of research to us now, but that is because our mentality does not accept the premises of Pharisaic reasoning: that the ancient texts were the revealed word of God, and that phrases or details in them which may not have been understood in the past were preserved by careful conservation of the exact words so that future generations might read and understand.

This was the reason for the insistence that 'not one jot or tittle of the Law' was to be changed or altered in any way (jot was the *yod*, the smallest letter of the Hebrew alphabet; a tittle was an ornamental flourish in a scribe's handwriting. Everything to be copied exactly to be valid.

As Muslims know, exactly the same care is taken with copies made of the Qur'an, and no translation of it is taken as authoritative. It has to be learned as it is, in its original and very idiosyncratic style of Arabic. There are numerous places where a translator might feel irritated and wish to smooth over words or phrases, but this is not allowed. Any tampering with the text could lose a vital part of the meaning that perhaps might only be understood by another generation, when the time is right.

The Gospel shows awareness of how religious schools in which the rabbis were trained were highly esteemed (7.15). And most significant of all, perhaps, is the fact that the author (or authors) was very familiar with the Jewish feasts, not just the obvious features that any well-informed Christian might be expected to know, but detailed background knowledge of their major themes. Unless the reader is aware of the ritual readings and ceremonies of these special occasions, a full understanding of many passages in the Gospel is impossible. For example, the setting for Jesus' speech on being the 'light of the world' was the Feast of Tabernacles. During these celebrations four massive candelabra were set up in the Court of Women, and every evening vast crowds assembled there with burning torches, in pious holiday spirit. Jesus made his speech 'in the Treasury' – this same Court of Women.

It would help if some firm conclusions could be drawn from these fascinating indications, but useful conclusions about the Fourth Gospel are elusive. We have to acknowledge that the mystery of its authorship and background must yet go unsolved, though we should maintain an open mind as to the authenticity of parts at least of its detail.

That having been said, we can now turn to the Fourth Gospel and see what it has to say about the opponents of Jesus.

In the very first chapter, v.19, it is reported that 'the Jews' sent priests and Levites from Jerusalem to question John the Baptist about his person and ministry in a conversation in which John declared that he saw himself as the forerunner of a Messiah who was about to make himself known publicly. It is specifically stated that these priests had been sent by the Pharisees (v.24). The intention of the author here must therefore have been to indicate the highly influential Pharisaic members of the Sanhedrin at Jerusalem, who had the authority to deputize Levites and priests of the lower orders.

Incidentally, this backs up the references in Mark's Gospel: 'scribes who had come up from Jerusalem', who challenged Jesus, and not his Galilean compatriots (cf. Mark 3.10–22; 7; etc.). Were these simply the less liberal-minded, 'nit-picking' southerners, or did the phrase imply that they were emissaries from the highest Pharisaic authorities in the land, those elite scholars who had been elected on to the Sanhedrin?

In chapter 3, one of those rulers is identified and named as Nicodemus, an eminent Pharisee who, it is implied, had been impressed and perhaps disturbed by the reports he had received about Jesus, and is most interested to discover for himself (and for those of like mind), whether or not this exciting new charismatic leader, Jesus of Nazareth, could really be the Messiah they had so long awaited.

The detail that Nicodemus goes to Jesus 'by night', under cover of darkness, is highly significant. Darkness is used throughout the Gospel as a symbol for 'the world', the realm of unbelief and unenlightenment (cf.8.12; 13.30).

All the discourses in the Fourth Gospel repay very deep and careful study, for the words given on the surface are like the tips of icebergs, and a whole vast depth of meaning lies beneath. Here, notice how it can be seen straight away that Jesus knows exactly what Nicodemus wants, and after the polite opening phrases plunges straight into a discussion on the vital but unasked question: what is it necessary for a person to do before he or she could be admitted into the kingdom Jesus had come to inaugurate?

> 'Rabbi, we know that you are a teacher come from God; for no one can do these signs that you do unless God be with him.' Jesus answered: 'Truly I say to you, unless one is born anew (or – from above) one cannot see the kingdom of God' (3.2–3).

This sort of narrative in the Fourth Gospel precisely illustrates the problems faced by those campaigning for the historicity of the work. Liberal scholars in the nineteenth century 'knew' Jesus and his miscellaneous contacts so well that clever edifices of characterization and motivation were set up, and became the staple fodder of religious education in schools and Sunday schools, and the inspiration behind numerous devotional novels.

Taking Nicodemus as an example, there was a considerable amount of material centred upon this person from very early times, yet he is not even mentioned in the Synoptics. Why did they leave him out? Or, why did the Fourth Gospel put him in? Was he no more than an invention? Was the content of his discourse with Jesus only a literary creation? Could he actually have been the unnamed Beloved Disciple? Did he exist at all?

None of these questions can be answered with any degree of certainty. Outside John's Gospel it would be difficult to prove his existence, unless one was prepared to accept that his real existence *had* to be the origin of all the apocalyptic material that shortly sprang up around him. Was he perhaps the famous Pharisee Naqdimon ben Gurion (see Chapter 7)? One is forced either into total scepticism or to take up a personal stance that invites charges of naivety. I would like to feel that there was a baby in the bath-water somewhere, and hesitate to pull out the plug.

In Chapter 3 Jesus begins his campaign of baptism in Judaea, a ministry running parallel to that of John who was working at Aenon, near the head-waters of the Wadi Fatah, where there were abundant springs. This suggestion is opposed by the Synoptic suggestion that Jesus did not commence his ministry until after the imprisonment of John. In 3.25–26, a 'Jew' opens a discussion with John's disciples over the issue of ritual purification, and although the discussion is not reported, one might assume from the subject-matter that this Jew was of the Pharisaic, or perhaps even the Essene, sect. Aenon is described as being 'near Salim', a place totally destroyed during the war of 70 CE.

In 4.1–4 it apparently comes to the attention of the Pharisees that Jesus is gathering more disciples that John, and this is given as the reason for Jesus's withdrawal from that area – a matter of tact!

A sabbath healing provokes 'the Jews' to question the actions of Jesus in 5.10. At the end of this episode, Jesus declares that just as his Father did not suspend his work in the sabbath, so Jesus might continue with his ministry, a statement which is supposed to have enraged 'the Jews', for it supposedly implied that he was the equal of God. In fact, the argument that God himself works on the sabbath to heal and mend wounds received the day before was acknowledged and accepted by all the rabbis. Here it is implied that

what they regarded as Jesus' arrogant appropriation of the authority of God for his own actions was what had offended them.
However, perhaps it is not the fact that Jesus had healed the man
that is challenged, but the actual reason given (although it may seem
trivial to a reader today): that the man was bearing a burden on the
sabbath.

Tradition stipulated that nothing more than the weight of one
dried fig might be carried on the sabbath day, and here was a man
bearing a stretcher. Jesus, as a Pharisaic rabbi, had a perfect right to
heal on the sabbath so long as he did not mix medicines which could
have been prepared the day before: indeed it was his Pharisaic duty
to do so. But he did not have the right to lay aside the sabbath
regulations as if he were possessor of an authority higher than
theirs, as if he were 'equal with God'.

Chapter 7 tells us that at the Feast of Tabernacles, Jesus remained
in Galilee and avoided Judaea, because 'the Jews' sought to kill
him. For this reason he did not at first go to Jerusalem. However,
after sending his brothers on ahead, he changed his mind and went
privately to the Feast, possibly hoping to be able to remain
incognito. This was not to be. While he was there he observed that
'the Jews' were looking for him, and that there was much speculation about him. For fear of 'the Jews' no-one dared speak openly
about him, or declare themselves on the side of his cause (v.13).

Then, suddenly, in the middle of the Feast, Jesus decided to show
his hand after all, and went into the Temple to teach in public. 'The
Jews' were amazed at his discourse, especially as he was known not
to have had the training usual for a Pharisee. ('How is it that this
man has learning, when he has never studied?' Jesus replied: 'My
teaching is not mine, but His who sent me.') This public appearance
caused the people of Jerusalem to debate whether Jesus might really
be the Messiah after all, on the grounds that he has come into the
open and the authorities have not arrested him. Verse 32 comments
that the Pharisees heard the speculations of the crowds, the
ignorant rabble, and were stirred up to do something about him
quickly. The 'chief priests and Pharisees' sent officers to arrest him
(v.32), but Jesus somehow avoided capture.

The last day of the Feast was the 'Great Hosanna' or 'Day of
Willows', when the special libation from the Pool of Siloam was
poured out on the altar. The priest came up from Siloam with his
golden pitcher and poured the contents on the base of the great

stone for the last time. Then the Hallel was sung, accompanied by the sound of the flute, the people responding and worshipping as the priests three times gave a threefold blast on their silver trumpets. Then the people would approach, waving lulabs, specially entwined leafy branches of willow and palm. The feast ended when the people beat their branches to shreds against the altar.

Apparently at some time during this ritual, possibly when the priest was poised to pour out the holy water, Jesus stood up and proclaimed: 'If anyone thirsts, let him come to me and drink, and from his inmost being rivers of living water will flow.' The Talmud similarly connected the water ceremony with the gift of the Holy Spirit, according to what is said: 'With joy shall ye draw water out of the wells of salvation' (J. Sukkah 5.1).

This very dramatic turn of events caused a sensation amongst the worshippers, and a great division – some saw this as a sign of his Messiahship but others were not convinced, because they thought that Jesus had been born in Nazareth in Galilee; and since the prophecy of Micah 5.2 stipulated Bethlehem as the birthplace of the Messiah, they did not realize that his claim could be seriously upheld.

Attempts were again made to arrest him, but the officers were impressed by him, and did not take him into custody. The Pharisees were furious, and pointed out that 'none of the authorities or the Pharisees believed in him' (v. 48). The crowd, who were ignorant *Amme ha-Aretz*, were accursed. This attitude of contempt for the people of the land was one of the less pleasant features of the extreme Shammaites. The statement that none of the Pharisees had believed in Jesus is immediately belied by Nicodemus, who attempts to defend him, but is speedily silenced, again on the grounds that Jesus was a Galilean. Nicodemus falls silent.

So, in this chapter, the 'Jews' seem to vary from a generalization of Jesus' enemies (vv. 1,11?,13,30) to the Pharisees, to the crowd that heard him speak (vv. 11?,15,20,25,31,35,40,43,49).

Jesus, however, does not shrink from the stir he is causing. It has been suggested that chapter 8 should really go before chapter 7, on the grounds that his declaration that he is the 'light of the world' (8.12) was made when the four enormous golden candelabra, the sacred lights, were being lit in the Court of Women on the *first* night of the Feast. This was a very moving occasion, when four youths of priestly descent holding pitchers of oil, shinned up the ladders which had been placed against the great candelabra with their four golden bowls each, the special wicks of which were economically made from the vestments worn just the once by the priests who had served within the sanctuary. The glow of light from the Temple lit up every courtyard in Jerusalem, and could be seen for miles around. It was intended as a symbol not only of the Shekinah, but also of the 'great light' which the 'people who walked in darkness' were to see (Isa. 9.40). According to tradition, the pillars of cloud and fire first appeared to guide Israel on the wilderness on 15 Tishri; and the dedication of Solomon's Temple and the descent of the Shekinah to it took place at this feast (I Kings 8; II Chron. 7).

The leading Pharisees danced before the people with flaming torches. The Levites stood on the steps with musical instruments and sang the fifteen Songs of Degrees. A three-fold trumpet blast was sounded at cockcrow, and another as they reached the tenth step. When they reached the magnificent gate that opened to the East, they turned round and faced the Holy Place and said: 'Our fathers who were in this place, they turned their back on the sanctuary of Yahweh and their faces towards the east; they worshipped towards the rising sun. But as for us, our eyes are towards the Lord.'

Again, it is possible that we have here an example of Jesus deliberately picking a highly-charged dramatic moment to turn the people's heads in his direction. 'I am the light of the world. He who follows me will not walk in darkness, but will have the light of life!' (John 8.2). The Pharisees immediately round on him for bearing witness to himself. By v. 22 his opponents have become 'the Jews' again, as also in vv. 48 and 57. In v. 31 'the Jews' are said to have included some who believed in him.

Linked to this theme of light, in chapter 9, on a sabbath day, Jesus heals a man blind from birth, a miracle of illumination both physical and spiritual. Again, there is more accuracy here than in the Synoptics, for what the Pharisees want to know was how Jesus worked the cure (v. 15). They are told that Jesus had mixed a kind of clay-poultice, with mud and saliva. In that way Jesus had broken the sabbath, not simply because he had performed an act of healing. The fact that he had ignored their tradition marked him off in their eyes as not being a 'man of God' but *Am ha-Aretz*.

By 10.31 we find that 'the Jews' are so incensed against Jesus that they are prepared to 'take up stones to stone him'. They feel obliged to go to these lengths because they now see Jesus as a very dangerous man, a blasphemer. Jesus does nothing to mollify them, and he is obliged to escape to a secluded spot across the Jordan.

When Jesus finds out that his friend Lazarus of Bethany (another person mentioned only in the Fourth Gospel and not in the Synoptics) has died, he travels back up from the wilderness to raise him. Bethany is only a short walk from Jerusalem, so Jesus knows that he will be in great danger once more. However, 'the Jews' are there to witness the event (11.36), and many of them are most impressed by what they see. The evidence of their own eyes overcomes their predjudice, and they are obliged to believe in him (v.45). Some go straight to the Pharisees of Jerusalem to tell them what has happened, and we need not assume that these witnesses were hostile to Jesus: they may have hoped to convince the authorities that Jesus really did have miraculous powers. But the Pharisees and chief priests call the Council together, and Caiaphas, 'who was high priest that year' (in fact from 18–36 CE), fearing the Roman reaction to a messianic surge of enthusiasm, suggests that it is expedient for one man to die, rather than the whole nation perish. Jesus, apparently well aware of the danger he is in, withdraws to the town Ephraim, which has been identified with El-Taiyibeh, a settlement that commanded an excellent view over the Rift Valley, from where he could easily see the approach of any hostile agents and take evasive action in good time.

As Passover approaches, the Pharisees and chief priests give orders that if anyone knows of his whereabouts, they should declare it. The warrant is out for his arrest. Any persons sheltering Jesus would themselves be in grave danger.

Nevertheless, six days before the Passover Jesus returns to Bethany, to the house of his friends, and a great crowd soon knows that he is there (12.9). The authorities immediately plan to arrest Lazarus also, the reason being that many of the Jews were believing in Jesus on account of his witness (12.11). Before anything can be done, Jesus sets out on his triumphal entry into Jerusalem, and a great crowd goes out to meet him and cheer him in. Jesus is flanked by loyal supporters who had witnessed the raising of Lazarus. The Pharisees are held in check by this popular enthusiasm and can do nothing. 'Look, the world has gone after him!' (12.19).

After speaking publicly, Jesus is again able to withdraw unmolested, and it is recorded that he now had adherents even in the ranks of the authorities, but they still did not dare admit it openly 'for fear of the Pharisees' (12.42). However, as we know, at least one of those persons of authority was himself a Pharisee, and there may have been many others by this time.

In the 'Farewell Discourses', Jesus does not once identify the Pharisees as being his enemies, but speaks in Pharisaic terms of 'the world' and 'the Prince of this world' – the Pharisaic expression for the Devil (14.17,19,30; 15.18; 16.8,11,33; 17.14,23,25). The 'world' could not receive the Spirit of truth, because it neither saw it nor knew it. The disciples were aware of its presence, for it dwelt within them. Likewise, after Jesus' departure from this earth, so far as the 'world' was concerned, he would simply cease to be: but again, the disciples would be aware of his presence. 'In that day you will know that I am in my Father, and you in me, and I in you' (v.20). Jesus is soon to return to the Father, and warns them beforehand so that when all he foretold comes to pass, they will believe. He knows that his arrest and demise are imminent, but the emphasis here is not on the personal enemies of Jesus who would have him put physically to death. It is on the cosmic struggle against the 'ruler of this world' in which Jesus, by his ultimate self-sacrifice, will emerge the victor and not the defeated party. Those who became possessors of the Holy Spirit will know and understand the true significance of what has happened, and in that the 'world' will not accept this, it will be judged.

Following these speeches, Jesus goes out across the Kidron Valley, and is arrested by a band of soldiers under a chiliarch, and some officers from the chief priests and the Pharisees, who arrive there guided to the spot by Judas. Jesus is seized and bound, and taken not to Caiaphas the high priest, but to his father-in-law, the previous high priest, Annas. Annas questions him about his teachings and his followers. Jesus is reluctant to bear witness to himself, and points out in his defence that he has 'always taught openly in the synagogues' (18.20), a very important statement of Jesus' rabbinic status in Galilee that is often ignored.

The trial before Caiaphas is omitted, and the sequence plunges straight into the interviews with Pilate in the praetorium, in which the accusers are stated to be 'the Jews'. Never once during these passages are the 'Jews' identified as the Pharisees (18.31,36,38; 19.7,12,14,20,21,31,38). Pilate himself states that it was the chief priests and Jesus' own nation that had handed him over for trial (18.35), and they are the first to shout for Jesus' crucifixion (19.6).

In fact, in these passages it is the chief priests who become virtually interchangeable with 'the Jews', and we should note that the word Pharisees does not appear again after 18.3, at the arrest.

Is this omission deliberate? It was the chief priests who cried 'We have no king but Caesar!' (19.5), a sentiment that would have fallen very strangely from the lips of Pharisees.

Joseph of Arimathea, who seems to have been one of those persons of authority who had been a secret disciple of Jesus, decides to come into the open, and, together with Nicodemus, he goes to Pilate and asks for Jesus' body (which was state property), and gives it honourable burial.

The last mention in this Gospel of the enemies of Jesus are the references in 20.19 and 26 that the disciples were meeting behind locked doors, for fear of 'the Jews'.

So, from this brief survey it can be concluded that whereas many people have assumed that the expression 'the Jews' could be safely taken to mean the Pharisees, there is not enough evidence to bear this supposition out. Nor is it really sufficient to conclude, with Bultmann, that an 'overall portrayal of "the Jews" viewed from the standpoint of Christian faith, as representatives of unbelief and thereby of the unbelieving world in general', presents them as the real enemies of Jesus, the darkness opposed to the light (*The Gospel of John*, 86).

Once again, a careful reading between the lines suggests that there was a strong lobby amongst the influential Jerusalem Pharisees in favour of Jesus, and that it was the Sadducean party, perhaps supported by extreme Shammaites, who acted against him, and those few Pharisees who chose uncharacteristically to side with them for political reasons.

One could also make a fair case that the Pharisees *did* dispute with Jesus, but *openly* – as was the normal practice amongst rabbis – and were often won over to his side by his deeds or his arguments. It was the Sadducees who saw Jesus as a major political threat to their peace and safety as Roman minions, and ruthlessly saw to it that he was removed. Or so they hoped!

11 · The Sermon on the Mount

Despite the attitude of the various Gospel writers towards the Pharisees, there is nevertheless a great deal of material in the texts which indicates a very powerful Pharisaic influence in the teachings of Jesus. This sometimes comes through quite unconsciously in the things Jesus is reported to have said and done, but often, as we have seen, when Jesus is occasionally presented as attacking the Pharisaic party, it is in precisely the same terms that the Pharisees would have used against *their* rivals, the Sadducees.

In other words, despite the interpretation that Jesus is supposed to be accusing his 'enemies' the Pharisees of not understanding the Law, or not taking it far enough, in those very passages he in fact teaches from a Pharisaic standpoint. The passages only make sense if one alters the position of 'Jesus attacking Pharisees' to 'Pharisaic Jesus attacking non-Pharisees'. Elsewhere, he seems to be taking the stance of a Pharisee attacking Pharisaic extremists.

Of course, the last thing the Gospel writers wished to do was to present Jesus as being sympathetic towards Pharisaism, but either a blissful or wilful ignorance of what the Pharisaic rabbis of the time of Jesus actually taught gives them away. Matthew's Gospel is particularly interesting in this respect, since it is widely believed and accepted by Christian scholars that this Gospel was written for a Jewish-Christian community, and had a vested interest in presenting Jesus as the fulfilment of Old Testament prophecy, the Son of David, the New Moses.

Aboth 3.2 preserves the saying: 'When two sit together and there are words of the Torah between them, there the Shekinah rests among them.' Matthew 18.20 gives: 'Where two or three are gathered together in my name, there am I in the midst of them.' In other words, for 'those who have eyes to see' and understand, Jesus has *become* the Shekinah, the symbol of the presence of God himself. Jesus never claimed to be greater than the Law (his reappraisal of the Torah in Matt. 5–7 only took what was taught to its logical conclusions); but as an embodiment of the presence of God, he was certainly greater than the Temple (Matt. 12.6); 'I tell you, something greater than the Temple is here.'

One of the most interesting sections in Matthew's Gospel is the block consisting of chapters 5–7, a carefully constructed passage known as the Sermon on the Mount. For various textual reasons, most scholars think it highly unlikely that it actually was one sermon, delivered on one occasion. Luke's Gospel includes much of its material in a different version, but the various items of teaching are scattered about the text. In Matthew's version we are given a series of moral principles which are often interpreted as being a deliberate contrast of Jesus' teaching with that of the Pharisees. Yet these supposed contrasts did not exist at all, and the whole tenor of the teaching in those chapters is precisely Pharisaic.

The passage about these moral principles begins with Jesus stating:

'Think not that I have come to abolish the Law and the prophets. I have not come to abolish, but to fulfil them. Truly I say to you, till heaven and earth pass away, not a jot [the smallest letter in the Hebrew alphabet] nor a tittle [a small decorative flourish in the handwriting] will pass away from the Law until all is accomplished (Matt. 5.17–19).

In rabbinic writings one finds: God spoke (to the Torah) and said:

Solomon and a thousand like him will pass away, but I will not permit the smallest stroke of you to pass away' (P. Sanh 2.20c; Ex. Rabba 6.2). Heaven and earth have measures, but the Law has none; heaven and earth will have an end but the law will not' (Gen. Rabba 10.1).

The dying words of Rabbi Johanan have already been quoted, which present the same idea (pp. 91f.); later, the Qur'an also reaffirmed the eternal and universal nature of God's Law:

If the waters of the sea were ink with which to write the words of my Lord, the sea would surely be drained before His words are finished, even if we were to add to it sea upon sea (surah 18.109).

One cannot help but wonder how the statement in Matthew's Gospel squares with the teaching of Paul, who considered the Law to be not only a burden but actually a *cause* of human downfall! When one looks across at the parallel passage in the Gospel of Paul's friend and disciple, Luke, one reads:

> The Pharisees, who were lovers of money(!) heard all this and they scoffed at him. But Jesus said to them: 'You are those who justify yourselves before men, but God knows your hearts; . . . the Law and the prophets were until John; since then the good news of the kingdom of God is preached, and everyone enters it violently. But it is easier for heaven and earth to pass away, than for one dot of the Law to become void' (Luke 16.14–17).

Matthew's version continued in a very different vein:

> Whoever relaxes one of the least of these commandments and teaches men so, shall be called least in the kingdom of heaven; but he who does them and teaches them shall be called great in the kingdom of heaven. For I tell you, unless your righteousness exceeds that of the scribes and Pharisees, you will never enter the kingdom of heaven.

The last sentence of the above passage might be interpreted as a criticism of Pharisees, but not as one that disparaged their particular attempt at living the submitted life. In Matt. 13.52 Jesus goes further, and praises the scribe:

> Every scribe who has been trained for the kingdom of heaven is like a householder, able to bring out of his treasure what is new and what is old.

A difficulty here is that form critics have argued that such passages as these are not authentic sayings of Jesus, but are pro-Jewish words that 'Matthew' has placed in his mouth, and that Luke has the more authentic version. What their grounds are for preferring Luke's presentation is not clear. It presumably stems from a lack of confidence in 'Matthew' as a result of its dubious historicity in the 'M' sections. One is at liberty to disagree with such outright scepticism.

The next section of Matthew 5 is almost pure Pharisaism, even if of a rather stern nature. Jesus acts on the principle of taking the written Law to its logical conclusions in people's hearts and motivation.

It was said to them of old, You shall not kill, and whoever kills shall be liable to judgment. But I say to you that everyone who is angry with his brother shall be liable to judgment; everyone who insults his brother shall be liable to the council; and whoever says 'you fool' shall be liable to the hell of fire. If you are offering your gift at the altar and there remember that your brother has something against you, leave your gift and go; first be reconciled to your brother, and then come and offer your gift (5.21–24).

According to the Pharisees, the spirit of the biblical Law suggested that while it was certainly in the province of the legislator to threaten severe punishment, nevertheless it was the duty of the judge to temper justice with mercy. There had been a gradual movement towards more humane methods of punishment when it came to the actual sentence of death. For example, although the following example may still sound pretty gruesome to us, in their legal system the Pharisees had abandoned burning people at the stake in favour of pouring a molten metal into the mouth of the condemned. This was a much quicker death, and in theory left the corpse intact for the expected resurrection, whereas cremation at the stake removed any such hope.

Another example of more humane sentencing was that of stoning. Simeon ben Shetah had insisted on this lesser penalty for witches, instead of burning. Moreover, the Pharisees altered the old method of stoning victims by hurling missiles to a method which included first the hurling down from a considerable height, which in itself might kill the condemned, followed by the crushing of the chest with a rock. It was specified that the rock had to be too heavy for one person to lift alone – so death should have resulted quickly.

Proceedings were tightened up in courts of law. A criminal could no longer be condemned on his own confession, and at least two witnesses were necessary in capital cases. A defendant could not be found guilty and convicted by a jury majority of one, but a majority of only one was sufficient to obtain an acquittal. Once acquitted, a criminal could not be retried, even if new evidence was produced (Sanh 4). In general, the principle was that it was far better for some guilty people to go unpunished than for any possibly innocent person to be convicted – a policy not attained in Great Britain until the trial abolition of hanging in the 1960s, for similar sentiments.

Jesus, in the Sermon on the Mount, considered the same question – murder, and the response to murder – but approached from a different angle. He was interested in the right motivation of a person's heart. Murder sprang from hatred and contempt, jealousy and resentment, and it was a believer's duty to overcome these in the heart, so that the extension of the malicious thought into malicious deed never became reality.

A law closely connected with these criminal proceedings was that of the *lex talionis*, which 'Matthew' gives later in 5.38–42.

> It was said: An eye for an eye and a tooth for a tooth. But I say to you, do not resist one who is evil. If anyone strikes you on the right cheek, turn to him the other also.

This old law of revenge, found in Exod. 21.24; Lev. 24.20; and Deut. 19.21, had already fallen under the Pharisaic hammer by the time of Jesus. A tradition survives that the Sadducaic house of Boethus still advocated the literal enforcement of it (Megillat Ta'anith 4), but there is no evidence that they ever gained their point. By the time of Jesus it was already accepted as a commonplace that the major principle of love for one's neighbour should take precedence over minor regulations in the law.

The original meaning, in any case, was of placing a *limit* on the amount of revenge a person could take on an enemy. If you had been wronged, you could not go and butcher your enemy's family and burn down his house, but only exact vengeance 'eye for eye' – no less, but *no more* than had been done to you. The Pharisees, however, considered that no one but God alone was in a position to know the full background to any case, and therefore justice should be left in God's hands alone. 'Vengeance is mine, says the Lord' (Deut. 32.35–36).

So the Pharisees arranged the strategy of a legal device, in which the right of the man who had suffered the loss of an eye was limited to the taking of an eye in vengeance *only if it was the exact copy of the one lost* in size and colour. This was obviously an impossibility, as it was in virtually every other case, so the *lex talionis* had in reality been abolished by the time of Christ, and a person could demand monetary satisfaction for his loss instead, including enough to cover medical care and compensation for pain, disability and humiliation too. The same principle still applies in the Islamic laws of retribution.

Jesus appealed to the conscience of the plaintiff, not to exact any vengeance at all, but to trust in God and leave the offender to God's judgment alone. He taught that we should look within our own hearts. If they were full of genuine love for God, then we should be prepared not to demand the 'eye for an eye', which signified the harbouring of malice and was the potential source of our own evil; but to resist evil by absorbing it within the scope of our own generosity, and not sink to the level of our enemy. This appeal to ethical conscience of individuals was simply taking Pharisaism to its logical conclusion.

Hillel argued that judges should certainly be extremely careful in the judgments they meted out, for they themselves would be examined and judged for their actions. They carried enormous responsibilities. 'In the measure in which a man metes, it is measured to him' (Mekilta 13.19; Sotah 1.7; T.Sotah 3.1, etc).

> Judge not, that you are not judged. For with the judgment you pronounce you will be judged, and the measure you give will be the measure you get' (Matt. 7.1–2).

Hillel thought that to have the responsibility for the death of any person, even a criminal, was extremely serious. A story was told of his seeing a skull floating in the river and saying ominously:

> Because you drowned others you have been drowned; but in the end those who drowned you will themselves suffer a similar fate' (Aboth 2.4).

Another example given in the Sermon is that of the adultery and divorce laws, also taken up in Matt. 19.3–9 and parallel passages. These laws were actually being hotly debated at the time of Christ by the schools of Hillel and Shammai. The old Law had allowed a man to divorce his wife if he had reasonable grounds, and it is all too obvious that many a discussion must have taken place of what these reasonable grounds might be. The Pharisees were very concerned about the practical happiness of marriages, and also the fate of women who had been cast out. They were particularly shocked by the older man who would 'put aside' the 'wife of his youth', simply because he wanted another, younger, woman – and could not afford to maintain them both.

The oral tradition confirmed the law of Deut. 24.1, which permitted divorce at the husband's discretion, but insisted on certain delays of procedure in the hope of there being reconciliation. It agreed with Jesus that the permission allowed in the Mosaic Law was only given because of human sin and weakness. It was not part of God's original plan, which clearly stated that a man and his wife should become 'one flesh'. However, although this was clearly the original intention, in practice marriages did not always work out. What was the fate of the marriage if a man found he no longer cared for his wife, or, as Akiba stated with very modern bluntness, he found one he liked better? In such circumstances the rabbis considered that it might be better for a couple to separate than live in misery, because it was God's basic principle to see people happy and contented. Therefore they reluctantly permitted divorce. It was a move to ameliorate marital conditions.

Shammai held that only adultery really justified divorce, but Hillel had apparently declared that a man might divorce his wife on the slightest of grounds, even for bad cookery. It is possible that he was speaking here in irony, the emphasis being on the word 'might', as the implication was that a husband wishing for salvation should be prepared to forgive even adultery in a wife, as God did figuratively in such passages as Jer. 3.1,12. It is possible that Matt. 19.6 has omitted the words 'lightly' or 'for slight cause'.

Matthew 6.27–28 proposed a fence around the Law, forbidding the lustful thoughts that were the initiators of lustful actions. Verse 32 goes much farther than the Law of Deut. 24.2, which actually sanctioned the subsequent remarriage of divorced women. Incidentally, the Pharisaic rulings permitted wives to divorce their husbands on such reasonable grounds as impotence, denial of conjugal rights, unreasonable restrictions of her freedom, loathsome ailments, and odorous occupations such as tanning! (Kethuboth 5.5; 7.2–5.9; Nedarim 11.12).

Islamic teaching is somewhat different in emphasis from that of Jesus, in that a person can be punished for an evil action, but not for an evil thought. Indeed, one could actually earn credit if one had evil thoughts, if the outcome was that the person overcame the temptations contemplated. The kind justice of God was such that one gained credit for a good intention (*niyyah*), even if the action was not done in the end for some reason, – but one did not gain discredit for a bad intention, so long as it was never carried out.

As regards marriage and divorce, the teachings are many and complicated, but the basic theory is that it cannot be right to cast out the wife of one's youth for no good reason; however, certain grounds are allowed for taking more than one wife – with a limit of four. So long as previous wives are satisfied with the arrangement and are cared for, a man may 'do as Christians do' and fall in love with more than one woman, but it is considered more honourable to keep earlier wives who do not wish for divorce rather than turn them out.

Islam regards marriage as the normal human status for adults, and discourages celibacy. Since the only true way for a Muslim to take part in sexual activity is within marriage, finding a good life-partner and building up a relationship together is regarded as 'half the faith'.

Whoever gets married has completed half of the faith; therefore be conscious of Allah in the other half of your faith' (Hadith).

Marriage is not seen as a sacrament but as a social contract which confers mutual rights and obligations on the couple, a partnership in which the pair play complementary roles. A true Muslim woman accepts only Allah as her Master, and does not therefore consider herself to be inferior to a husband. The couple contract only a mutual commitment to live together according to the revealed teachings of the Qur'an. If husband or wife subsequently depart from the Qur'an, their marriage is considered automatically null and void.

A man may marry polygamously rather than break up an existing marriage, but the permission for this is conditional. If he commits any injustice, then that marriage can be declared illegal and against the principle of Islam. The man *must* deal with justice for his household. He should give equal quality and amount of food, clothing, medication, recreation, housing, time, compassion and mercy. The only one area where complete justice is impossible is in the degree of emotional feeling that the man can have for more than one woman.

The Prophet prayed: 'O Allah! This is my justice in what I could control; do not blame me for what only You control, that which is out of my hands' (Hadith).

Some Muslims argue that since surah 4.129 states, 'You will never be able to do justice', polygamy was intended to be prohibited. However, this argument is not well-founded, since it is a fact of history that the Prophet and all his companions practised polygamy (as did Old Testament personalities) and it is inconceivable that they should have done so in violation of Qur'anic law. Muslims maintain that the Western practice of insisting on having one wife at a time leaves care for women open to abuse, since it encourages divorce and dishonourable sex outside marriage.

Islam is, however, against a woman having more than one husband, because of a child's prior right to know who its father is, which would be impossible in a polygynal marriage.

Islam also recognizes that human nature is such that not every pairing will be successful. In some societies divorce is forbidden completely, resulting in much distress; in others it is too freely available, and there are no checks on its abuse. Neither of these extremes is helpful in solving the problems of human suffering. Also it is patently obvious that some human beings choose to ignore, abuse or defy the laws of their societies. Rather than condemn people to lifelong misery, the Qur'an makes provision for legal divorce as a last resort – although it is highly discouraged:

> If a wife fears cruelty or desertion on her husband's part, there is no blame on them if they arrange an amicable settlement between themselves; and such a settlement is for the best (surah 4.128).

> Either keep your wife honestly, or put her away from you with kindness. Do not force a woman to stay with you who wishes to leave. The man who does that only injures himself (surah 2.231).

It should always be the last resort, after all attempts to put things right have failed.

> The most detestable act permitted by God is divorce (Hadith).

Jesus was perhaps concerned about the fate of women who had been cast out, who in many cases might then be condemned to a life of shame, perhaps, even prostitution or starvation. He seems to have considered that divorce should not be granted at all, except on the grounds that a man had found his wife not to be a virgin when he married her – a stipulation found only in Matthew's version (5.32; cf. Mark 10.11–12; Luke 16.18). Presumably the point behind the clause was that 'in the eyes of God' the girl was already married to the first man who had enjoyed her, and therefore the legal husband had unwittingly committed an adultery for which he could not be blamed – unless he continued in his marriage to the girl.

So far as adultery was concerned, the Pharisees had ruled that it was only the *act* that was an offence, not the thought about it. To think lustfully of a woman and be able to overcome those thoughts might even count in a man's favour. The sin of coveting a woman, a 'mental' crime, was in the province of God's judgment, not human law. Jesus, however, following his theme of right motivation, appealed to people who had been tempted to think lustfully to see their thoughts themselves as a prime cause in the breakdown of marriage, and urged them to resist temptation. It is very unlikely that the Pharisees would have disagreed with this.

The pericope of the woman taken in adultery, which appears in various places in Luke or John, but usually as John 7.53–58 or 8.1–11, gives an instance in which Jesus was deliberately confronted by scribes and Pharisees in a challenge to his personal authority. If Jesus admitted that nothing should hinder the full vigour of the Law, the woman would have been sentenced to death, and this would have contradicted his stance of compassion and leniency. If he excused the woman, this would have been at the cost of a denial of the validity of the Law of Moses. Thus, they reckoned they had caught Jesus in a trap.

If Jesus had shown compassion, it would not only have indicated that he accepted the law of Rome in preference to the Torah, since they obviously intended to stone the woman with or without Rome's permission, but it would have laid Jesus open to the charge of being a 'rebellious elder'. In fact, Jesus found a way of excusing the woman without actually incriminating himself, and his opponents were the ones who retired hurt: 'Let him who is without sin amongst you cast the first stone!' (John 8.7).

In *Law in the New Testament*, J. D. M. Derrett pointed out that the pericope omits to mention any witnesses to the woman's act, yet she could not have been condemned without them. And if there had been witnesses who had found her lying with another man, where was the man? Had this girl simply been condemned on hearsay? If so, her accusers were in no way free of sin themselves, indeed, their sin was arguably worse than the woman's. They were made to face themselves, and found themselves wanting, so they discreetly withdrew.

Adultery and magic were closely associated in those times (cf. II

Kings 9.22; Nahum 3.4; Mal. 3.5), and if this were so in her case, she *would* have been subject to the law of Deut. 17.2–7 which specified stoning. However, here it was pointed out quite clearly that only 'on the evidence of two or three witnesses shall the one to die be put to death; a person shall not be put to death on the evidence of one witness alone'. It further specifies that 'the hand of the witnesses shall be first against him to be put to death, and only after that the hand of other people'. The witnesses had to cast the first stone.

An added insight to the passage was given by Joachim Jeremias in *The Parables of Jesus*, who suggested that possibly the woman here was only a girl of some twelve years of age, since the Law of Deut. 22.24 stipulated that it was an unfaithful *betrothed* who could be stoned (p.158). Betrothals were normally converted to marriages soon after the age of thirteen, so it may well have been a young girl, a child, who was brought before Jesus. (One cannot help, of course, thinking of the mother of Jesus himself – who according to the Proteveangelion of James was only twelve years old when she became the betrothed wife of Joseph the Carpenter.) However, this is only speculation. The reference in Deut. 22.24 actually refers to the case of virgins who were raped within earshot of people. As in Islamic law, they were not considered blameless but guilty, and were condemned – because they did not cry out for help. If a girl had been raped out in the country there would have been no penalty against her, because even if she cried out, no one would have come to help her. As regards older women, the actual penalty for unfaithful wives was not specified in Deut. 22.22, but one would probably be safe to assume that it might also have been stoning.

Another possibility was that the adulterous woman was a young girl who had just been given in marriage and was found not to be a virgin. She could have been stoned for this (Deut. 22.20–21). Whatever the truth, Jesus acted with dignity and compassion, and the woman was not condemned.

Next, in the Sermon, Jesus took the business of the swearing of oaths.

It was said: You shall not swear falsely, but shall perform to the Lord what you have sworn. I say to you: Do not swear at all, either by heaven, for it is the throne of God, or by the earth, for it is his footstool . . . let what you say be simply 'yes' or 'no'. Anything more than this comes from evil (Matt. 5.33–37).

To swear by one's head (v.36) was not a Jewish oath, but a popular Graeco-Roman one at that time.

This seems to have been an anti-Sadducaic attack. The Pharisees, like Jesus, insisted that the Sadducaic idea of the relative importance of various vows was nonsense. The Sadducees would regard a vow as being more binding if it was made by the Temple, or a part of it, or some part of the Temple paraphernalia. Both Jesus and the Pharisees saw *every part* of the earth as being God's, and therefore all speech and all promises were made in God's presence, and all vows were equally binding. One's word *was* one's promise. One should fulfil every word spoken and not let people down.

According to the Torah, once a person made a promise, then that oath was binding and had to be 'paid to God'.

When a man vows a vow to the Lord, or swears an oath to bind himself by a pledge, he shall not break his word; he shall do all that proceeds out of his mouth (Num. 30.2).

When you make a vow to the Lord, you shall not be slack to pay it; for the Lord will surely require it of you, and it would be sin in you (not to perform it). If you refrain from vowing (and then change your mind about what you intended to do) it shall not be a sin to you. You shall therefore be careful to perform what has passed your lips, for you have voluntarily vowed to the Lord what you have promised with your mouth (Deut. 23.21–23).

Sifre on Deut. 23.23 has:

It were good that you vow not at all.

Gittin 35a counselled the devout to beware of swearing even on a truth. The schools of Shammai and Hillel were involved in rather a peculiar discussion as regards the use of vows as a means of protecting honest men from victimization. The Shammaites suggested that when confronted by tax-gatherers, robbers or murderers, men might 'declare that what they carry is an heave-offering, although it is not a heave-offering; and that it belongs to the king, although it belongs not to the king'. The school of Hillel assented to this, and added that the false declaration might even take the form of an oath (Ned. 3.4). However, Sifre on Leviticus 19.36 stated, virtually in the words of Jesus,

Let your 'no' be an honest 'no', and your 'yes' an honest 'yes'. Say not one thing in your heart but another with your mouth.

The Pharisees, always practical, had realized that occasionally a person might make a vow under certain circumstances, as we have seen in the *Corban* procedure, and then come to regret it bitterly. Although there was no Torah basis allowing them to 'loose' vows, they had worked out a legal device to enable people to get themselves out of these situations, and protect them from their own foolishness:

> I will give you the keys of the kingdom of heaven; whatever you bind on earth shall be bound in heaven, and whatever you loose shall be loosed in heaven (Matt. 16.19).

Mishnah Hagigah 1.6 admits that the practice of loosing vows 'floats in the air, and has no verse on which to depend', but the principle was one of practical kindness. For example, Rabbis Eliezer and Meir went so far as to state later that if a man had vowed no longer to associate with his wife and then wished he had not been so hasty, he could be reminded of the obligation to pay back his dowry. If he could assert that he had forgotten that condition when he made the vow, or that had he remembered it he would never have made the vow, then he could be released from it, as the vow as only valid when he was in full possession of all the provisos. Jesus took the view that it would be more sensible by far for vows not to be made at all, but for a person to live at all times according to his word, so that he could be trusted and be known to be reliable without having to resort to oaths.

Jesus' mind also ranged over the 'law' of loving one's neighbour and the implication that one should hate one's enemy. He insisted that we were to love our enemies also, and pray for those who persecute us. In support of Pharisees, and spiritual Judaism in general, it should be made crystal clear that in fact there is *no such law* about hating one's enemy in the whole of the Old Testament. The closest one can come to the law to which Jesus is supposedly referring is Leviticus 19.17–18, which specifically states:

> You shall *not* hate your brother in your heart, but you shall reason with your neighbour lest you bear sin because of him. You shall not take vengeance or bear any grudge against the sons of your own people, but you shall love your neighbour as yourself.

It seems quite plain that there was no intention at all that they should 'hate their enemies', and that injunction occurs absolutely nowhere in the Bible or in any Pharisaic literature.

On the other hand, the appeal 'to love your neighbour' is a frequent theme. Tobit 4.15, for example, states 'what you hate yourself do not do to any other person', a statement repeated in the delightful story about Rabbi Hillel in Shabbath 31a.

One sees the teaching illustrated in the story of the Good Samaritan. A scribe stood up to put Jesus to the test saying: 'Teacher, what shall I do to inherit eternal life?' Jesus said to him: 'What is written in the Law? How do you read?' And he answered in the words of the great *kelal*: 'You shall love the Lord your God with all your heart, soul, mind and strength; and your neighbour as yourself.' And Jesus said to him: 'You have answered rightly; do this, and you will live.' But the scribe, desiring to justify himself, said to Jesus 'And who is my neighbour?' (Luke 10.25–29). In response Jesus told the famous parable, ending with the question, 'Who proved to be neighbour to the man who fell among thieves?' The scribe said: 'The one who showed mercy on him.' And Jesus said to him: 'Go and do likewise.'

In Mark's Gospel, this same summary of the Law occurs as the answer to the fourth question Jesus was asked on the Tuesday of Holy Week. One of the scribes had asked, 'Which commandment is the most important of all?' The answer given by Jesus to this vital question is of paramount importance, especially to those who claim that Jesus was Muslim, and had no belief in himself as part of a Trinity. In fact, Jesus answered in more or less the same words as those given to the scribe in the Good Samaritan passage: there was only one God, the Absolute, and he alone was to be adored and served. In Matthew's version interesting details are added. The scribe answered:

> 'You are right, Rabbi. You have truly said that God is One, and there is no other but he; and to love him with all the heart, and with all the understanding, and with all the strength, and to love one's neighbour as oneself, is much more than all whole burnt offerings and sacrifices.' And when Jesus saw that he answered wisely, he said to him: 'Truly, you are not far from the kingdom of God' (Mark 12.28–34).

12 · The 'True' Pharisee

The main theme of the teaching of Jesus was that the Kingdom of God was at hand, and within the grasp of ordinary people.

> The kingdom of God is not coming with signs to be observed; nor will they say 'Here it is!' or 'There!' For behold, the kingdom of God is within you (Luke 17.20f.).

It was not something far distant and way beyond their understanding, but there – waiting to be discovered, a new and deeper awareness of life. It was obviously not an earthly, political kingdom, but a brotherhood of people with a certain kind of insight, people who accepted the sovereignty of God in their hearts and spirits.

In the so-called Sermon on the Mount, Jesus set out the characteristics of the people who would find the kingdom and become part of it. Any true Pharisee of the time of Jesus, or *any* submitted person, would find themselves in complete accord with his beautiful teachings. The Beatitudes of Matthew 5.1–12 are a prime example, and would find ready acceptance in the heart of any true Pharisee.

> Blessed are the poor in spirit, for theirs is the kingdom of Heaven. Blessed are those who mourn, for they shall be comforted. Blessed are the meek, for they shall inherit the earth. Blessed are those who hunger and thirst for righteousness, for they shall be satisfied. Blessed are the merciful, for they shall obtain mercy. Blessed are the pure in heart, for they shall see God. Blessed are the peacemakers, for they shall be called sons of God. Blessed are those who are persecuted for righteousness' sake, for theirs is the kingdom of Heaven. Blessed are you when people revile you and persecute you and utter all kinds of evil against you falsely on my account. Rejoice and be glad, for your reward is great in Heaven;

for so people persecuted the prophets who were before you . . .
You are the light of the world . . . Let your light so shine before
people that they may see your good works and give glory to your
Father who is in Heaven.

The Latin word *beatus* from which 'beatitude' comes means
'blessed' or 'happy' – and the key feature of a citizen of the
kingdom of heaven is personal happiness – a sense of fulfilment
and rightness. In these verses Jesus outlined the necessary qualities a person had to develop in order to achieve true happiness.
What are the people like who will gain entry into his kingdom?
They are the humble, the straightforward, the self-controlled, the
merciful, the peacemakers, those who accept wrong done against
them for the sake of the right. Truly, their reward will be great –
they will be filled, they will inherit the earth, they will find
happiness, joy, forgiveness and peace.

Notice how Jesus draws *all* believers, *all* who submit, into one
companionship. They are all to be one, and shall be called 'sons of
God'. When people submit to the will of God, then their light will
shine out clearly before everyone. The thanks and the praise for
this, stated Jesus, was not to be given to him – heaven forbid that
he should have entertained any such thought of personal glory! He
saw himself as the pure representative of all humanity, showing
them the way to the Father. He was the Son of Man, a messenger,
showing the way of truth for those who had eyes to see. Everything
that he did, he did for the glory of God, the divine Father.

There is a variant version of these Beatitudes in Luke
6.17,20–23.

Blessed are you poor, for yours is the Kingdom of God. Blessed
are you that hunger now, for you shall be satisfied. Blessed are
you that weep now, for you shall laugh. Blessed are you when
people hate you, and when they exclude you and revile you, and
cast out your name as evil, on account of the Son of Man.
Rejoice on that day, and leap for joy, for behold, your reward is
great in heaven; for so their fathers did to the prophets. But woe
to you that are rich, for you have received your consolation!
Woe to you that are full now, for you shall hunger. Woe to you
that laugh now, for you shall mourn and weep. Woe to you
when all people speak well of you, for so their fathers did to the
false prophets (Luke 6.20–26).

Muslim readers will notice immediately how Jesus deliberately called himself 'Son of Man', as he did so often, and not the trinitarian title given to him by Christian believers.

Which was the original version? Which gives us the actual words of Jesus? Who can say? Maybe neither does, but both versions are the creations of the authors of the two Gospels, developed out of their own interpretation of something Jesus had said which was along these lines. Luke's version seems to be Ebionite in nature, praising the poor and hungry simply because they were in those devout states.

He who eats and drinks while his brother goes hungry is not one of us (Hadith of Muhammad).

How can you call yourself a believer, while your brother goes hungry? (Hadith).

It is difficult to know exactly what Jesus meant by 'the poor in spirit'. Being poor-spirited does not sound very attractive at all. Most likely, what Jesus had in mind was the sort of person whose spirit was not cluttered up with pride, ambition, greed and self-seeking: one who has an attitude of detachment and serenity. No earthly possession or ambition should be so valuable to a person that it cannot be given up. To cling to such things does not always bring happiness; it can bring quite the contrary. The Muslim idea of acceptance is probably exactly what Jesus had in mind. God sends us good or bad fortune, not according to what we might desire, but according to his will. The truly submitted person will accept both with equanimity, well aware that neither state is permanent, and that God's will lies behind even seeming disasters.

Be firm and patient in pain or suffering and adversity, and throughout all periods of panic. Such are the people of truth, the God-fearing (surah 2.177).

How can you reject faith in God? – seeing that you were without life and He gave you life; then He will cause you to die, and will bring you again to life; and again to Him will you return' (surah 2.28).

The people who are capable of mourning will find true happiness because they are capable of knowing deep feeling and compassion.

Because they have known hurt, they can share sympathy in a way that people who have never suffered cannot.

The phrase 'blessed are the meek' is the subject matter of Shabbath 30b, which counsels that 'a man should always be as meek as Hillel' (and not as quick-tempered as Shammai!). Hillel himself said: 'He who is quick-tempered cannot be a teacher' (Aboth 2.5). Quick-tempered teachers were certainly not unknown, as was illustrated in later times by a casual statement of Rabbi Johanan ben Nuri, an overseer in the academy conducted by Rabbi Gamaliel II, that Akiba ben Joseph was flogged more than five times at his instance (Arakim 16b; Sifre Kedoshim 4.9.89b). This dreadful villain Akiba was the saintly rabbi-to-be!

'Meek' is a word that has almost completely lost its meaning nowadays, and usually means 'timid' or even 'cowardly'. Really, it implies a person who is so self-controlled and patient that he or she has the strength not to hit back when provoked, but is content to leave any retribution to God, who is alone the judge. It means true and complete acceptance.

> They can have no real faith until they make You judge in all disputes between them, and find in their souls no resistance against Your decisions, but accept them with fullest conviction (surah 4.65).

The concept of righteousness implies a longing to see justice and mercy prevail, both in our lives and in society in general. Any truly righteous society must begin with individuals caring about their own standards and actions, and not just leaving the responsibility to others. No one can alter the state of 'the world' until they are themselves as far beyond reproach as possible.

> Truly, God will never change the condition of a people until they change it themselves with their own souls (surah 13.11).

Any people who are consciously doing their best are not a burden on others, but the strength of the community rests in them.

The merciful are those in a position to hurt others who do not take advantage of their opportunities to do so. They try, on the contrary, to overcome evil with good. The pure in heart are those who do not compromise, as far as God is concerned. The nearer one draws to the kingdom of heaven, the more important it is to have the right motives and actions as regards the smallest details of life, and not

give way to the temptation to take it easy. The peacemakers are
those who are not only at peace in themselves, but actually manage
to radiate peace in others. They have the type of character to which
people in trouble will turn for refuge and strength. To live in such a
way is bound to invite persecution, for the world is full of people
overcome by jealousy, malice and depression. All those who
attempt to put right injustice and selfishness and oppression are
bound to run into opposition, sometimes even physical torment.
Yet who suffers most: the people who die for their faith because
they will not be untrue to what they firmly believe is right and good,
or the people who bow to their enemy and give in? Those who are
shahid, the persecuted martyrs, may suffer, but they will know
peace of mind and happiness of soul.

This standard of submission to the will of God has often been
criticized as being too high, too demanding, too difficult for the
average person to keep. But Jesus believed that the power and faith
of any submitted person, with God's help and reassurance, was
enough to bring success: 'not as the world gives', but success of soul
and spirit.

Matthew 6 develops the themes of submitted life along several
lines. It commences with 'Beware of practising your piety before
people in order to be seen by them', and then goes on to accuse the
Pharisees of showing off in the most blatant fashion, walking about
the streets with people sounding trumpets, so that all might know
that they were there to dole out charity. In fact, the Mishnah
mentions one of the Pharisaic innovations in the Temple, the
'Chamber of Secrets'. This was filled with donations for the poor,
and constructed in such a way that the poor could avail themselves
of help 'in secret' without being seen or having to confront the
donors (Shek 5.6). The tactful benefactors were determined to
exclude even the remote possibility that they were vainglorious or
wished to humiliate their fellows. Yet Matthew 6 suggests that these
'hypocrites' did their good deeds publicly, sounding trumpets when
almsgiving, praying on street corners, and fasting with 'disfigured
faces' so that their goodness might be noticed and approved of by
people. The scholar J. B. Lightfoot took the trouble to go through
the entire texts of rabbinic literature with a fine-toothed comb, but
could find no mention whatsoever of these wretched trumpets.

Jesus thought it vital that a person's motives were carefully
examined. If one was merely doing acts of kindness and holiness in

order to get human praise, then one would surely get the appropriate reward. No doubt such persons would be well thought of, by those who did not know them well; but they must be completely unaware of the presence of God who can read the heart and the innermost thoughts.

Those who are aware that God knows their motives do not bother with self-seeking, and do not desire praise from others. In fact, it becomes an embarrassment if anyone else knows what they are doing. As soon as any good deed becomes public property, the special relationship between the doer and God is in danger of being lost.

Fasting was a regular act for pious Jews, the object being to discipline and purify the body, and improve the concentration for acts of worship. Inevitably, going without food could make a person look pale and drawn. Jesus despised the kind of hypocrisy that drew attention to this. To want people to notice how good you are is a sign of weakness and insecurity in your character, not a reason for merit.

Similarly, prayer should not be performed in a public manner in order to impress others: it should be done only out of love for God. God was not subject to flattery, like an oriental potentate. It should be an honest attempt to bring our minds into harmony with God's mind, so that God's will can be done on earth as it is in heaven. Unless our minds are in this state of harmony, we will not 'see' what is God's will. So, there should be no barriers caused by guilt or selfishness or unwillingness to serve in whatever situation we find ourselves. The resignation of our wills to God's must be complete, with no holding back.

What is important is that the Pharisaic writings themselves condemned any hypocrisy of the above-mentioned sorts, and threw light on what Jesus was talking about. The Babylonian Talmud (Sotah 22b) not only gave the story of Alexander Jannaeus on his death-bed warning Queen Salome to beware the dangers of those who were hypocrites, but even listed seven sorts of Pharisees; and their own criticism of themselves is worth examining in detail.

The first was the 'Shoulder Pharisee': the man who wore his good deeds on his shoulder in order to be seen. He thoroughly enjoyed his reputation, precisely as Jesus indicated in Matthew 8. The Pharisees themselves condemned persons like that. They laughed at them! The second sort was the 'Wait-a-little' Pharisee. Yes, he would do what was requested of him, but first he must just go and do

something else. Jesus criticized just such a person when he said that
'no man who put his hand to the plough and then looked back is fit to
enter the kingdom of heaven' (Luke 9.62). The same thought lies
behind the passage where Jesus tried to call various disciples, but
they all made excuses; also the parable of those invited to the feast,
who all had reasons why they could not attend.

The third sort was the 'Bruised' or 'Bleeding' Pharisee. This was
the man who was too pious even to look at a woman, in case he
might be tempted; so whenever he was in danger of seeing one, he
shut his eyes and walked into the wall – hence the bruises! Fun was
made of him, as he was so anxious to gain credit for his piety that he
wished his blood or bruises to be seen, and nothing pleased him
more than to be asked how he had gained them. This was rather like
the person mentioned by Jesus who liked to look thin and grey and
ill, and rubbed ashes on his face, so that everyone could assume he
had been fasting (Matt. 6.16). The true believer should leave his
piety as a matter between himself and God; the faster should anoint
his face with oil, make it shine, so that no one would know about his
private discipline.

Every Muslim will know the man who makes a show of complete
avoidance of contact with women; not only will such a man not
touch the hand of a woman, or meet her eye, but he will not even
look at her while speaking. No one objects to his purity, his
righteousness, his attempt to live the good life – but how embarrassing and unnecessary the behaviour of such people can be at times!
One wonders what the down-to-earth Prophet Muhammad would
have made of such followers!

The fourth sort was the Uriah Heep of the Pharisaic world, the
'Pestle-and-mortar' or 'Hump-backed' or 'Tumbling' Pharisee.
This one, unbearably serious, bore on his shoulders the whole
weight of the Law. He was hump-backed or tumbling because he
never lifted his eyes to people's faces, or his feet from the ground.
He advertised his holiness by adopting these obvious poses. His
excuse was that this gave ample warning to any 'unclean' people, so
that they should not defile him by touching him or accidentally
bumping into him. This was of vital importance, since he was in
continuous prayer for them, and so forth.

Then came the 'Ever-Reckoning' or 'Compounding' Pharisee,
the man whose life was ruled by the obsession of looking out for
something extra to do, to make up for something that he might have

neglected. He was not too bad a chap, however – at least he erred on the right side! – nor was the 'Timid' or 'Fearing' Pharisee, who was for ever trembling in awe of God and living in dread of punishment. No matter what they did, or how good they were, they could not believe that they had really earned their place in the heaven to come. The deathbed discourse of Ben Zakkai might suggest that he suffered in this way – maybe Paul did too. Perhaps these were just psychological hang-ups. Certainly people who thought in this way were ripe for conversion to trinitarian Christianity, which taught that no matter how good people might have been, or how noble their efforts, they could *never* be good enough to earn their place in God's kingdom – and therefore the sacrifice of an incarnate God-man became necessary for their salvation. The true Pharisee, or later true Muslim, thought that such an attitude was a *lack* of faith, and really an insult to the God who was supreme compassion, and always ready to forgive the penitent.

The final sort was the 'True' Pharisee, known and loved by everyone, the 'Born' or 'God-Loving' Pharisee. Such submitted and committed people could never lose confidence in the God they knew and loved, who was their dear Father and Lord, and who loved and had compassion on all his created children, no matter what their failings and weaknesses. He knew them all, and yet still He loved them.

> If God punished us according to what we deserve, there would be left on earth not one created being' (surah 16.61).

When one goes through that list, ascribed in Sotah 3.4 to Ben Zakkai's pupil Rabbi Joshua, one cannot help but feel that Jesus' criticisms of the Pharisees as given in Matt. 6, and again in those terrible 'woes' in Matt. 23, were precisely what the 'Born' Pharisees might have thought of those of their membership whom the caps fitted.

Similar criticisms occur in the Pharisaic book *The Assumption of Moses*:

> And in the time of these, destructive and impious men shall rule, saying that they are just . . . devourers of the goods of the poor, saying that they do certain things on the grounds of their justice, but in reality to destroy them [cf. Luke 20.46–47: 'They devour widows' houses, and for a pretence make long prayers']; com-

plainers, deceitful, concealing themselves lest they should be recognized, impious, filled with lawlessness and iniquity from sunrise to sunset, saying: We shall have feastings and luxury, eating and drinking, and we shall esteem ourselves as princes. [cf. Luke 20.46: 'They love the best seats in the synagogues and the places of honour at feasts']. And though their hearts and mouths touch unclean things, yet their mouths shall speak great things, and they shall say furthermore: Do not touch me in case you should pollute me.

The Qur'an has a good comment about this sort of person:

Those who love the life of this world more than the Hereafter, who hinder people from the path of God . . . they are astray by a long distance! (surah 14.3).

What about that sublime piece of teaching, the Lord's Prayer?

Our Father in heaven, may your name be glorified, your kingdom come, your will be done on earth as it is in heaven. Give us every day our daily bread, and forgive us our sins as we forgive those who sin against us. Lead us out of temptation and deliver us from the evil one.

Muslims will notice how similar it is to their own chief prayer, the surah al-Fatihah.

Praise be to You, O Allah, Lord of the worlds, the Most Compassionate, the Most Merciful, Master of the Day of Judgement. You Alone do we worship, from You Alone do we seek help. Show us the next step along the straight path of those who are seeking Your favour, not the path of those who are going astray.

Both prayers commence with the sentiments of the Kaddish: 'Father, let your great name be magnified and hallowed' (cf. Matt. 6.9). The prayer 'Your will be done, as in heaven, also on earth', and the words of the angelic chorus in Luke 2.14, 'Peace on earth to men of goodwill', find a ready echo in T. Berakoth 3.7: 'Do thy will in the heavens above, and give tranquility of spirit to those who fear thee on earth.'

Next comes the petition 'Give us this day our daily bread', or, according to some readings, 'our break for the morrow'. Probably the first reading is to be preferred, as meaning 'let each day be taken as it comes, we will have faith that our needs will be met and taken care of', or, as it is expressed in Matt. 6.34: 'Do not be anxious about tomorrow, for tomorrow will be anxious about itself.' The Muslim sentiment is that one should always put one's trust in God that he will provide if it is his will; and if it is his will that one should finish life on earth and return to him, then the Muslim accepts the time, and is ready:

He is my Lord! There is no God but He! In Him do I trust, and to Him I return' (Surah 13.30).

The test of manna when the Jews were wandering in the wilderness was the test of their faith in the providence of God, and of their patience. It was specifically forbidden for the Jews to store up food supplies for the morrow. They were to trust in God and accept His will. In a surfeit of piety, sometimes it is possible to go against the spirit of the Law. For example, it was said of Shammai that he spent all his life in preparation for the sabbath, putting things aside for it, and then finding better things with which to replace them; but such was the faith of Hillel that he would never prepare for the sabbath until Friday actually came. 'God is to be blessed each day for the day's goods' (Bezah 16a). Rabbi Eliezer summed up Hillel in c.10 CE by saying:

Whoever has sufficient food for the day and says: What shall I eat tomorrow? is lacking in faith (Mekilta Beshallah, Masseket Vayyassa 2.161).

Again, one can compare this with Christ's teachings on anxiety in Matt. 6.25–34.

Do not be anxious for your life, what you shall eat or what you shall drink . . . your heavenly Father knows that you need all these things. Seek first his kingdom and his righteousness, and all these things will be yours as well.

Matthew 6.26–29 gives us:

Look at the birds of the air: they neither sow nor reap nor gather into barns, and yet your Heavenly Father feeds them. Are you not of more value than they?

Kiddushin 4.14 reads:

Did you ever in your life see an animal or a bird which had a trade? And they support themselves without trouble. And were they not created to serve me? And I was created to serve my Maker. Does it not follow that I shall be supported without trouble?

Again, Matt. 7.7–12 reads:

Ask, and it will be given to you . . . if you who are evil know how to give good gifts to your children, how much more will your Father in heaven give good things to them that ask him! Whatever you wish that people would do to you, do so to them; for this is the Law and the Prophets.

Just as Peter declared: 'Have we not left all for thy sake?' And Jesus replied:

There is no one who has left house or brothers or mother or father or children or lands for my sake and for the gospel, who will not receive a hundred-fold now in this life . . . and in the age to come, eternal life (Mark 10.28–30).

The Qur'an gives us:

He who forsakes his home in the cause of God, finds in the earth many a refuge, wide and spacious; should he die as a refugee from home for God and His apostle, his reward becomes due and sure with God; for God is the Compassionate, the Merciful (surah 4:100).

For any submitted person, the whole of life should be an act of faith, and love.

13 · Postscript: 'Pharisaism'

As a postscript to the text, let us consider the subject of what is now called 'Pharisaism' as opposed to the examination of facts about the real Pharisees. 'Pharisaism' is something totally different, and a trait easily recognizable in individual representatives of any religion. I had the experience of arguing the toss with countless Christian Pharisees while I was a member of the Christian faith, and now, in Islam, I encounter no less a number of the same brigade. Indeed, in Islam, the strain of 'Pharisaism' is far stronger than it is at present in the church, simply because the faith is 'on the boil', and undergoing a similar kind of persecutive reaction to that faced by the Christians in earlier centuries.

I have tried to argue that Jesus was himself a Pharisee in thought, word and deed. He represented the very best flowering of that movement. I have also tried to argue that what is now generally regarded as 'Pharisaism' – an overwhelming obsession with legal minutiae to the detriment of faith – is not the same thing as being a Pharisee, and has cast a virtually ineradicable slur upon those believers who were 'muslim', submitted in every aspect of their lives – like Jesus (peace be upon him!) – to the will of God.

What Jesus did attack seems to have been that over-stress on the minutiae that lay like a web over the whole concept of ritual holiness. He cut through it like a knife. Jesus quite probably did not regard himself as an anti-Pharisee at all, but as a reformer of the movement. The Essenes had taken separation and submitted lives to the extreme that no one could join them unless they went through no less than seven years of apprenticeship and training, and very stringent tests and oaths; some Muslims argue that a person's prayers and 'religious attempts' are invalid because they are performed in the wrong way or at the wrong time. Jesus, peace be upon him, took believers to a different kind of extreme. He taught that the open and loving arms of God were available to all: tax-collector, prostitute, Samaritan, peasant or Gentile. The exclusive extremist would not eat with such people because of the rules of purity in the service of God. Jesus, on the other hand, drew many of his followers from the ranks of these 'untouchables', people who longed to quench their spiritual thirst but who thought they were totally beyond the appropriate qualifications because they could not perform the rules of separation.

Jesus said: 'Those who are well have no need of a physician, but those who are sick' (Mark 2.17). The Pharisaic Midrash on Eccl. 1.7 agreed absolutely: 'If two men came to you to borrow money, one of them rich and the other poor, to which of them would you lend – the rich or the poor?'

There is one beautiful hadith of the prophet Muhammad that tells of a simple shepherd who was making his prayer in 'totally inappropriate terms' that a passing mullah found ridiculous and offensive. He sent the poor man off with a stinging rebuke. Then came the most privileged moment of that mullah's life – a personal Bath Qol from Allah. But it was not what he expected. 'Who gave you the right to prevent my servant from worshipping me?'

It is undoubtedly true that the main bulk of Pharisaic writing was concerned with all sorts of ritual practices, all considered to be of vital importance if the 'holiness' or 'separatedness' of the submitted person was to be genuine. These rules were probably never intended to become 'tyrants'. When later teachers expressed the view that if you loved God, you could 'do as you liked', they did not sanction freedom for bad or irresponsible behaviour. What they meant was that those who genuinely loved God would always wish to behave in a way that *God* would like, so that God's will would be done on earth as it was in heaven. It meant that so long as your heart was directed aright, the details would take care of themselves.

For those whose hearts and minds were fixed upon God in a more mystical and contemplative way, the minutiae could be devastatingly irritating, and it is even possible to interpret the obsessive detraction of the mind from God into a slavish devotion to these minutiae as the very clever and subtle influence of the 'devil', occupying and worrying devout persons with trivia that were completely irrelevant to the good life, and yet which had taken over and now ruled their every moment.

The rabbinic literature is full of examples. Water-baths had to be regularly cleaned and repaired for the reason that if soil fell into them, then they would contain less than the required amount of water for the cleansing of the ritually unclean. There was an interesting discourse on the 'cleanness' or otherwise of spittle encountered in the streets. If found in Jerusalem, it was probably 'clean' because the people there were scrupulous in matters of purity. Outside Jerusalem it was presumed to be 'defiled'. Also suspect was spittle found in the market-place, since that was frequented by 'heathen launderers' and 'people with an issue'. If found in the middle of the road it was counted as unclean, since that was where the bulk of pedestrians walked along. At the sides of the road it would probably be the spittle of persons scrupulously avoiding contact with the crowds, and therefore ritually pure! However, since at festival times it was assumed that the bulk of pedestrians would be pure and going to the Temple to worship, the situation about the centre and sides was reversed. It was expected that the 'unclean' would courteously get themselves off to the sides. Sadly, Jesus had no comment to make on this fascinating subject! (It reminded me of the instruction given in one convent that 'nuns were not to spit on the stairs'!)

One of the most difficult aspects of Islam with which people coming to that faith from 'outside' have to grapple is the same blindness, almost a wilful blindness, which has arisen out of the devotion of some Muslims to not only the Qur'an itself, but also to their own calling as Muslims. It is as if the most important lesson taught by the Prophet Jesus had never been learned at all.

Just as George Bernard Shaw once remarked of youth that it was wasted on the young, so Islam sometimes seems to be wasted on the Muslims! In frustration, some leading scholars in Islam have claimed – particularly in Shi'ite Iran – that only their peers have the intellectual equipment necessary to determine if any other such scholar has the ability to the same degree – therefore only a mujtahid is qualified to appoint another safely (an important point behind the Iranian 1980 Constitution).

But did God intend this exclusiveness? Should the exercise of *ijtihad* be limited to none but qualified jurists? Or should the consensus of saintly laymen in the community also be allowable, and if not, why not? Are not jurists, although experts, actually out of touch with the real needs and feelings of ordinary people? Should the 'gate of *ijtihad*' be locked or open?

Over-fastidious concern with ritual precision makes many devout believers suffer from pharisaism, or *'waswas'* – agonizing about the validity of personal purity and the desire to correctly carry out the will of Allah, an agony so destructive that it can actually *prevent* them from achieving their objectives. *'Waswas'* implies hesitation, or doubt, and some *mujtahids* have taught that it is nothing less than the plotting of the Devil, since we should always place our trust in God's lovingkindness and mercy. God desires heaven for us, not difficulties beyond our scope. The Qur'an teaches that God will never place upon us a burden greater than we can bear – and therefore we should never despair but live in an attitude of trust and hope, and the certain knowledge that we are forgiven our short-comings if we are sorry for them.

There is a story of Sheikh Mortaza Ansari once observing a student making the same round at the pool, over and over again. He asked what on earth he was doing. The youth said that his intention was to pray with full intention (*niyyah*), but he was not sure at what stage his intent had to come into force, and since he doubted at every step, he was literally going backwards! Mortaza asked angrily who his teacher was, and when told it was himself, declared curtly: 'I do not hold *niyyah* to be mandatory (*wajib*); get on with it, get it done!'

There is one famous Iranian story involving a dog and a goat that certainly 'opens the gates'. Supposing a person had become ritually clean by performing *wudu*, but was then splashed by water from an unseen source above? Looking up, one can see a wet dog shaking itself on the roof of the house. If the water has come from this dog, the person has been defiled, since the dog is a contaminating animal. But maybe the water did not come from the dog? Who knows? Don't make assumptions based on ignorance. Maybe there is also a wet goat on the roof which, being a clean animal, would not render the person ritually unclean? The continuity of the known condition (the person's cleanliness) takes a merciful legal precedence over an assumption based on an uncertain point (that the water came from the dog) – therefore one could say *'Insha' Allah, buz bud'* – 'God willing, it was the goat.'

To cynics, however, the expression soon became the saying for all occasions when someone did not want to face reality!

In fact huge areas of Muslim law are uncertain, and there are two ways of dealing with them. One can assert that the regular sources of the law give 'overwhelming likeliness', or that less certain areas can be treated according to the procedural principles for those necessarily uncertain situations.

Coming to Islam from a background which is not of the Middle East offers certain advantages and disadvantages. Among the many disadvantages, of course, are ignorance of and perhaps discomfort with the cultural background out of which the religion has grown. However, people converting to Islam from Christianity do not usually feel completely lost: after all, Jesus was born very few miles geographically away from the Prophet Muhammad (peace be upon both of them!). On the contrary, until they come up against Islamic 'Pharisaism', Christian converts usually feel overwhelmed by a sense of rightness, of *fitra*, that they are 'coming home' to something they have always known to be true in their hearts. They do not regard themselves as blasphemous renegades, turning their backs on all the Christian values they used to hold dear, nor do they feel that they are forsaking the love of their first religion for the enticements of a new one. On the contrary, most of what was incomprehensible in Christianity falls neatly into place, and there is often a 'flash of light' experience that what they have suddenly found is really the truth that can be compared to any Christian 'born again' experience.

In the Western world, one of the dangers in the Christian faith has been that Jesus has been interpreted almost entirely as a Western phenomenon – with many innocent souls honestly thinking of him as an 'Englishman'. Life and worship in these countries now bears very little resemblance to the land of origin of all three 'religions of the Book' – Judaism, Christianity and Islam – which Muslims claim strongly are all revelations from the same Absolute God.

One of the advantages, however, is that Western converts – like a whole series of Islamic reformers throughout their history – tend to learn Islam from the Book itself (the Qur'an), and are not bogged down by the centuries of tradition encrusted upon it, which may or may not be helpful.

It is only human nature, of course, for the expert scholars steeped in the traditions of their faith to react strongly against any attempt to criticize or alter part of it, particularly when that attempt comes from newcomers, usually untutored ones at that, who are openly ignorant. Islam has resistance to any alteration of the Qur'anic Arabic built into it as part of its dogma, and rightly so. Nevertheless, sometimes the fresh mind, coming upon a subject, can see straight away what are the things of value and what the clutter of dross. Sometimes, in an attempt to keep pure what is holy, a building set aside becomes a dust-covered museum instead of a living and breathing shrine. We all know this. Instead of devotion to the Power who makes the shrine holy, a dangerous veneration grows for the shrine itself. This holy object must never be moved; this holy ritual must always be done like this; no one must ever do such-and-such a thing in that area; teacher so-and-so has said that this is the one true interpretation of this particular rule – and so on.

'Pharisaism' implies that a certain set of opinions or interpretations have become so sacrosanct in themselves that vast oceans of academic ink can be spilled and whole academic lifetimes be spent in tracking down every last possible detail concerning them, with the result that in the end the interpretations become more important than the revelation, the letter can become more important that the spirit, and the real aim of what Allah intended be lost and submerged beneath this welter of irrelevant detail.

How do we judge what is irrelevant or not? Is it not for us to impose *our* judgment either – for then we would be guilty of the same fault. This is the major reason why 'pharisees' are so careful to keep faithfully every single detail. No individual person in any particular generation can understand the motivation of the whole. If they make a judgment as to the importance or otherwise of *any* of the laws, no matter how seemingly trivial, they could be damaging the repository of faith for another generation that might be led towards seeing with different eyes. It is indeed vital *that not a jot or tittle be changed.*

Any convert coming into Islam *has* to accept that the Qur'an is the revealed word of God, and that every word of it is true; and that no human has the right to decide whether one verse of it is superior to another – for it is *all* the word of God. What irritates such converts, and where they are apparently at such an enormous disadvantage to those born and bred in Islam, is that they are not familar with what has become known as the *sunnah*, the extra expectations laid upon Muslims that have grown out of the teaching and practice of the Prophet Muhammad (peace be upon him!).

Yet, appalling though the thought must be to a Muslim, the study of the *sunnah* can become a monster, and the Muslim can be affected by 'pharisaism'. It is only natural that Muslims will be outraged at this statement and deny it, usually quoting two passages from the Qur'an:

> O you who believe! Obey Allah *and the Messenger* and those charged with authority among you, and if you differ in anything among yourselves, then refer it to Allah and the Messenger' (surah 4.59).

> They cannot be believers until they make you judge in all disputes between them, and find in their souls no resistance against your decisions, but accept them with the fullest submission (surah 4.65).

However, one only has to ask the opinion of, say, a Pakistani Deobandi Muslim about the other Muslims to get the full flavour of what I have been talking about. Muslims usually deny that there is any sectarianism in Islam – except the Sunni-Shi'ite split – but there are at least seventy 'strains', many of them as rampantly intolerant as good old Oliver Cromwell!

The main reason for this is that the *sunnah*, no matter how revered, *is not the Qur'an*. No one can be certain of the content of the *sunnah* (in the same way that one can of the Qur'an), since so much legendary and unreliable material has been generated about the Prophet since the days he walked the earth. Just as most Muslims do not even bother to study the Christian Bible on the grounds that it is all legendary material and not reliable (and certainly not the pure revelations from God that the great Prophet Jesus taught – the Injil) the same arguments can be made regarding the hadith (sayings of the Prophet Muhammad), despite the protestations of the scholars. Christian scholars who become converts to Islam, who take the Muslim point about their own old texts, cannot really see the difference between that and the way the Muslims regard the content of the various collections of *hadith*. Muslims usually argue that there is no comparison, but few have read more than a simple pamphlet on the subject of Christian form criticism.

It ought to be taken as axiomatic by every Muslim that if God had intended any instruction, or verse, or minute detail, to form part of his Holy Revelation – the Qur'an – then *he would certainly have given it as part of that Qur'an*, and not left it to the chance interpretations of human brains to pick over down the centuries. Any important aspect would be part of that unalterable revelation, no jot or tittle of which should ever be changed. If any matter is not part of that revelation, then it must stand to reason that it *is* open to interpretation, and is not binding as a matter of compulsion of any believer. Any Muslim submitted to God should be free to apply sense and reason. Of course, one can make recourse to the *hadith* and *sunnah* as the very highest examples of the working out of that reason, coming as they mainly do from the life and teachings of the Prophet – but the Muslim must not elevate the word of any human, no matter how exalted, into the same category as the word of God! And this countless Muslims have done.

Any Muslim scholar worth his salt will admit readily that there are literally thousands of *hadith* in circulation that are not reliable, although many of them are extremely interesting, venerable, and teach a worthwhile lesson. They usually maintain that the earliest collections, especially those of 'Bukhari' and 'Muslim', are entirely reliable, but that there is doubt over the later material. Others make a point of collecting up as many obscure sayings as possible, and basing teachings upon them.

Sometimes, since this is all done with the best of motives, it doesn't matter at all. But sometimes the results can be quite overwhelming, especially when the accepted culture of any particular country is presented as being 'Islam', when in reality it is not. Sometimes this can lead to terrible cruelty and illogical repression. Free and equal Muslim women, who were enjoined to behave modestly and 'veil their eyes' (surah 24.31) as befitted women submitted to the will of God of their own free will (for let there be no compulsion in religion!, 2.256), are sometimes forced into purdah on the grounds that *this* is Islam, when there is no evidence whatsoever of God issuing any such unreasonable command anywhere in the Qur'an. (They were simply required not to show off the outlines of their bodies when outside by wearing 'outer garments', surah 33.59. Modest behaviour required that they did not flaunt their bosoms, 35.60.) *Nowhere in the Qur'an does God specify the type of complete black covering often seen in Muslim countries.* If Muslim women don this garment from choice, well and good. But one can be modest and devout without it, and I have seen plenty of women whose complete *hejab* did nothing to improve their public behaviour!

To throw in another highly controversial example: prayer-times in the UK and similar countries could be another result of 'pharisaism'. Mosques are usually meticulous in keeping lists of exact times at which the five compulsory prayers should be offered, and this is of course a necessity if any kind of organized gathering is intended. However, some Muslims then go on to regard prayers said at any other moments of the day as being certainly inferior, if not actually invalid – though quite who gave them permission to decide what God accepts or does not accept as pleasing to him is a bit of a mystery!

A study of the Qur'an surely reveals that the intention of the five obligatory prayers was to set one's mind upon God at certain natural points during the day – on waking, before sleeping, during the mid-day break from labour, and before and after sunset. Over and over again in the Qur'an Allah requests his submitted people to make *regular* prayers. Not once does the Qur'an lay down the specific times accepted now as being *sunnah* – times which are quite sensible for those living in the Middle East, but nonsensical for those living far from the equator but at the 'ends' of the earth.

It can surely hardly be the case that those who always made prayer to God their first act on waking should be castigated because they did not deliberately get up and make that prayer at around 2.30 a.m. on an English summer morning, and then go back to sleep until it suited them! Any Muslims suffering from 'pharisaism' must ask themselves how much of the above-quoted commands *as actually given in the Qur'an* they actually keep, as well as their set routine of prayer times.

What brought home the 'pharisaism' of Islam to me, perhaps more than anything else, stemmed from the fact that I am a woman, and a Western woman at that. Brought up more or less in a tradition of female freedom and equality, I assumed without any hesitation that the commands and revelations God gave to Muslims through the Qur'an were addressed to *all* Muslims. The word Muslim meant simply a 'committed person, submitted to the will of Allah'. It never occurred to me for one moment that it should apply less to the females of the species, especially since a careful study of the Qur'an showed no evidence whatsoever of sexism. One of the strongest appeals of Islam to the rational human mind must be that it speaks directly to men and women as they are: equals, created for the mutual comfort and sustenance of each other. Different, but equal. This equality is always pointed out by Muslims, usually with great pride and satisfaction – but sadly, often with appalling ignorance of the reality of what freedom and equality means.

When conversations turn to the employment or place of women, there is usually an outraged raising of hands in pity and dismay for the lot of the exploited Western woman, and a horror at the results of the breakdown in family life in Western society, which is usually thought to be the inevitable result. It is observed, quite justifiably, that men who have allowed their women equality are often insecure, violent, dissatisfied, shaken up in many ways. They are often extremely disgruntled, having lost the facility of a cheap 'slave', who may actually have turned out to have more earning potential than themselves. The whole business of what is the best and most satisfying way of life for men and women is thrown into the melting pot.

All Muslims are called upon to serve God as best they can; it makes no difference to the God who created everything 'in pairs' whether submitted people are male or female.

As this book has been about the Pharisees, and has been an attempt to defend them, and show them to be true Muslims, let a Pharisaic quotation take the final words. A splendid outline of the Pharisaic standpoint was made by Josephus in '*Against Apion*', 2.187–191. It could almost have come from the mouth of Jesus himself, or from any devout and understanding Muslim.

What are the commands and prohibitions of the Law? They are very simple, and familiar. At their head stands one of which God is the theme. The universe is in God's hands; perfect and blessed, self-sufficing and sufficing for all. He is the beginning, the middle and the end of all things. By his works and blessings he is plainly seen, indeed, he is more manifest than anything else; but his form and greatness surpass our powers of description. No materials, however costly, are fit to make an image of him; no art has skill to conceive or represent Him. The like of him we have never seen, we cannot imagine, and it is impious to guess at. We behold his works: the light, the heaven, the earth, the sun, the waters, the reproductive creatures, the sprouting crops. These God created, not with hands nor with toil, nor with assistants of whom he had no need: he willed it so, and forthwith they were made in all their beauty. Him we must worship by the practice of virtue; for that is the most saintly manner of worshipping God.

Amen. Amen.

APPENDIX 1

The Holy Texts Quoted in This Book

The holy texts referred to or quoted in this book fall into three categories.

First, there are extracts from the Bible. The Hebrew Bible, the sacred scriptures of the Jews, was taken over by Christians as the *Old* Testament. However, for Jews it is *the* Bible, consisting of Torah, prophets and writings. The Torah, the first five books (Genesis, Exodus, Leviticus, Numbers, Deuteronomy) contains an account of the creation of the world and the origins of the Jewish race, and the revelations and legal guidance granted to the prophet Moses. It is the ground of Jewish belief. The prophets and writings are seen as the first comment on it; they contain the works of prophets and wise men, and books which look like history books. The earliest parts of the Hebrew Bible may date back to around 1200 BCE.

The New Testament, formed by the Christian church, consists of four Gospels or 'lives' of Jesus of Nazareth, the Messiah; an account of the growth of the earliest church, almost certainly in a simplified and partly misleading form; a book of eschatological visions; and various letters written either by some of the first Christians, or by later writers using these famous Christians' names. Much of the New Testament seems to have been written between 65 and 90 CE. Most scholars accept that many of these texts as we now have them are the product of a complex process, which began either at the time of their original compilation or at a later stage. There is a great deal of academic interest in trying to discover 'original source' material, but the whole business is fraught with difficulties.

Then there are quotations from the Qur'an, the holy book of the Muslim faith. This book is not considered by Muslims to be in any way similar to the other scriptures quoted here, but is believed to be the actual series of revelations from God delivered verbatim to the Prophet Muhammad over a period of twenty-three years, ending with his death in 632 CE. The revelations are divided up into surahs and ayats, or chapters and verses, and are not in any chronological order, but a special order as God directed Muhammad. Muslims believe that not one word is of human origin, but is the direct and unaltered revelation of God.

The other Muslim sayings are hadiths, wise words uttered by the prophet Muhammad himself, and not to be confused with the revealed word of the Qur'an.

The third type of scripture quoted here is the Talmud, ('study' or 'learning'), a name applied to two massive collections of academic discussions and judicial decisions made by Jewish rabbbis over a period of several centuries.

Any statement of a rule of right conduct is known as a halachah, and the rulings cover the whole of practical life. Haggadah is the interpretation of scripture in general, and not specifically for the regulation of personal conduct; it is the 'drawing-forth' of the content of the Torah from which one was intended to deduce lessons. The Mishnah was the authoritative statement of the halachoth, a classification of rulings initiated in the times of Hillel and Shammai, continued principally by Akiba and Meir, and completed by Judah the Prince (ha-Nasi) at the end of the second century CE.

The scholars working on it from c20–200 CE were called Tannaim, and the scholars that came after and completed the Mishnah were known as Amoraim. The Tannaim were mentioned by name in the Mishnaic collections, and held the same kind of honour afforded in Islam to the first four khalifas, or successors of the Prophet Muhammad. The Amoraim were not permitted to dispute any of their statements.

Once put into written form, the Mishnah itself then became a prime object of study, and results of this study were called Gemara. The Talmud, was the compilation of the Mishnah plus the Gemara. There are in fact two Talmuds, one compiled towards the end of the fourth century in Palestine, and one in Babylon a century later. Each Talmud consists of the Mishnah, together with a gemara or comment on the Mishnah, which often contains supplementary material. The authorities named in the Palestinian Talmud all lived before 400 CE, those in the Babylonian Talmud all lived before 500

CE. The Talmuds also include some material believed to have been introduced by later authors.

The Palestinian Talmud developed in the academies of Eretz Israel, and has a commentary of thirty-nine of the sixty-three tractates of the Mishnah. The Babylonian Talmud is around three times the length of the Palestinian, and according to tradition, it was finally edited by Rabbis Rav Ashi and Ravina. It comments on thirty-seven of the sixty-three tractates. Since it is a record of oral discussions, it is neither systematic nor concise. The English 'Soncino' version, edited by I. Epstein, runs to thirty-five volumes.

Details about the Talmuds can be found in the *New Standard Jewish Encyclopedia* (ed. Cecil Roth and Geoffrey Wigoder, W. H. Allen 1975; and *Everyman's Judaica* (ed. Geoffrey Wigoder, W. H. Allen 1975).

The full list of Orders, Tractates (or Mishnah) and Gemara is given on the pages following.

Orders and Tractates of the Mishnah and Talmud

	Mishnah No. of Chapters	Babylonian Talmud No. of Folios	Babylonian Talmud Folios Munich Ed.	Jerusalem Talmud No. of Folios	Subject matter
ORDER ZERA'IM					
Berakhot	9	64	19	14	Benedictions
Pe'ah	8	–	3	7	Gleanings (Lev. 19.9–10)
Demai	7	–	3	6	Doubtfully tithed produce
Kilayim	9	–	4	7	Diverse kinds (Deut. 22.9–11)
Shevi'it	10	–	4	7	The Sabbatical Year (Ex. 23.10–11)
Terumot	11	–	4	9	Heave offering (Lev. 22.10–14)
Ma'aserot	5	–	2	5	Tithes (Num. 18.21)
Ma'aser Sheni	5	–	3	5	Second tithe (Deut. 14.22ff.)
Hallah	4	–	2	4	Dough offering (Num. 15.17–21)
Orlah	3	–	2	4	The fruit of young trees (Lev. 19.23–25)
Bikkurim	3	–	3	3	First fruits (Lev. 26.1–11)
ORDER MO'ED					
Shabbat	24	157	28	18	The Sabbath
Eruvin	10	105	17	9	The fusion of Sabbath limits
Pesahim	10	121	18	11	Passover
Shekalim	8	–	6	7	The Shekel dues (Ex. 30.11–16)
Yoma	8	88	16	8	The Day of Atonement
Sukkah	5	56	9	5	The Feast of Tabernacles
Bezah	5	40	11	5	Festival laws
Rosh Ha-Shanah	4	35	7	4	Various new years, particularly Rosh Ha-Shanah
Ta'anit	4	31	8	7	Fast Days
Megillah	4	32	9	7	Purim
Mo'ed Katan	3	29	7	4	The intermediate days of festivals
Hagigah	3	27	6	5	The Festival offering (Deut. 16.16–17)

ORDER NASHIM

Tractate					
Yevamot	16	122	24	16	Levirate marriage (Deut. 25.5-10)
Ketubbot	13	112	20	12	Marriage contracts
Nedarim	11	91	10	7	Vows (Num. 30)
Nazir	9	66	8	8	The Nazirite (Num. 6)
Sotah	9	49	11	9	The suspected adulteress (Num. 5.11ff)
Gittin	9	90	16	7	Divorce
Kiddushin	4	82	14	9	Marriage

ORDER NEZIKIN

Tractate					
Bava Kamma	10	119	22	7	Torts
Bava Mezia	10	119	20	6	Civil law
Bava Batra	10	176	21	6	Property law
Sanhedrin	11	113	24	14	Judges
Makkot	3	24	5	3	Flagellation (Deut. 25.2)
Shevu'ot	8	49	9	7	Oaths
Eduyyot	8	–	4	–	Traditional testimonies
Avodah Zarah	5	76	13	7	Idolatry
Avot	5	–	2	–	Ethical maxims
Horayot	3	14	4	4	Erroneous ruling of the court (Lev. 4.22ff)

ORDER KODASHIM

Tractate					
Zevahim	14	120	21	–	Animal offerings
Menahot	13	110	21	–	Meal offering
Hullin	12	142	25	–	Animals slaughtered for food
Bekhorot	9	61	13	–	Firstlings (Deut. 15.19ff)
Arakhin	9	34	9	–	Vows of valuation (Lev. 27.1-8)
Temurah	7	39	8	–	The substituted offering (Lev. 27.10)
Keritot	6	28	9	–	Extirpation (Lev. 18.29)
Me'ilah	6	22	4	–	Sacrileges (Lev. 5.15-16)
Tamid	7	9	4	–	The daily sacrifice (Num. 28.3-4)
Middot	5	–	3	–	Measurements of the Temple
Kinnim	3	–	2	–	The Bird offering (Lev. 5.7ff.)

ORDER TOHOROT

	Mishnah No. of Chapters	Babylonian Talmud No. of Folios	Babylonian Talmud Folios Munich Ed.	Jerusalem Talmud No. of Folios	Subject matter
Kelim	30	—	11	—	Uncleanness of articles
Oholot (Ahilot)	18	—	7	—	Uncleanness through overshadowing (N. 19.14–15)
Nega'im	14	—	7	—	Leprosy (Lev. 13,14)
Parah	12	—	5	—	The Red Heifer (Num. 19)
Tohorot	10	—	5	—	Ritual cleanness
Mikva'ot	10	—	5	—	Ritual ablution
Niddah	10	73	14	4	The menstruant
Makhshirin	6	—	3	—	Liquid that predisposes food to become ritually unclean (Lev. 11.37–38)
Zavim	5	—	2	—	Fluxes (Lev. 15)
Tevul Yom	4	—	2	—	Ritual uncleanness between immersion and sunset (Lev. 22.6–7)
Yadayim	4	—	3	—	The ritual uncleanness of the hands
Uzkin	3	—	2	—	'Stalks': parts of plants susceptible to uncleanness

APPENDIX 2

A Brief Chronology of Jewish History from the Exodus from Egypt to the First Crusade

(For want of conclusive evidence, many of these dates are approximate)

BCE

Thirteen century(?)	Exodus from Egypt
Twelfth/eleventh centuries	Settlement in Palestine/period of the Judges
1020–1004	King Saul
1004–965	King David
965–928	King Solomon
928–720	Divided kingdoms of Israel and Judah
720	Israel destroyed and exiled to Assyria
586	Destruction of Jerusalem. Exile in Babylon
538	Return from exile on orders of King Cyrus
520	Building of Second Temple begins
Mid-fifth century	Activity of Ezra
332	Conquest of Alexander the Great
From 301	Eretz (land of) Israel (the term 'Israel' by itself was applied to the people, not the land) ruled over by Ptolemies . . .
c.270	Death of Simon the Just
From c.198	Eretz Israel ruled over by Seleucids. Gerouisa or 'New Sanhedrin' established.
168	Beginning of Maccabaean revolt
160–142	Reign of Jonathan ben Mattathias
142–135	Reign of Simeon
135–105	Reign of John Hyrcanus. 'Pharisees' become 'Separatists' or 'Expelled Ones'

104–76	Reign of Alexander Jannaeus. Persecution of Pharisees
76–67	Reign of Salome Alexandra. Activity of Honi the Circle-Drawer
67–63	Reign of Aristobulus II
63	Roman conquest under Ptolemy
63–40	Reign of Hyrcanus II. Activity of Shemaiah and Abtalion
37–4	Reign of Herod the Great. Activity of Hillel and Shammai
CE	
6–14	Judah and Samaria become Roman provinces
c.5–30	Life of Jesus
26–36	Pontius Pilate procurator of Jerusalem. Hillel's grandson Gamaliel I teaches the apostle Paul (?)
c.30	Cruxifixion of Jesus
66	Revolt against Rome. Activity of Johanan ben Zakkai and his pupils
70	Fall of Jerusalem to Romans. Johanan ben Zakkai moves spiritual centre to Yabneh
c.80–130	Gamaliel II strengthens Yabneh, succeeded by Joshua as leader of Sanhedrin. Activity of Akiba
c.131–5	Revolt of Bar Kokhba
135	Aelia Capitolina located on site of Jerusalem
140	Sanhedrin located at Usha, under Simeon II, son of Gamaliel II
170	Sanhedrin at Beth Shearim
200	Sanhedrin at Sepphoris
210	Redaction of the Mishnah
235	Sanhedrin at Tiberias
320	Death of Judah the Prince, grandson of Simeon II
324	Eretz Israel under Byzantine rule
390	Palestinian Talmud completed
500	Babylonian Talmud completed
533–628	Growing persecution of Jews in Europe
c.570	Birth of the Prophet Muhammad
614–618	Jerusalem conquered by the Persians
632	Death of the Prophet Muhammad

632–663	Period of the first four khalifas: Abu Bekr, Umar, Uthman and Ali, the Prophet's nephew
638	Jerusalem conquered by Ummayad Muslims
750	Eretz Israel conquered by Abassids
1070–8	Eretz Israel conquered by Seljuks
1096–9	First Crusade. Jerusalem conquered by Crusaders

BIBLIOGRAPHY

This is a selection of the many books which I have found relevant and useful.

I. Abrahams, *Studies in Pharisaism and the Gospels*, Cambridge University Press 1917

R. A. Banks, *Jesus and the Law in the Synoptic Tradition*, Cambridge University Press 1958

C. K. Barrett, *New Testament Background: Selected Documents*, SPCK 1958

– , *Jesus and the Gospel Tradition*, SCM Press and Fortess Press 1967

– , *The Gospel of John and Judaism*, SPCK 1975

M. Black, *The Scrolls and Christian Origins*, Nelson 1961

– , *An Aramaic Approach to the Gospels and Acts*, Oxford University Press 1967

J. Blinzler, *The Trials of Jesus*, Mercier Press 1959

G. Bornkamm et al., *Tradition and Interpretation in Matthew*, SCM Press and Westminster Press 1963

J. Bowker, *The Targums and Rabbinic Literature*, Cambridge University Press 1969

– , *Jesus and the Pharisees*, Cambridge University Press 1973

R. Bultmann, *Primitive Christianity in its Contemporary Setting*, Thames and Hudson 1956

– , *The Theology of the New Testament* (two vols), Scribners and SCM Press 1952, 1955

– , *The History of the Synoptic Tradition*, Blackwell and Westminster Press 1971

– , *The Gospel of John*, Blackwell and Westminster Press 1974

D. Catchpole, *The Trial of Jesus*, E. J. Brill, Leiden 1971

D. Daube, *The New Testament and Rabbinic Judaism*, Athlone Press 1956

W. D. Davies, *Christian Origins and Judaism*, DLT 1962

– , *The Setting of the Sermon on the Mount*, Cambridge University Press 1964

– , *Paul and Rabbinic Judaism*, SPCK 1972

J. D. M. Derrett, *Law in the New Testament*, DLT 1970

James D. G. Dunn, *The Partings of the Ways*, SCM Press and Trinity Press International 1991

A. Finkel, *The Pharisees and the Teacher of Nazareth*, E. J. Brill, Leiden 1964

L. Finkelstein, *The Pharisees*, Jewish Publishing Society of America 1962

D. Flusser, *Jesus*, Herder and Herder 1969

R. T. France, *Jesus and the Old Testament*, Tyndale Press 1971

B. Gärtner, *The Temple and Community in Qumran and the New Testament*, Cambridge University Press 1965

J. Goldin, *The Thinking of the Rabbis*, Judaism 5, 1956

M. D. Goulder, *Midrash and Lection in Matthew*, SPCK 1974

A. T. Hanson, *Grace and Truth*, SPCK 1974

E. Hennecke, W. Schneemelcher, R. McL. Wilson, *New Testament Apocrypha*, (two vols), Westminster Press and Lutterworth Press 1963, 1965; reissued SCM Press 1974

J. Jeremias, *The Parables of Jesus*, SCM Press and Scribners1967

– , *Jerusalem in the Time of Jesus*, SCM Press and Fortress Press 1969

M. Kadushin, *The Rabbinic Mind*, Jewish Theological Seminary of America 1952

J. Z. Lauterbach, *The Pharisees and their Teachings*, Bloch Publishing Co, New York 1930

J. Le Moyne, *Les Sadducéens*, Études Bibliques, Libraire Lecoffre 1972

H. Maccoby, *Revolution in Judaea*, Ocean Books 1978

– , *The Mythmaker*, Weidenfeld and Nicolson 1986

R. Marcus, 'The Pharisee in the Light of Modern Scholarship', *Journal of Religion* 32,3, 1951

J. L. Martyn, *History and Theology in the Fourth Gospel*, Harper and Row 1968

G. F. Moore, 'Christian Writers on Judaism', *Harvard Theological Review* 14, July 1921

– , *Judaism in the First Centuries of the Christian Era*, Harvard University Press 1954

J. Neusner, *The Rabbinic Traditions about the Pharisees before AD 70*, E. J. Brill, Leiden 1971

– , *The Modern Study of the Mishnah*, E. J. Brill, Leiden 1973

– , *From Politics to Piety*, Prentice-Hall 1973

– , *The Development of a Legend*, E. J. Brill, Leiden 1970

James Parkes, *Jesus, Paul and the Jews*, SCM Press 1936

D. W. Riddle, *Jesus and the Pharisees*, University of Chicago Press 1928

A. T. Robinson, *The Pharisees and Jesus*, Duckworth 1920

– , 'Jesus and the Pharisees', *The Expository Times* 28, 1971

E. P. Sanders, *Paul and Palestinian Judaism*, SCM Press and Fortress Press 1977

– , *Jesus and Judaism*, SCM Press and Fortress Press 1984

– , *Jewish Law from Jesus to the Mishnah*, SCM Press and Trinity Press International 1990

S. Sandmel, *We Jews and Jesus*, Gollancz 1965

H. J. Schoeps, *Paul*, Lutterworth Press 1961

B. Schechter, *Some Aspects of Rabbinic Theology*, A. & C. Black 1961

G. Schofield, *In the Year 62*, Harrap 1962

H. T. Schonfield, *According to the Hebrews*, Duckworth 1937

Morton Smith, *Tannaitic Parallels to the Gospels*, Journal of Biblical Literature Monograph Series 6, 1951

R. Travers–Herford, *The Pharisees*, Allen and Unwin 1924

G. Vermes, *Jesus the Jew*, Collins 1973; reissued Fortress Press and SCM Press 1985

Paul Winter, *On the Trial of Jesus*, De Gruyter [2]1974

S. Zeitlin, 'The Origin of the Pharisees Reaffirmed', *Jewish Quarterly Review* 59, 1969